1984

LANGUAGE IN MODERN LITERATURE:

Innovation and Experiment

HARVESTER/BARNES & NOBLE STUDIES IN CONTEMPORARY LITERATURE AND CULTURE

General Editor Patrick Parrinder, Department of English, University of Reading

This is a new series of original, full-length studies of modern literature and its cultural context. Although a variety of historical, theoretical and critical orientations will be encouraged, each title will aim to illuminate the common themes and conditions of twentieth century writing, rather than to explicate the work of an individual author. Taking 'literature and culture' to indicate the whole of organized verbal expression, the series will extend to include studies of modern criticism, the press and the communications media, as well as offering new and stimulating approaches in the fields of English and comparative literature.

LANGUAGE IN MODERN LITERATURE:

Innovation and Experiment

JACOB KORG

Professor of English Literature, University of Washington

THE HARVESTER PRESS · SUSSEX

BARNES & NOBLE · NEW YORK

First published in Great Britain in 1979 by
THE HARVESTER PRESS LIMITED
Publisher: John Spiers
16 Ship Street, Brighton, Sussex

and in the USA by
HARPER AND ROW PUBLISHERS, INC.
BARNES AND NOBLE IMPORT DIVISION
10 East 53rd Street, New York 10022

© 1979, Jacob Korg

British Library Cataloguing in Publication Data

Korg, Jacob
    Language in modern literature. –(Harvester
    studies in contemporary literature and culture; 1).
    1. English literature–20th century–History and
    criticism   2. English language–Style–Case
    studies
    I. Title
    820′.9′00912   PR478.S/

    ISBN 0–85527–965–6

    Barnes and Noble
    ISBN 0–06–493892–1
    LCN 79–53297

Photosetting by Thomson Press (India) Ltd., New Delhi.

Printed in Great Britain by
Redwood Burn Limited, Trowbridge and Esher

CONTENTS

ACKNOWLEDGEMENTS

The author wishes to express his thanks for permission to quote copyrighted material from the following sources:

Complete Poems and Plays, 1909–1950 by T. S. Eliot, copyright T. S. Eliot and Harcourt, Brace, Jovanovich. Reprinted by permission of Harcourt, Brace, Jovanovich and Faber and Faber, Ltd.

Poems 1923–1954 by E. E. Cummings. Reprinted by permission of Harcourt, Brace, Jovanovich and by permission of Granada Publishing Company, Ltd.

Speculations by T. E. Hulme. Reprinted by permission of Harcourt, Brace, Jovanovich and Routledge and Kegan Paul, Ltd.

The Collected Poems of Wallace Stevens, copyright Wallace Stevens. Reprinted by permission of Random House, Alfred A. Knopf, Inc., and Faber and Faber, Ltd.

Selected Writings of Gertrude Stein. Reprinted by permission of Random House, Alfred A. Knopf, Inc., and David Higham Associates.

A Portrait of the Artist as a Young Man and *Finnegans Wake* by James Joyce. Reprinted by permission of Viking Penguin, Inc., and the Society of Authors.

Ulysses by James Joyce. Reprinted by permission of Random House, Alfred A. Knopf, Inc., and John Lane, The Bodley Head.

The Philosophy of Symbolic Forms by Ernst Cassirer. Reprinted by permission of Yale University Press.

James Joyce, Finnegans Wake: A Symposium. (Our Exagmination ...) Copyright Sylvia Beach. Reprinted by permission of New Directions.

Personae, copyright 1926 by Ezra Pound and *The Cantos of Ezra Pound*, copyright 1934, 1938 by Ezra Pound. Reprinted by permission of New Directions and Faber and Faber, Ltd.

Imaginations by William Carlos Williams, copyright 1970 by Florence H. Williams; *Collected Earlier Poems* by William Carlos Williams, copyright 1938 by New Directions Publishing Corporation; *Paterson* by William Carlos Williams, copyright 1949 and 1958 by William Carlos Williams; and *Selected Essays* by William Carlos Williams, copyright 1954 by William Carlos Williams. Reprinted by permission of New Directions.

Selected Letters 1907–1941 by Ezra Pound, D. D. Paige (ed.), copyright 1950 by Ezra Pound, Reprinted by permission of New Directions.

INTRODUCTION

THIS BOOK takes the view that linguistic experiment is an essential element of literary modernism. To be sure, not all modern writers were innovators in language, and many who were had nothing new to say. But none of the themes and methods identified with modern literature is more indicative of the modern spirit than its treatment of language. New forms, new ideas, and attacks on tradition are features that modernism shares with other periods; but there is no precedent in English or American literature for the radical, principled, and extensive renovation of their medium of expression that writers attempted between about 1910 and the outbreak of World War II.

Verbal experimentation was a symptom of thoughts and feelings that influenced Western culture as a whole in the first few decades of the twentieth century. All forms of expression were coming under investigation, the relation of language to logic and reality was a central theme in studies ranging from philosophy to anthropology, and modernists in every field agreed that a work of art ought to be a dialogue between the artist and his medium. In June 1929, *transition* magazine, in a notorious announcement, proclaimed the advent of a 'revolution of the word', declaring that the autonomy of the poetic imagination justified writers in deviating from the rules of textbooks and grammars. *Transition's* flamboyant phrase was treated with sarcasm by contemporary critics, but it has risen to a position of acceptance, and has acquired a more general meaning than the one *transition* assigned to it. There is now no doubt that a revolution occurred, and that it was primarily a verbal revolution, manifesting itself in new uses of language.

It was not, however, a concerted or coordinated effort. The writers I have focused on in this study—Gertrude Stein, T. E. Hulme, Ezra Pound, Wyndham Lewis, T. S. Eliot, James Joyce, William Carlos Williams and E. E. Cummings—do not form a group and cannot be treated collectively; the differences among them are easily as important as the resemblances. The verbal revolution in which they participated radiated in many directions, claiming functions and possibilities for language that can be classified as both classic and romantic, objective and subjective, representational and abstract. The form of my book is determined, for the most part, by this situation. I have not dealt with the authors as individual figures, nor with whole books or poems; there has already been much interpretation of this kind, and I am heavily indebted, as will be obvious, to earlier analysts and explicators. Instead, I have devoted each chapter or section (with the exception of the last, which is on *Finnegans Wake*), to a specific experimental principle. Since most of the works and authors employed a number of these, each is approached repeatedly over different ground, and in connection with a different topic, in chapter after chapter; the resulting effect is that of a recursive, but non-repetitive conformation that might be compared with that of Browning's *Ring and the Book* or the double helix.

For help in illuminating my subject, I have turned to contemporary developments in other fields of art and literature in other languages. It has long been recognized that there are close relationships between the graphic arts and the literature of the modern period. The Anglo-American writers befriended artists, worked with them, followed their leadership, and some were painters themselves; but the nature of their connections with European experimental writers remains controversial. Most of them were hostile or indifferent to the literary aspects of such movements as Dada, Futurism and Surrealism, and literary historians have been reluctant to concede that any meaningful influences existed in this area. But Ford Madox Ford insisted on the cohesiveness of international modernism in the 1920s, writing, 'all over the Anglo-Saxon world . . . there is in motion a very definite creative impulse that is pretty well kindred throughout, and that is pretty well akin to the larger world movements'.[1] And Octavio Paz, in *Children of the Mire*, has supplied a long-needed corrective to the established version of literary history by showing that the Anglo-Americans must be seen as participants in a single complex and widely-ranging transformation of the arts that encompasses many oppositions. 'Anglo-American "modernism,"' he declares, 'is *another* version of the European avant-garde.'[2] The two are not the same; but they shared many technical interests, including imagery as a means of reconciling mind and matter, irrational thought, the influence of urban life and technology on consciousness, and such new kinds of structure and articulation as the metonymic, the analogical and the spatial. Modernism was not a unified cause, but as Ford called it 'a movement', and the attitudes Renato Poggioli has attributed to avant-garde movements in his definitive analysis, namely hostility to tradition, adventurism, nihilism and self-destructiveness, all played their parts in motivating verbal experiment.[3]

The modern period has been described, not only as a revolution, but as 'a reign of terror'. The term is intended to be depreciative, but the aesthetic standard of terror is as old as Aristotle, and also, in another sense, one of the modern inventions. In 1918 T. S. Eliot wrote that he found Wyndham Lewis's *Tarr* and James Joyce's *Ulysses*, a part of which he had just read in manuscript, 'terrifying,' and added: 'That is the test of a new work of art. When a work of art no longer terrifies us we may know that we were mistaken, or that our senses are dulled: we ought still to find *Othello* or *Lear* frightful.'[4] Unlike Aristotle, however, Eliot believes that art should arouse apprehension, not to resolve it, but to sustain it. The Shakespearean tragedies frighten us (or ought to) because they expose moral dangers whose existence we are forced to admit; but the modern works project visions of life that transcend our awareness of actuality. They do not submit themselves to our judgment. Instead, the observer who stands before a disciplined and well-proportioned Mondrian or an apparently uncontrolled Kandinsky feels that he is himself being judged by some enigmatic intelligence, some representative of a world of values to which he is a stranger. Like Leontes before the supposed statue of Hermione in *The Winter's Tale*, he asks himself, 'does not the stone rebuke me,/ For being more stone than it?' In graphic art, perceptions too radical for overt expression are embodied in non-representational elements; in modern literature they are expressed through deviations from the conventional idiom.

The verbal revolution is often described as an attack on language, or an attempt to destroy coherence; but among the Anglo-American writers the demonic components of modernism were enlisted in an effort that amounts, in the final analysis, to a search for new expressive resources and new ways of understanding the world. Claude Bernard characterized the scientific experimenter as 'the examining magistrate of nature', and the experimental writer might be regarded as the examining magistrate of language. He deforms and probes it, not to destroy it, but to achieve a decreation that releases new powers of articulation. By setting aside the usual rules of language, he makes the discovery that Michel Foucault attributes to the culture that frees itself from traditional concepts of order, learns that they are not indispensable, and 'then finds itself faced with the stark fact that there exists, below the level of its spontaneous orders, things that are in themselves capable of being ordered, that belong to a certain unspoken order; the fact, in short, that order *exists*'.[5] In the same way, the revolutionary writers reached below the conventions imposed on language by time, place and custom in an effort to locate the essential sources of meaning. In *The Chequer'd Shade* John Press attributed the obscurity of English poets writing after 1930 to a desire to imitate the meaninglessness of their world, and contrasted them with the writers of the previous generation, who hoped to shape their materials into coherent visions. This view would have astonished the early readers of experimental literature, but we now understand that the literary revolution and the verbal experiment it involved were not a thrust into chaos but a search for alternative concepts of order.

Lamenting the futility of discussing the corrupt state of language in language itself, Coleridge observed: 'Our chains rattle even while we are complaining of them.' His image applies perfectly, I am afraid, to the term 'experimental' as it appears in literary contexts. The word is usually used in the careless and degraded sense, 'something new', even in such sources as the Preface to *Lyrical Ballads*. The concept itself has often been dismissed as directionless and superficial, even by critics who have analyzed it with some precision. Yvor Winters devoted a chapter of *Primitivism and Decadence* (1937) to a valuable discussion of experimental poetic modes, but concluded that they were of little importance. Renato Poggioli concedes that experimentation is capable of enduring achievements, but he minimizes its value, warning that the novelty of technical means may end in sterility, and is often irrelevant to artistic purposes. Experiment, he declares, is only preliminary to creation, not identical with it, and the finished work, if it is successful, absorbs the experiments that have gone into it.[6] Poggioli's point may explain why I have found it more natural, in this study, to deal with isolated aspects of works that bear upon specific techniques. Experiment may not have been a sufficient condition for art, but it was often considered a necessary one by modernists like Pound, who wrote: 'Willingness to experiment is not enough, but unwillingness to experiment is mere death.'[7]

Modern writers experimented in order to exploit the authority of science and to maintain their contemporaneity; but there was also a widespread conviction that beauty could be identified with novelty. The tenet that a work of art must embody some crucial increment in awareness is at least as old as Romanticism, which usually conceives the aesthetic experience as a sensation of discovery or transformation. In poetry, said Eliot, expressing a view representative of modernism, 'there is always the communication of some new experience, or some fresh understanding of the familiar, or the expression of something we have experienced but have no words for, which enlarges our consciousness or refines our sensibility'.[8] Since on the one hand, the modern writers took experiment seriously, and it was, as Poggioli acknowledges, an indispensable component of modernist thinking, and since, on the other, it has always suffered a certain disrepute, I have tried to rehabilitate it as a critical concept by defining it more narrowly and developing some affinities between artistic and scientific experiment.

There is an unavoidable paradox connected with the study of the new, or what is considered new. On the one hand, novelty is one of the commonest literary qualities, for every meaningful word in a work of literature may usefully be regarded as a new word that cannot be fully explained by tradition, but acquires a new identity in its particular context. Yet there is probably no innovative use of words, not even the distortions of Joyce and Cummings, that is without precedent. Such disturbances of the normal printing conventions as Pound's Chinese ideograms and Guillaume Apollinaire's *Calligrammes*, whose poems are shaped like their subjects, bring us back to the pristine act of writing, making marks on a surface. Parody used without satirical intent, to demonstrate the ambiguity of language, is, as we shall see, a characteristic modern device; yet some of Homer's notorious repetitions have exactly this effect. In literature, the old and the new are indispensable to each other. Its revolutions are nearly always reactions against the recent past, and a search for lost traditions. As Northrop Frye has said, 'Originality returns to the origins of literature, as radicalism returns to its roots.'[9] For the purposes of this study, therefore, I will assume that the new was what was felt to be new, even if it must often be understood in terms of its relations with the old.

I am indebted, for help of various kinds, to Maurice Beebe, Vincent Brome, Donna Gerstenberger, Donald Kartiganer, Michael Magie and Naomi Pascal, as well as to my wife, Cynthia, who shared much of the work. Most of my research was done in the British Library and in the various libraries of the University of Washington, whose staff members performed many services for me. I wish to thank the *Journal of Modern Literature*, and its editor, Mr Beebe, for permission to reprint material about literary experiment originally published there.

I EXPERIMENTAL MOTIVES

> If we never write anything save what is already
> understood, the field of understanding will never
> be extended.
>
> Ezra Pound
> *Thrones*, Canto 96

I AM not at all sure that so diversified a phenomenon as the Anglo-American literary revolution can be attributed to any one cause. But if we seek an underlying source for it, a plausible one, I believe, is to be found in the conviction that the revolutionary writers shared with such neo-idealistic philosophers as F. H. Bradley, Henri Bergson and Ernst Cassirer: that man, his universe and the reality he inhabits are largely products of his own conceptual activities, and that the nature of his experience is strongly controlled by the resources he uses for making it available to conciousness. The revolt against literary convention is linked to a general sense that art, literature and, in fact, all forms of knowledge and expression contain radically creative energies which cannot avoid shaping the material they deal with, and must not be allowed to operate in darkness, or to fall prey to obsolete motivations.

Cassirer's *Philosophy of Symbolic Forms*, which was written in the 1920s, and therefore belongs to the period of *Ulysses* and *The Waste Land*, is a magisterial theoretical statement of the beliefs which were imposing new responsibilities upon the arts of the time. Cassirer explains the self-constitutive power of thought, and its relation to external reality by saying:

Every authentic function of the human spirit has this decisive characteristic in common with cognition: it does not merely copy but rather embodies an original, formative power. It does not express passively the mere fact that something is present but contains an independent energy of the human spirit through which the simple presence of the phenomenon assumes a definite 'meaning', a particular ideational content. This is as true of art as it is of cognition; it is as true of myth as of religion. All live in particular image-worlds, which do not merely reflect the empirically given, but which rather produce it in accordance with an independent principle. Each of these functions creates its own symbolic forms. . . . They are not different modes in which an independent reality manifests itself to the human spirit but roads by which the spirit proceeds towards its objectivization, i.e., its self-revelation.[1]

He places language squarely among the forms of expression that shape the human condition:

> Cognition, language, myth and art; none of them is a mere mirror, simply reflecting images of inward or outward data; they are not indifferent media, but rather the true sources of light, the prerequisite of vision, and the wellsprings of all formation.

The perceptions among which we live are often mistaken for objective existences; in actuality, says Cassirer,

> ... they are image-worlds whose principle and origin are to be sought in an autonomous creation of the spirit. Through them alone we see what we call 'reality', and in them alone we possess it: for the highest objective truth that is accessible to the spirit is ultimately the form of its own activity.[2]

Cassirer's views reflect the process of secularization that is so conspicuous in recent cultural history; the tradition that God created the world through his utterance is replaced by the idea that it is created by the utterances of man. Ezra Pound, who is perhaps the least subjective of the figures we will be dealing with, claimed for art a controlling power not generally associated with it when he wrote in an essay characteristically called 'The Serious Artist' published just before World War I, that 'the arts bear witness and define for us the inner nature and conditions of man', and said, in another piece, that, while man does passively receive impressions, he can also be thought of as 'directing a certain fluid force against circumstance, as *conceiving* instead of merely reflecting and observing'.[3] And a recent critic of *Ulysses* has attributed two of Joyce's contributions, his aesthetic theory and the stream of consciousness style, to the same motivation. 'Both the theory and the technique', says S. L. Goldberg, 'arise from, and point to, the central theme of the work itself: the activity of the human spirit through which, in which, life continually seeks to understand itself, and, understanding, to re-create.'[4]

Language does not seem to be a promising medium for this sort of renewal because it is essentially conservative, a structure of consensus, a fabric held together by a vast number of historical and communal agreements. The materials of the other arts have almost no innate meaning; the paint in a tube and the stone in a raw block are very close to being neutral substances which the artist can fully control within physical limits. But language has commitments that take priority over its aesthetic potentialities; it must represent or articulate something; and it must embody some notion of regularity. Linguistic innovations can be meaningful only against the backdrop of the inherently systematic nature of language. A text can depart from the specific conventions of the prevailing idiom only if it subscribes to the principle of convention itself. Most of the experimental writers were, in spite of their radicalism, traditionalists who understood these limitations, and who expected the new forms they invented to derive their significance, in part, from their relationships to established ones.

Linguistic deviations are invariably deviations in depth which abrogate agreements accepted by the community of the past and present speakers of a language, and arbitrarily displace them with new ones proposed by an individual author. It is therefore natural that the experimental writers should have encountered resistance and incomprehension among their contemporaries. But recent speculation about language and its relation to culture has occasioned renewed scepticism about linguistic experiment from a different point of view. Roland Barthes and Michel Foucault have warned that language, like all the modes of expression mentioned by Cassirer, is controlled by forces originating in the depths of history, and threatens to master, rather than serve the writer, forcing him to enter into the involuntary agreements which Benjamin Lee Whorf described as conditions attached to the use of all language, and making him a victim of the bewitching power which Ludwig Wittgenstein regarded as a threat to philosophy. The writer or speaker may have the illusion that he is using words, not that they are using him, but he is in reality confronted with a Chinese wall of established, though unconscious ideas that runs through the syntax, vocabulary and rhetorical practices of his medium, and he is fortunate indeed if he is able to penetrate this density with some elements of his own individuality. Everyone who uses language critically has felt something of this sort. The meeting between the writer's ideas and the language available to him may result in a collision that is destructive and creative at once, but it is much more likely to be a surrender, in which the originality of thought is swallowed in the quicksand of conventional usage, making it nearly indistinguishable from what has been said before. The author, says Barthes, seeks to fulfill or essentialize himself through individual expression, but society betrays him by transforming him into the priest of an ineffective linguistic rite.[5]

The experimental writers were motivated by exactly this acute sense of the tyranny exercised by conventional language. Some of their innovations correspond with principles the structuralists were later to develop, and there are many parallels between their critique of the conventional literary idiom and the structuralist reading of linguistic history. However, it is not surprising that there is also considerable difference between the views of Anglo-American writers of the early century who were seeking to undo the influences of Romantic poetry and the realistic novel and those of French critics writing forty years later who were occupied mainly with the specialization literary French had undergone since Mallarmé and Rimbaud. They are sufficiently out of phase with each other, in spite of a common dissatisfaction with the state of language, to be mutually illuminating.

According to Foucault's history of the encroaching hegemony of language in *The Order of Things*, the 'classical' seventeenth century accepted language as a transparent representational medium which disclosed the realities of the world, and no rationale was needed to demonstrate the resemblance between words and their referents. However, in the fifty years bisected by the beginning of the nineteenth century, a change that Foucault describes as a great rift, and one of the major events of Western cultural history, disturbed this harmony. The assumption that language was attached to external reality was replaced by the idea that it was a system sustained by inner relationships, primarily autotelic rather than representational. Among those primarily responsible for this change were Mallarmé, the Symbolist poets and the nineteenth-century philologists, whose work had the effect of demonstrating that language operated according to principles unrelated to human interests. 'From the nineteenth century', says Foucault, 'language began to fold in upon itself, to acquire its own particular density, to deploy a history, an objectivity and laws of its own.' He describes the present situation as one in which man, uncertain of his identity, and newly aware of areas impenetrable to knowledge both within and around him, turns to the mysterious formal properties of language as a source of order, and unconsciously accepts the linguistic categories as models of his thoughts and activities, surrendering his independence to them, and becoming a helpless particle in the field of alien linguistic energies.

Pound, Eliot and their contemporaries had something very much like Foucault's diagnosis of the pathology of language in mind when they complained, during and after the period of World War I, that the literary idiom of the recent past had lost its signifying power. However, they attributed this, not to Foucault's deep cultural change, but on the contrary, to the failure of language to absorb developments in the state of knowledge. They found that conventional syntax and vocabulary silently insinuated assumptions about time, space, matter, causality, the mind, the self and other elementary concepts which were becoming obsolete. Journalism and popular literature circulated a debased linguistic medium, limited to the expression of simple, familiar ideas through stock phrases and trite, sensationalizing rhetorical devices. The current forms of language had few resources for conveying the insights into the nature of external reality which science was disclosing, or the experiences of a machine age, whether they were the sense of power praised by the Futurists, or the boredom and monotony in Eliot's poems of city life. They were not adapted to expressing irrational psychological processes, the paradoxical interweaving of subject and object that takes place in the act of perception, or states of mind that fail to correspond with recognized patterns of consciousness.

But the very existence of linguistic experiment asserts another and much deeper disagreement with Foucault's analysis of the condition of language. The structuralists, as a group, while agreeing in principle with Cassirer's belief that language is among the prime agencies of human self-realization, assume that its only significant dimensions are those that are socialized; they discount the importance of idiolects, and, by implication, of radical departures from the communicative function. In Foucault's view, the autonomous linguistic medium sponsored by the Symbolist movement was a futile, self-serving business of gesturing in empty space, and was one of the main sources of the alienation of language. But the Anglo-Americans felt that Symbolism offered the writer the freedom to devise, and to embody in his work, verbal orders capable of supplanting the order imposed by conventional language. They felt that it enabled literature to become an expression of the writer's mind rather than a pale reflection of actuality, and that under these conditions the literary idiom could afford to seek out representational powers and contact with empiric experience again. In a passage describing the intentions of the French modernists, some of whom the experimentalists admired, Roland Barthes sketched aims that correspond to the kind of writing the experimental movement as a whole aspired to produce. Such writing disengages itself from social commitments, regains the instrumental function it had in the classical period, and becomes an independent object capable of purposeful manipulation. It does not express a substantive philosophy as literature did in classical times, but rather a 'new situation of the writer, the way a certain silence has of existing'. Barthes employs an image often used by Ezra Pound when he says that language overturns convention by achieving the pure state of an equation in relation to man's deepest feelings. When that happens, 'the problematics of mankind is uncovered and presented without elaboration, the writer becomes irretrievably honest'.[6] The revolutionary writers did not, with the exception of Gertrude Stein, conceive of this honesty in terms of Barthes' 'zero degree', in which words acquire significance by divesting themselves as far as possible of meaning; this was a development of the post-modern period, the time of Beckett, Ionesco, Pinter and Robbe-Grillet. The moderns themselves were moving in another direction, toward Pound's language 'charged with meaning to the utmost possible degree'. Their work is not alien to humanism, as Barthes says modern poetry is, but embodies a renewed humanism. Yet when it renounces predication and strives to project meaning through its formal properties, it clearly offers a counterpart of the neutrality and 'silence' Barthes praises as the attributes of writing fully conscious of its position.

Foucault perceives that an effort to recover the truths that lie behind the facade of language has been going on in recent times, but he locates it in exegetical writing, which undertakes the tasks 'of disturbing the words we speak, of denouncing the grammatical habits of our thinking, of dissipating the myths that animate our words, rendering once more noisy and audible the element of silence that all discourse carries with it as it is spoken'.[7] The revolutionary writers carried out a programme of this kind within literature itself, exposing the rigid habits of mind and deceptive silences Foucault speaks of by turning words out of their moulds and re-assembling them in new conformations and for new purposes. They tried to evade what Foucault calls 'the trap of philology' by setting aside traditional and communal rules, and devising new ones adapted to modern or individual consciousness, in the spirit of Blake's 'I must Create a System or be enslaved by another Man's.' Their innovations were not mere stylistic ventures, but deviations which transformed consciousness by altering the syntactic, structural and lexical foundations of language, and the premises embodied in them.

The renovation of the literary idiom they undertook involved two separate, though related motivations. As we shall see, much of their inventive energy initially went into devising methods for bringing language into an immediate, revelatory relationship with externals, so that it could achieve the clarity and exactness found in such models as the poems of H.D. [Hilda Doolittle] and Joyce's *Dubliners*. But during the investigation of techniques arising from efforts of this kind, the thrust toward reality was deflected by the consciousness that the language of poetry and literature was not merely a record of reality, but a 'substantial medium' to use Gerald L. Bruns' term, capable of generating rather than merely reflecting meaning. This led to the concept of the autonomous work, a verbal space cleared of referential responsibilities where language is free to deploy its inherent energies. Pound advised, 'don't represent—present', but in the face of this demand for immediacy, the external subject could never be more than a 'referent', and the thing presented could only be the poem itself. As we shall see, this shift occurred in the development of many of the experimentalists, recapitulating Foucault's history of the shift in language use from representational to autotelic functions. The first was not superseded by the second, but remained a powerful influence on modern poetry, and the two are seen side by side in the theories and literary texts of the experimentalists, complementing and cooperating with each other.

Improved imitation was the original aim both of Gertrude Stein and of the group of young writers who assembled around T.E. Hulme and Ezra Pound in London in the years before World War I, and among whom the roots, first of Imagism and then of the general literary revolution are to be found. They meant to restore some version of the transparent representationalism which Foucault describes as characteristic of seventeenth-century language, in which the relation of word to thing was so clear that one could serve as a surrogate for the other, and the order of words could be considered equivalent to the order of things. In its early phases, Imagism was possessed by a dream of a language so firmly locked into reality that it would both satisfy the intuitions and survive scientific verification. Pound is at his most characteristic when he calls for precision, accuracy and concreteness, as he does in the 1913 statement on 'Imagisme' published in *Poetry*. When he argues, in *How to Read* (1929), that the writer performs a service to the state by preserving the integrity of language as an instrument of ideology and legislation, he makes it clear that he is thinking of its referential function, for he identifies the 'very essence' of the writer's work as 'the application of word to thing', and declares that 'the whole machinery of social and individual thought and order' depends upon the clarity of this relationship.[8]

Mere naming, however, does not grasp the reality of an object, but simply fixes it within the space of conventional language, clogging the doors of perception. In order to discover verbal forms so inevitably representational that they become identified with their referents in a definitive, revelatory union, the writer must resort to deviations from conventional language. Theorists of this radical form of mimesis often speak of the object revealing itself, or unfolding itself in words, but it is clear that these are metaphors, and that whatever is perceived must address some perceiving consciousness. The poet is not absent, as he is sometimes figuratively said to be, but is submerged in an act of attention so complete that a sense of the object fills his mind, controlling his use of language, and displacing conventional and habitual techniques of representation.

Four of the prominent critical formulations of the modern period are efforts to identify this relationship and specify a means of expressing it. All are based on the traditional conviction that language, mind and reality share a common nature and can therefore share the task of reflecting objects of perception. The earliest of these critical concepts, Hopkins's 'inscape' is nowhere clearly defined, but it involves a sense of the individuality of the object, together with an accompanying appreciation of its pattern or form of organization. Pound's 'image'—'that which presents an intellectual and emotional complex in an instant of time'—is the concrete presentation of some external that defines a feeling, not merely a depiction of it. Joyce's 'epiphany' is the radiant selfhood an object acquires when its particularity and the structure that gives it that particularity are manifested to perception. The short compositions Joyce called 'epiphanies' are stringently objective renderings of scenes whose language does nothing more than let the subject speak for itself. Eliot's 'objective correlative' finally, is an external that is treated as the surrogate for some emotion. While these terms and the techniques they refer to are not identical with each other, (though critics have often used them interchangeably), all of them affirm that reality can project meaning only through consciousness, and that consciousness can find meaning only in reality. The general idea is conventional; but the doctrines associated with the four modern tropes declare that particular instances of this interdependence can only be adequately expressed through means that escape the conventional formulations.

In their efforts to touch reality more directly, the revolutionary writers sometimes resorted to techniques for establishing a substantial, rather than a symbolic presence, such as the representational typography of Cummings, various versions of *collage*, the Chinese characters found in the *Cantos*, and other graphic effects later to become common in concrete poetry. Paradoxically, these devices invariably call attention to themselves as media of signification rather than to their referents, a reversal which is perfectly appropriate to the self-conscious, self-exploratory nature of verbal experiment. Language, which seems, on the one hand, to flood the space about us, identifying each element of the environment, is also contained within various polarities, such as the mimetic and the abstract, the metaphoric and the literal, the denotative and the emotive. We recognize that it cannot actually attain any of these extremes in a pure state, but as it moves closer to any of them, a tension exerted by its opposite is often felt. An especially objective description is likely to make us feel the absence of emotion, and nonsense, as Gertrude Stein noticed, has a mysterious power to awaken dormant reserves of signification in words. She could declare, with some justice, that in 'A rose is a rose is a rose' the rose at last bloomed again, and William Carlos Williams pointed out that another sentence of hers, 'The envelopes have been tied to all the fruit trees', made the envelopes and fruit trees perfectly visible.[9]

While the idea of autonomy in literature had been available to the English-speaking public since 1899 in Arthur Symons's *Symbolist Movement in Literature*, the first decisive turn in that direction seems to have been stimulated by the appearance of abstract, non-imitative works of painting and sculpture in the years just before the war. It seems to be identifiable especially with Pound's shift from Imagism to Vorticism in 1914. In 'The Serious Artist', which appeared in *The Egoist* late in 1913, he speaks of literature as if it shared many of the scientific values, and emphasizes precision, communication and expression; but in the important 'Vorticism' essay of September 1914, he turns for his model from science to the 'new arts' of Picasso, Epstein and Gaudier-Brzeska, speaks of art as 'an arrangement of planes' and 'the organization of forms' and compares the poetic image to a quadratic equation on the ground that it has the power to define universal feelings as the equation defines universal geometric forms, without committing itself to a specific content.[10] By 1925 E.M. Forster could explain the nature of the autonomous work with extraordinary directness and simplicity, as if no contradiction were to be expected. He argued that anonymity was an advantage to literary creation because it made a poem more autonomous, freeing it from the personality of the author and the function of conveying information. 'Information', he said, 'is true if it is accurate. A poem points to nothing but itself. Information is relative. A poem is absolute.'[11] The later motivations can be seen taking their place, side by side with the referential ones Pound had championed in his Imagist phase in a letter written to Iris Barry in 1916. He says here that the 'whole art' of poetry can be divided into two things, which we should count as three; first, 'concision', or clarity and economy; second, 'the actual necessity for creating and constructing something', the formal aspect of the poem regarded as an autonomous work; and third, presenting images of concrete things that move the reader, or representation.[12]

The shift from radical mimesis to comparative autonomy, and the effect of this change on the functioning of language is illustrated with some clarity in the poetics of Gerard Manley Hopkins, the most important English forerunner of the experimentalists (the only others are Browning and Lewis Carroll). It was natural for Hopkins to think of poetry as representational, because he believed in the continuity of thought and matter, internal and external, language and reality. His poetic innovations, like his poetry generally, are based on the conviction that existence and thought are animated by the same divine energy, that 'To be and to know or Being and thought are the same', and that 'All words mean either things or relations of things.'[13] His contribution to the techniques of radical mimesis, 'inscape', which involved the perception of the object as a distinctive variant of a generic pattern, is a form of the more fundamental Hopkinsian principle of rhyme, which identifies beauty with the conjunction of likeness and difference. To 'inscape' an object is to gain a particularly intimate sense of its individuality by seeing it as a specific and particularized manifestation of a general design. The language that seeks to render inscapes therefore itself becomes individual and peculiar, verging, as Hopkins admitted, on eccentricity.

But the formal and phonetic patterns which Hopkins developed so intensively in order to capture inscape exhibit the Being of the poem, making it less a representation than an object suitable for the aesthetic response that Hopkins called 'contemplative enjoyment'. It becomes a counterpart of reality, not because it imitates some object, but because it acquires an inscape of its own, a self-sustaining individuality that distinguishes it from all other realities. One result of this is that Hopkins's words, while borrowed from the common stock for the most part, surrender a good part of their referential force as they become parts of a unique artifact with a unique meaning. Another is that his subjects, instead of standing forth vividly as they would in genuinely imitative poetry, seem swaddled in language, muffled in a virtuoso design of multiple patterns and meanings. In Hopkins's poems about the windhover, Felix Randal, the redcoat soldier, and the bugler boy at his First Communion, the dense structures of technical effects obtrude themselves instead of delineating their subjects. Form and design are emphasized, not as aids to communication, but as aesthetic values in themselves, engaging a range of feelings different from those involved in imitation, and competing with them. The poem's resemblance to reality is based, not on the weak capacity words may have for imitating things directly, but on a quality language is eminently fitted to achieve, the patterned, organized individuality or inscape through which all things manifest their existence.

During the World War I period, radical mimesis, the correspondence of word to thing, or Gertrude Stein's aim of finding words that would make things look more like themselves, remained a prominent experimental motive, but it became less significant than the correspondence of the poem as a whole to the self-constitutive, independent, autotelic condition of things we call reality; '... not "realism"', said William Carlos Williams, 'but reality itself—'.[14] Poetry aspired, not only to the condition of music, but more specifically to the condition of the Cubist painting, in which forms taken from the external world are reshaped in the interests of order and cognition.

The development of Cubism is a classic illustration of the revolutionary consequences of radical representationalism. Its earliest, or analytic stage, which is usually assigned to the period between 1907 and 1912 when Georges Braque and Picasso were developing the new style, embodied the consciousness that the visible universe is only the simplified abstraction of a dense, continuous reality, the jungle of process envisioned by Whitehead. The Cubist painter feels that a painting ought to be, not merely a record of the eye's superficial interpretation of this world, but an image of the reality opened to the mind by modern science and philosophy; not the momentary glimpse offered by conventional pictures, but reality in its essential nature as a complex, ongoing interweaving of multiple relationships. The Cubist paints what he knows and feels as well as what he sees. His first principle is a spirited assertion of the reality of the canvas itself as a two-dimensional, static surface, not the fictional window earlier painters had devised to counterfeit the depth, light effects and other physical properties of actuality. He lifts his objects out of the perspectival depth of conventional paintings and brings them into relation with the level of the canvas, moving foreground and background shapes into a single plane so that they abut on each other, sharing the same dividing lines, or intersect in ways that suggest a blending together in the same flat space. Intent upon capturing the interconnectedness and continuousness of things, he links various objects to each other, brings forward parts of the model that are below or behind to give them a place in the visual field, or depicts its past and future aspects at once, building up his images with fragments that are incompatible with each other in terms of ordinary perception. Aspects that can be seen only successively as one walks around the object, or turns it from side to side, are presented simultaneously.

Because he is interested in his objects as instances of process rather than in their separate individuality, the Cubist is reluctant to close his forms; he is likely to interrupt his outlines by breaks or overlappings, to display the inside of an object as well as the outside, or to show how it looks in more than one position. *Collage*, a very early development in Cubism, has as one of its many values a rejection of conventional illusionism. All of these techniques assert the claim that the painting is real, that it shares the space of the room or gallery in which it is displayed with the mouldings and the wallpaper. They tend to suppress the sense of the model, which is, after all, absent, and a fiction, in favour of the lines, shapes and colours which constitute the real design that is actually at hand.

Yet this research into the nature of reality generated revolutionary ideas of design and the vigorously expressive form and colour which dominated later stages of Cubism, in a development parallel with that of radical mimesis in literature. The methods that led to abstraction and autonomy had been devised, originally, as resources for recognizing new kinds of order in external reality.

This motivation corresponds exactly to what Roland Barthes was later to call 'structuralist activity', a 'mimesis' undertaken, not to copy reality by imitating its substance, but to make it comprehensible by replicating its functions.[15] Barthes acknowledges that the work of structural analysts who perceive specific relationships in such fields as anthropology and economics is exactly like that of modern artists who create works of art in accordance with independent principles of unity. Their characteristic procedures are selection and arrangement; some unit of reality is selected, not for its inherent meaningfulness, but because it is capable of entering into crucial relationships with other units; this is taken out of its normal context and put into a structure reflecting deliberate organization. The result is not a picture of externals as they are conventionally seen, but an exhibition of the process by which things are endowed with meaning. The idea that literary works could project meaning independently in this way suggested that the medium in which they were written could differ radically from the referential language of daily life, and opened the way to the possibility of innovations designed, not to emulate reality, but to exploit the inherent expressive potentialities of language itself. In 1925, Edwin Muir, after reading Joyce's *Portrait of the Artist as a Young Man*, gave a name to a venerable idea that became a commonplace in the modern period. Commenting on the way in which the dialogue of the novel participates in the design of the whole, Muir said: 'That pattern of speech seemed complete in itself, a thing of different nature from, but as real as, the events and experiences, many of them sordid, which it described. There were thus two values in the novel, separate, yet necessary to each other: the value of language and that of life, the value of art and that of experience. . . . '[16] These speeches, said Muir, constituted a 'second language' that varied and complemented the general form of the book.

The view that the idiom of literature is a 'second language' removed from ordinary language is connected with the theory that the writer creates in his work a 'second nature' distinct from the actual world. M.H. Abrams has shown how the latter, developed in the eighteenth century and in earlier periods to explain the appearance of monsters and supernatural beings in literature, led to the view that the process of literary creation is analogous to that of cosmic creation.[17] Just as the world within a poem need not correspond with actuality, but should, in fact, be idealized or ordered by the imagination, so the language of literature need not resemble ordinary language, but should have expressive capacities of its own.

This division is one of the major linguistic themes of the modern period. Hopkins, trying to maintain that the language of poetry ought to be no more than 'current language heightened' was compelled to add that it might be 'to any degree heightened and unlike itself' as long as it was not obsolete. Renato Poggioli regarded the obscure idioms of avant-garde texts as one of the manifestations of 'antagonism', the militant opposition to accepted practices characteristic of many modern artists. But he pointed out that unconventional language could also serve the more serious purpose of correcting the colourless and denatured idiom of habitual perception through a metaphoric, ambivalent medium that amounted to 'a game of multiple, diverse and opposing meanings' whose most characteristic effect would be an Empsonian ambiguity.[18] A deeper motivation for the differentiation of literary language from ordinary speech is to be found in the conviction that external reality is inaccessible to perception, and that the poem can be no more than a manifestation of the power of language to shape consciousness. Ortega y Gasset believed the artist's feeling that he is cut off from external reality, and his acceptance of inner life as a substitute for it to be among the determining characteristics of modern art. The fact that it is impossible to 'walk barefoot into reality' as Wallace Stevens has put it, to jump over the wall erected around the objective world by conceptions and ideas and know it as immediate experience, means that material actuality is forbidden to cognition, and that the mind must turn to itself in its search for knowledge.

These feelings were especially strong among the experimental writers. The imagery of isolation found in *The Waste Land* for example, owes much to Eliot's study of the philosophy of F.H. Bradley, who located reality in individual minds, 'finite centres', and argued that the universe men think they experience in common is only a fiction resulting from their tacit agreement to equate their private experiences with each other. In works written on this understanding, the world of facts and ideas is no more than a patient etherized upon a table; Wyndham Lewis testified that the dominant impression created by the external world was one of deadness; William Carlos Williams called it 'a world of stones'. The modern artist, according to Ortega, tends to meet this situation by endowing his subjective ideas with the validity usually reserved for actuality, so that they replace the objective knowledge he can never attain. Instead of using thoughts to grasp reality, he turns away from it, and treats his thoughts as if they were objective things; he 'realizes the unreal', tries to 'objectify the subjective . . . "worldify" the immanent'. While it is prominent in modern metaphors, says Ortega, 'This inversion of the aesthetic process is not restricted to the use made of metaphors. It obtains in all artistic means and orders, to the point of determining—in the form of a tendency—the physiognomy of all contemporary art'.[19]

Language that is under the influence of this inversion may either generate new modes of signification or undertake to create the form of a literary work out of its own properties, using the non-verbal universe as an element of its design. In an autonomous work, language becomes metalanguage, discourse that takes discourse itself rather than any referent external to language as its subject. Wittgenstein, in one of his discussions of names, offers the incidental insight that the predicating effect of language may be reversed, so that it is exerted upon the proposition itself instead of its reference. 'Red exists' is not a message about the external world, for whatever referential meaning it may have is already inherent in the assumption that the word 'red' has an accepted significance. Lévi-Strauss notes that a similar reversal occurs in the names given to dogs, which often tell nothing about the animals, but can hardly fail to reveal the owner's idea about how dogs should be named. The subjects of self-reflexive statements, therefore, are not external facts, but the terms they employ; the message they convey is primarily a linguistic one, and a text composed of them presents itself primarily as a system of verbal processes and relationships. One finds numerous anticipations among the experimental writers of the structuralist view that literature should be interpreted as a form of behaviour whose patterns are indicative of underlying ideas.

In Muir's 'second language', the language of design, imitation and self-expression are assimilated into formal configurations which project their significance through a kind of silent radiation. It does not compete with the first, or referential language, but rather conforms to such specifications as those inherent in Mallarmé's observation that poetry exists to compensate for the faults of language, and Wallace Stevens's view that 'A poet's words are of things that do not exist without the words.'[20] In an ironic footnote, Lévi-Strauss observes that non-representational art does not produce objects co-eval with reality, as it claims to do, but is simply a demonstration 'in which each artist strives to represent the manner in which he would execute his pictures if by chance he were to paint any'.[21] Many of the experimental artists and writers would have no objection to this way of describing their work; it simply says that the artist takes as his subject the possibilities of his medium.

Among the revolutionary writers both motives served as bases for deviation from conventional language and literary form. The merits of each, their interrelationship, and their compatibility with each other are questions that are still being debated.[22] It is enough to point out that in most of the experimental works— *Ulysses* and the *Cantos* are good examples—both the representational and contextual functions of language, intensively developed and newly explored, work well together, and that this coexistence is not as inconsistent as it might seem. The representation that survives in an autonomous work no longer has the parasitic dependence on non-verbal reality found, for example, in the realistic novel. Instead, it functions contextually, as the language in an autonomous work ordinarily does, participating in a design that is distinctively linguistic or literary. Foucault has observed that even at its most autonomous, language remains inescapably representational to some degree, and that its most abstract forms depend on the function of articulation.[23] The same point has been made about non-verbal art. Wassily Kandinsky, the least representational of painters, who believed that the imitation of externals is, in the final analysis, impossible, and that art can express only inner life, nevertheless felt that abstract forms retain 'the Timbre of the Organic', an echo of the world of nature.[24] In his introduction to *A Window to Criticism*, Murray Krieger has proposed a critical position which sees the poem as both referential and self-constitutive, drawn from the world, yet also bringing to the world something new and substantial which it would not otherwise contain. Among the experimental writers a similar duality is found, as especially severe doctrines of imitation lead to an emphasis on internal formal relations and autonomy.

There is an illuminating parallel to this shift in the development of Ludwig Wittgenstein, the philosopher who thought most tenaciously about linguistic questions during a period that overlapped and followed the experimental one. His *Tractatus Logico-Philosophicus* was published in book form in 1922, the year of *The Waste Land* and *Ulysses*, two works which may be said to refute the theory of language it presented. Wittgenstein attempted to solve the problem of how language can be relevant to reality by a deceptively simple 'picture theory' which says that ordinary language shares with reality in general an attribute called 'logical form', that it contains elementary propositions whose structure in some way duplicates that of the facts they represent, and offers a 'picture' of them. The *Tractatus* is quite unequivocal about the accuracy with which 'pictorial form' represents actuality: 'It is laid against reality like a ruler.'[25] In spite of this terminology, Wittgenstein does not mean that the correspondence is visible, or even easily determinable. As other examples of this sort of relationship, he mentions the phonograph record and the musical score, which do not obviously resemble their originals, but must nevertheless possess features that correspond to them in some way. So pervasive are the requirements of 'logical form' that it is impossible, according to Wittgenstein, for thought to depart from it, or for language to express anything that conflicts with the nature of reality, just as it is impossible to draw a geometrical figure that conflicts with the laws of space.

The 'picture theory' is at once the best possible justification for the imitative use of language and a demonstration of its futility. Its argument that there is an inescapable relation between language and reality, and that they are bound by the same structural principles applies, not to the existing conditions of actuality, but to its nature, to the possibilities inherent in it. A thought or statement must be true, not with respect to what actually is, but with respect to what can be. Clearly, it is perfectly possible to make misstatements about actual conditions; but it is not possible to describe intelligibly conditions that could not exist. 'Logical form' connects language to the structure, not to the facts of reality; it has nothing to do with questions of truth and falsehood. In fact, a statement which is true under all conceivable conditions, says

Wittgenstein, is perfectly meaningless, a mere tautology that communicates nothing. This perception implies that there is an inverse relation between the success of a statement as representation, and its capacity for expressing independent meaning.

Wittgenstein's critic and interpreter, Max Black, has demonstrated that Wittgenstein was mistaken in believing that the logical form of propositions is relevant to reality.[26] According to Black, their relevance is purely internal, for they follow the rules of logic, which are invented rules, like those of chess. Just as a particular game of chess demonstrates nothing about war, which it vaguely resembles, but must illustrate the rules of the game, so propositions demonstrate nothing about reality, to which they may have some connection, but cannot avoid illustrating the standards we find acceptable for making propositions.

Wittgenstein himself ultimately found the 'picture theory' unsatisfactory, and in *Philosophical Investigations* (1945) offered a view of language which corresponds, in many ways, with the one implied by the conception of the autonomous poem. In these later speculations, language is considered a self-contained entity separate from material reality and organized according to rules of its own (here, too, chess is the analogue) with an indefinite potentiality for change and renewal. It is not a single system of rules, but an assemblage of such systems, to which Wittgenstein applies the term 'language games'. Within the context of these systematic, limitless and constantly changing sets of rules, utterances have no fixed meanings. Their meanings depend on tacit assumptions, a view which corresponds to Whorf's observations about primitive languages, and to what Bergson called 'the motor diagram', the basic understanding that must exist between speaker and hearer if discourse is to take place. These 'rules' are often far subtler than those of grammar, and need not be indicated by morphological clues, but may depend entirely on the interplay between a word or expression and its context.

Far from serving as a guide to reality, language is thought of in *Philosophical Investigations* as a force generating complex and ephemeral internal relationships which obscure our understanding of reality unless they are carefully examined. Since it is systematic (though not uniformly so) it cannot be understood piecemeal, a word at a time, as if it were referential; words are understood, not by locating some meaning to which they always refer, but by defining their positions in the systems within which they appear. Further, the rules governing these systems are not imitated from reality (as Wittgenstein thought they were in the *Tractatus*), but are purely linguistic. Experimental writers as early as Hopkins and Gertrude Stein had grasped and applied the idea that the meanings of words depend upon the system that contains them, but they saw no reason why such systems could not be the products of deliberate invention as well as historical development. Perhaps the single most important principle common to *Philosophical Investigations* and the thinking of the revolutionary writers is the insight that language is not controlled by the phenomenal world, but is free to organize experience in collaboration with the imagination. Wittgenstein's dictum, 'to imagine a language is to imagine a form of life' might serve as one of the definitive formulations of the spirit of experimental literature, together with Mallarmé's 'Donner un sens plus pur aux mots de la tribu', Eliot's 'last year's words belong to last year's language', and Pound's 'Make it new'.

Many of the innovations introduced by the revolutionary writers in exploiting the possibilities of the autonomous literary work correspond to the principles Wittgenstein perceived when he recognized that language itself is largely autonomous. In a work of this kind, words regain a certain freedom, drawing away from their dependence on the non-verbal world, and projecting meanings as words, through their own history, and through their relationships with other words. On the aesthetic plane, formal properties shift into the central position traditionally occupied by the content or the subject, and the work becomes a self-contained design rather than a representation. On the linguistic one, reference is absorbed into contextual relation, meaning is transformed into being, the medium of signification into the signified. The language of the poem becomes an opaque, intrusive, informing presence, and the ideas embedded in its structure and vocabulary bear 'messages' antecedent to any its discursive aspect may contain. It is not divorced from content, but is related to it through such intransitive modes as symbolization or embodiment. It is less a medium of cognition than a counterpart of it, a model of an approach to the basic facts of reality. And since it is comparatively free from such traditional commitments as reference, syntax and particular conceptions of style, its formal properties are open to deviations capable of reflecting wholly new premises about the fundamental conditions of existence and perception.

The linguistic innovations of the modern period are so diverse, not only because they arise from both representational and contextual motives, but also because autonomy itself has opened varied possibilities to language. In *Modern Poetry and the Idea of Language* Gerald L. Bruns has shown that the idea of the primacy of language, a conception related to that of the autonomous work, has diverged into two theories of poetic speech; one, which he calls 'hermetic', views the poem as a self-contained aesthetic fact independent of actuality; the other, which is called 'Orphic', sees it as maintaining a semantic function by embodying or defining experience rather than imitating it. In the first, the word exists primarily as a member of a linguistic system, in the second as part of a lexical repertory that creates, instead of merely reflecting, a conception of reality. The first is descended from the formalism of Mallarmé (whose work does not, according to Bruns, correspond to his own definition of the poet as one who gives an Orphic explanation of reality), and appears in the 'depersonalization' of Eliot, the 'stylization' of Worringer, the 'dehumanization' of Ortega y Gasset, the 'defamiliarization' of the Formalists, and the wide range of techniques that separate the word from its familiar applications. The second is exhibited in Gertrude Stein's feeling that there is an intimate link between word and thing, in the tendency toward radical mimesis in the work of Pound and the Imagists, and in Williams's view that words exercise control over reality. These two related, but separable impulses are scattered throughout the work and thinking of the revolutionary writers, often generating innovative uses of language that collaborate with or contradict each other.

Both theories of the dominance of language appear, for example, in Williams's acute speculations on the poetic medium. He believed, as we shall see in a later chapter, that the poem needs a clear initial relationship with actuality as it is revealed to the senses, but that when these perceptions enter the poem, they are taken over by the imagination, which releases them from their referential functions. The world of the poem is not the actual world, but a counterpart, equally authentic, which has the advantage that it can speak directly to intuition and be fully possessed by it in an act of true cognition. Speaking of writing that is both mimetic and imaginative, and corresponds to Bruns's 'Orphic' category, Williams said: 'There is not life in the stuff because it tries to be "like" life. First must come the transposition of the faculties to the only world of reality that men know: the world of the imagination, wholly our own.'[27] In this other, truly accessible life, perceptions acquire meanings and relationships they do not have in the world of matter. Hence, they may be fragmented and rearranged in accordance with the insights of the imagination: ' ... a poem is tough by no quality it borrows from a logical recital of events nor from the events themselves but solely from that attenuated power which draws perhaps many broken things into a dance giving them thus a full being.' Copying reality as it is is pointless, for 'The world of action is a world of stones'. Instead of imitating it, 'the poet in desperation turns at right angles and cuts across current with startling results to his hangdog mood'.[28] But when the poet creates a self-sustaining form, its words are freed from their referential functions to become parts of its design, not simply reflections of something else, acting according to Bruns's 'hermetic' principle. It is clear why Williams should identify this process with the paintings of Cézanne and the Cubists. 'The only realism in art', he says, 'is of the imagination. It is only thus that the work escapes plagiarism after nature and becomes a creation.'[29] Williams specifies, however, that this 'is not an escape from reality, but an opportunity to grasp the essentials of reality instead of merely describing it, so that it has an "Orphic" power as well. His image for this union is again the dance. When the poem is taken as a virtual, rather than a literal representation of reality, and the meanings of its words are taken as virtual meanings, '... the author and reader are liberated to pirouette with the words which have sprung from the old facts of history, reunited in present passion. To understand words as so liberated is to understand poetry. That they move independently when set free is the mark of their value.'[30] And it is also a mark of their return to a 'hermetic' rather than an 'Orphic' function. Williams himself does not make these distinctions, but we can see that his deviations from convention take him in somewhat different directions as he unconsciously crosses back and forth over the line between the two uses of the independent poetic medium Bruns has specified.

New ventures in art are often described as 'experimental', but in the modern period a somewhat more responsible and scientific concept of experiment was adopted by writers as part of a general tendency to exploit scientific methods. Pound's 1913 essay, 'The Serious Artist' illustrates the acceptance of scientific principles among the theoreticians of the time, for it relies heavily on scientific analogues to define ideas about the nature of art and the role of the artist. Pound felt that a kind of testing reminiscent of laboratory work might be of some use to artists, that art could treat feelings with scientific precision, and that 'without constant experiment literature dies'.[31] The image of the catalyst in Eliot's 'Tradition and the Individual Talent' was intended to illustrate the point that poetry can approach the 'condition of science'. And William Carlos Williams, whose medical training gave him some authority over the conjunction of these two fields, declared that 'The imagination uses the phraseology of science.'[32]

In spite of their differences, which are, of course, more obvious today than they were in the revolutionary period, the parallels between literary invention and scientific experiment are genuinely illuminating. Fortunately, Claude Bernard, the early theorist of experimental science, formulated its principles so lucidly and humanely in his work *La Médecine expérimentale* (1865) that they can be transposed into literature, where they assume the aspect of a modern *ars poetica*. The experimental method, as Bernard explains it, introduces deliberate variations into the processes of nature, creating unprecedented situations within which their mechanisms are exposed to analytic scrutiny. An experiment begins with an imaginative perception called a hypothesis, and culminates in a direct experience of new facts, which becomes a basis for valid action. This firsthand encounter with the new is essential, for 'experience', says Bernard, 'is the one source of human knowledge'. He regards as significant the fact that the French *expérience* and *expériment* are cognates, both derived from the Latin *experiri*, to test. (The history of the English word displays this affinity even more clearly, for 'experimental' once meant simply 'based on practical experience'.) In science, as in poetry, the experience of a new condition of things demands new explanations, opens the mind to new possibilities, and, at its most extreme, launches a new state of consciousness. Bernard warns, however, that the conclusions that may be reached cannot be regarded as absolute, and that doubt alone can preserve the independence of mind necessary for escaping the bondage of involuntary assumptions and assimilating the unexpected truths experiment may reveal. This doubt is not nihilistic. Bernard, who was, of course, a firm nineteenth-century determinist, counselled that nature follows regular rules, and that the experimentalist is called upon to believe that 'in nature, what is absurd . . . is not always impossible'.[33]

Bernard's way of approaching nature parallels a number of general values prominent in the poetics of modern literary experiment: the illuminating power of departures from familiar patterns; the importance of concrete or direct experience; the collaboration of the hypothesizing imagination and the world of fact; and the contingency or relativeness of conclusions. Two of these, innovation and scepticism, seem to condemn art and literature to the state of permanent revolution which some critics have predicted for it. This was a possibility which was welcomed by the more extreme modernists, who equated beauty with novelty, or felt that novelty was an indispensable component of beauty.

Various rationalizations of this idea are to be found among the modern poetic theorists. The Russian Formalist critic, Victor

Shklovsky, defined art as the restoration of perceptive capacities that have been lost through habit by means of a process of 'defamiliarization'—the Russian word is *ostraneniye*—which encourages us to attend to objects we no longer notice by making them appear strange. Art should not seek to enclose its elements within coherent frameworks, but should offer them as enigmas, so that they awaken the perceptions and open the mind to experience.[34] Shklovsky's idea that the strange is also the beautiful was anticipated by Baudelaire, has its contemporary counterparts in Surrealist theory, and in the *Verfremdungseffekt* of Bertolt Brecht, and is echoed in Gary Snyder's principle of 'riprap'—the notion that poetry should obstruct and divert familiar currents of thought in the way that rocks in a stream resist the current of water. Owen Barfield, in *Poetic Diction*, a book written in the 1920s, argued that a conscious sense of the difference between the rational and poetic uses of language is indispensable to the poetic experience. The poetic pleasure, he said, consists of a 'felt change of consciousness', which can take place only if the reader is aware of the manner in which poetic language departs from accepted prose norms. This awareness is not available to primitive people, who use expressions which we consider metaphoric as literal statements of fact. Only after the development of rational thought can metaphors appear 'poetic', that is, imaginative alternatives to the prevailing mode of cognition. Hence, for Barfield, a firmly rational orientation and a capacity for assimilating violations of rationality are both necessary for the change of consciousness poetry effects.[35]

The importance of new and unassimilated elements in art is interestingly confirmed from a psychoanalytic point of view by Ernst Kris, who regards art as an interplay between the powerfully charged but inchoate emotions of 'primary process' and the rational control of the ego. According to Kris, the artist moves back and forth between inspiration and discipline, between fantasy, wishfulfillment and other regressive thought-processes on the one hand, and the directing power of the ego which adjusts these energies to external reality on the other. In confronting the work of art, the audience shares the 'shift in psychic levels' embodied in this collaboration.[36] Like Barfield, Kris emphasizes the emergence of irrational feelings within a rational context as a central element in aesthetic experience, and the power of the artist to close up the split created by the different levels of thought. Kris's 'shift in psychic levels' corresponds to Barfield's 'felt change of consciousness'. What is especially interesting in both arguments, for our purposes, is the psychological basis they provide for the motivations expressed in such statements as William Carlos Williams's:

'We must invent, we must create out of the blankness about us, and we must do this by the use of new constructions .... We've got to experiment with technique long before the final summative artist arrives...'[37]

Bernard's reminder that the conclusions drawn from scientific experiment can never be more than provisional usefully calls our attention to an important and little understood aspect of literary experiment. Contemporary audiences, misled by the belligerent manifestoes issued by the revolutionary artists, regarded them as reckless dogmatists; but their works are far less positive. Just as scientific inquiry is concerned with particular facts only for the sake of the general principles they illustrate, experimental art is concerned less with specific insights about life than with the nature of the world (or the medium) they illuminate. Some of the experimental writers did express opinions about social and political matters in their books; but they were far less successful in advancing substantive ideas than in devising methods of decreation that freed the raw materials of thought and experience from the patterns in which they had been fixed. 'Modern art', Octavio Paz has said, 'is modern because it is critical.'[38] And experiment is the most radical of its critical modes. It is not occupied with ideas, but with the fundamental perceptions of time, space, personal identity and existence on which ideas must be based. By experimentally dividing what was unified and combining what had been considered irreconcilable, the revolutionary writers exposed aspects of man's condition that undermined the familiar ideological structures. Their works illustrate Foucault's contention that the movement away from representation disclosed a more fundamental world of chthonic realities. His formulation of the situation sounds exactly like a programme for *The Cantos*, *The Waste Land*, *Paterson* or *Finnegans Wake* :

... European culture is inventing for itself a depth in which what matters is no longer identities, distinctive characters, permanent tables with all their possible paths and routes, but great hidden forces developed on the basis of their primitive and inaccessible nucleus, origin, causality, and history. From now on things will be represented only from the depths of this density withdrawn into itself, perhaps blurred and darkened by its obscurity, but bound tightly to themselves, assembled or divided, inescapably grouped by the vigour that is hidden down below, in those depths. Visible forms, their connections, the blank spaces that isolate them and surround their outlines—all these will now be presented to our gaze only in an already composed state, already articulated in that nether darkness that is fomenting them with time.[39]

The traditional notion of form, as it is reflected, for example, in Yvor Winters's *In Defense of Reason*, is that it is assertion carried on by other means; but the loose, baggy monsters of experimental literature are cast in forms capable of embodying the limitation, paradox and contradiction, as well as the multiplicity of the modern consciousness. Experiment is a prime expression of the 'agonism' which Renato Poggioli has perceived as one of the identifying modes of the avant-garde, a phase of extreme tension generated by radical dissatisfaction, whose energies are directed against the self as well as external conditions. It embodies the urge to proceed indiscriminately beyond whatever is known, with results that may be sacrificial, destructive and tormenting. Thus, the shocking and illuminating effects of experimental works should be understood within the context of the selfnegating irony which Octavio Paz has identified as a central trait of modern art. Dada, it has been said, is without meaning, as Nature is. Joyce, explaining the elaborate construction and symbolism of the 'Oxen of the Sun' episode in a letter to Frank Budgen, ended with the self-mocking 'How's that for high?'[40] Further, as Phillip F. Herring points out in his edition of the *Ulysses* notesheets, it cannot be shown that Joyce followed the complex plan he outlined for the chapter and Herring thinks it possible that he did not take his own explanation seriously. Literary experiment carries the scepticism recommended by Bernard to an extreme by refusing to trust its own methods as instruments of cognition, using them, not to communicate, but to offer direct experiences of the agonizing emotions the artist feels as he strives toward absolute truth. This excessive form of autonomy involves painful, self-defeating and reckless conflicts, but it may also express itself through absurdity, the irresoluble self-contradiction that makes the experimental work indistinguishable from a hoax.

In *The Banquet Years*, Roger Shattuck shows how the principle of autonomy led to a fusion of art and life, so that the two universes of reality and imagination 'engaged in mutual interference'. His phrase recalls the stage device which Bergson calls 'reciprocal interference of series', an event which may belong equally well to two entirely different plots, and is comically misinterpreted by the characters as belonging to one rather than the other. The meeting between two lines of action, and the implication that two irreconcilable situations may actually be mistaken for each other generates comedy; but the effect depends on a clear knowledge of the true and false interpretations.

Most of the experimental works might be called comic in this sense. Like the stage comedies Bergson takes as his examples, they are structures for embodying contradiction, for demonstrating that the elementary constituents of art and life which the pre-modern mind accepted as fixed are equivocal and problematic. They expand the consciousness by asking the reader to bear in mind two or more possibilities that may very well seem inconsistent with each other, each of them implying its own general vision of reality. 'We have to take reality as many,' said F.H. Bradley, 'and to take it as one, and to avoid contradiction.' The experimental works seem first to resolve contradiction by blending disparate things, and then to emphasize their incompatibility, vibrating deceptively between definition and enigma in an effect as crucial to experimental art as the ambiguity of situation is to the comedies in Bergson's analysis.

The most prominent example of this aspect of experiment is no doubt Joyce's *Ulysses*, which is, among other things, both a natural-istic novel and an abstract verbal design. These two modes co-exist in a separation so distinct that, on the one hand A. Walton Litz has complained that the novel's leitmotifs and Homeric correspondences often seem to be superficial ornamentation, while Robert M. Adams, on the other, has said that the details which he discovered to be drawn from actuality fail to coalesce into structural patterns. These comments miss the *tertium quid* of the irony generated by the conjunction of realism and formalism. The enormous virtuosity with which Joyce pursued each of these modes, and which has so often been taken for a commitment to them is not misplaced; it gives a corresponding force to the ulti-mate irony that calls both of them into question.

Thus, the characteristic experimental methods embody the contradictions and ambiguities of the modern ontological comedy. The fragmented syntax of the interior monologue and other paratactic styles, the problematic sequence of the individual poems in Pound's *Mauberley*, the group of quotations at the end of *The Waste Land*, and many similar constructions suggest that reality, too, can be seen as both continuous and discontinuous, homogeneous and chaotic. Parody duplicates a style of conscious-ness, together with an ironic awareness of its limitations or its absurdity. The discordant imagery related to Surrealism gains its effect by asserting an identity between two things in the face of their radical difference from each other. Literary *collage* is on the one hand an image of the sharp disjunction between the real and the imagined; but, on the other, by combining the two in a single text, it shows that they can exchange attributes, and tempts us to believe that art and reality can intersect and co-ordinate with each other. It is perhaps the archetypal experimental technique, for its basic effect is that of an ambivalent magical feat in which the two fundamental possibilities of the work of art, meaning and being, are endlessly transformed into each other.

II TOWARD REALITY

I hold that the ultimate appeal is to naive experience and that is why I lay such stress on the evidence of poetry.

Whitehead, *Science and the Modern World*

In T.S. Eliot's *Murder in the Cathedral*, Thomas Beckett observes that 'Human kind cannot bear very much reality.' The modern age as a whole did not share this tragic consciousness, but was innocent enough to lust for reality, complaining only that the means of reaching it were inadequate and unreliable. The urge to depict life as it is that manifested itself in nineteenth-century realistic fiction lost none of its force in the twentieth century. Even writers strongly interested in the abstract and non-representational, such as T.E. Hulme, Joyce and Eliot, passed through periods of concern with the problems of objective depiction. Wyndham Lewis, who was one of the radical innovators in both art and literature, declared, 'I am for the physical world.'[1] This passion for the authentic is satirized in Louis Aragon's little poem, 'La Réalité', which, after some sketches about banal realities in historical settings, resorts, in a 'Coda', to linguistic invention as a way of conveying the ambiguities of the modern mind's relation to actuality:

> Ité ité la réa
> ité ité la réalité
> La réa la réa
> Té té La réa
> Li
> Té La réalité
> Il y avait une fois LA RÉALITÉ[2]

It is clear that reality exercises an irresistible attraction, that the poet is obsessed with it, and that he refuses to mention any subject of less importance. But since language offers no closer approach to it than the word itself, the problem of celebrating it in a poem without descending to something else is best solved by sticking to this truest of all words, simply re-arranging its syllables. The result suggests that reality discloses itself only in a stammering, incoherent, perhaps ridiculous fashion. This, however, is only a consequence of the modern spiritual condition; in simpler times, says the last line, such as those in the historical sketches that precede this 'Coda', reality was clear and obvious, as it is written here, in capital letters.

Balzac, Flaubert and Zola had pursued reality through a heroic empiricism that confronted life, penetrated its secrets, and laid them out for display on the cold, neutral slab of objective art. But mere imitation, as Wilhelm Worringer observed, though a fundamental human need, is not art.[3] William Carlos Williams insisted that mere representation could not solve the writer's eternal problem of getting ordinary externals to participate in the work of the imagination. 'The senses witnessing what is immediately before them in detail see a finality which they cling to in despair, not knowing which way to turn. Thus the so-called natural or scientific array becomes fixed, the walking devil of modern life.'[4] According to Wyndham Lewis, the clearest impression reality makes is one of deadness. Attacking the version of reality proposed by the neo-idealist philosophy of the early twentieth century, he complained:

Thought or perception has tended to be entirely cut off from this new absolute. We, the forlorn *subjects* of this objective drama, and all our phantasmagoria of quality and sense, are left suspended nowhere, high and dry in a No Man's Land of 'common-sense': or left turning in our circular, many-coloured, primitively furnished, maze. The reality has been pushed infinitely far away, and the severance between it and us is complete.[5]

New conditions of knowledge were disclosing that even the truths of the material world were too elusive for the methods of the realists. Modern representationalists were compelled to think of art, in Cassirer's terms, not as an imitation, but a discovery of reality, for science was transforming familiar things that had once served as models into insoluble riddles by reshaping their elementary constituents. Wyndham Lewis, a leading exponent of the view that modern artists would have to take their subjects and techniques from the technological scene which was to be modern man's environment, perceived that the task of representation was becoming problematic: 'Science began as hard and visible truth: but now that which began as a hard and visible truth has become a fluid and infinitely malleable one. It flows out everywhere. There is the tacit assumption that truth *can* be reached, other than symbolically and indirectly; with the habit of the fluidity comes just as firmly the belief that it cannot.'[6]

Lewis blamed the 'fluidity' to which he objected on figures like Bergson, Whitehead, Alexander, Spengler and others who defined reality as a process, and who, he correctly complained, dominated the early modern period. For, while science was remoulding the nature of the objective world, philosophy and psychology were showing that the traditional perceptive and conceptual capacities were inadequate as ways of grasping it. Such techniques as impressionism, *pointillisme*, and *trompe l'oeil* had already exploited the discrepancies between appearance and reality, calling attention to the limitations of vision as a way of registering reality. If the senses were obviously not a reliable bridge to external actuality, the mind itself was equally suspect. The emerging reality was not only imperceptible, it might also be unthinkable. New varieties of idealism argued that even the most objective view of externals must be tainted by the limitations inherent in the act of observation.

This was the position of F.H. Bradley, whose philosophy was the subject of the dissertation Eliot wrote between 1911 and 1916. Eliot, explaining the implications of Bradley's view, maintains in his opening pages that it is impossible to disengage immediate experience from 'ideal construction', the process of selection and interpretation which the mind imposes on perceptions. Hence, 'although immediate experience is the foundation and the goal of our knowing, yet no experience is only immediate'.[7] Discussing this view in one of his early articles, Eliot inferred further that it meant that an external has two entirely separate aspects: one which is experienced privately and cannot be communicated, and another, composed of those properties communally ascribed to it, 'a common intention of several souls', which forms its public aspects.[8] In this analysis the solid object of common sense has been reduced to a more or less cohesive grouping of shadowy sensory stimuli, some of which are selected, for the sake of convenience, to stand for the object in the marketplace of communication. Bergson, who was unwilling to grant a monopoly over reality to subjective perception, admitted that the latter played an important part in conceptualization, but felt that this fact led away from, rather than toward an accurate notion of actuality. The division of the continuous flow of experience into distinct particulars is, for Bergson, not a movement toward accuracy, but simply a functional necessity of life. Naive perceptions can be grouped together to give a sense of the unity of some object only under the influence of education. 'The distinct outlines which we see in an object, and which give it its individuality, are only the design of a certain kind of *influence* that we might exert . . . it is the plan of our eventual actions that is sent back to our eyes, as though by a mirror, when we see the surfaces and edges of things.'[9] It is the need for coping with the material world, not a desire for true knowledge that leads us to entertain the fiction that individual things exist. 'All division of matter into independent bodies with absolutely determined outlines is an artificial division.'[10]

Alfred North Whitehead, another of Wyndham Lewis's villains of process, was opposed to the subjectivism represented by Bradley and Bergson, because he felt that cognition parallels actuality and shares its structure, so that there is no radical disparity between the perceiver and what is perceived. According to Whitehead, the external object and the perceiving consciousness share a common world as equals.[11] He therefore sees no such difficulty in gaining access to this common world as the subjectivists do. The aspect of his philosophy that probably attracted Lewis's opposition was his view that reality is essentially a complex process which transcends knowledge, and that what we perceive as objects and events acquire their appearance of unity and independence through the act of perception itself.[12] Ernest Fenollosa, whose speculations on the poetic qualities of written Chinese played an important part in Ezra Pound's development, was struck by a similar insight while thinking about a very different matter. Criticizing the justifications usually given for the sentence form, Fenollosa argued that since all processes are interrelated, no sentence could satisfy the grammarian's standard of completeness, 'save one which it would take all time to pronounce'.[13] Whitehead called his view an 'objectivist' one, but the limiting tendencies of the perceiving mind are fully as important in it as the expansive tendencies of external process.

Thus, ordinary assumptions about man's relation to the material universe were undermined, from different directions, by the investigation of material reality and speculation about the nature of conceptualization. Neither the constitution of external reality nor our means of possessing it intellectually were understood. Further, neither of these mysteries could be detached from the other; externals could be known only in a form distorted by the very act of knowing. Similar intimations were circulating in the world of graphic art, where they produced the situation that André Breton called 'the crisis of the object'. Scepticism about the traditional notion that objects are unified and independent is suggested in the paintings of Cézanne, Monet and the Impressionists generally, and becomes perfectly visible in the earliest canvases of the Cubists and Futurists where fragmentation, multiple images, interlocking planes, abstraction and *lignes-forces* imitate, not the appearance of objects but their status in reality as the modern mind was beginning to perceive it.

These changes in the perception of objective reality made changes in the use of language necessary. Even the most conservative view of the relation between language and reality led to this conclusion. Wittgenstein's assurance in the *Tractatus* that language is inescapably representational, that it cannot avoid expressing itself in ways that correspond to objective reality, means that shifts in such elementary assumptions as the existence of distinct objects, the possibility of fixing time, the unity of the self and its separation from the external world, the reliability of sense-perceptions, and the distinction between things and processes must inevitably lead to radical deviations from conventional language.

Representation thus became one of the motivations for such innovations as the elimination or curtailment of syntax, the refinement of vocabulary, new kinds of imagery, and even for the reform of punctuation and unconventional uses of typography. The single aim of rendering reality accurately expressed itself in a variety of ways because there was now considerable variation in the ideas of what reality is and how it is apprehended. It produced radical changes because the new writers felt on the one hand that the language of the past could not meet the new standards of immediacy, accuracy, precision and clarity; and on the other, that it could not capture such properties as ambiguity, complementarity, indeterminacy and psychological depth which a newly-examined universe was beginning to manifest. If the public did not recognize the imitative intention at work in the new art and literature, that was because it had not yet perceived the world it was trying to imitate.

1 GERTRUDE STEIN

Gertrude Stein is a crucial figure in modern experimental literature because she was the first to write English in a style that rejected fundamental ideas about words, sentences and the function of literary language, and to transfer to literature the influence of modern painting. Her work has much in common, in the way of sources and theoretical principles, with the writing of other experimentalists, and she is a convincing example of the fact that, in the cultural environment of the early twentieth century, re-presentationalism, diligently pursued, was bound to produce eccentric results. Although a number of other interests appear in the books she wrote before 1930, Gertrude Stein's main motive during these years was that of conveying her impressions, first of the people in *Three Lives* (1909) and *The Making of Americans* (completed 1911; published 1925) and then of the 'Objects Food Rooms' that are the material of *Tender Buttons* (1914).

There will always be something mysterious about Gertrude Stein's early and effortless assimilation of the modern spirit. 'A new world of the mind had been constituted', said John Malcolm Brinnin. 'Gertrude Stein had come to its threshold, folded her umbrella, and crossed over as easily and naturally as if it led into a house she knew.'[14] Her literary innovations were suggested by two fields that were to become familiar sources of new ideas for experimental writers: psychology and art, especially the work of the Cubist painters. The psychology that influenced her was the experimental variety she had encountered while a student at Radcliffe rather than the Freudian and Jungian principles that were soon to infiltrate literature. At college she had conducted some experiments involving automatic writing, and found that she was less interested in what they demonstrated about the nature of attention or consciousness, than in what they revealed about the people who took part in them as subjects. Yeats and the French Surrealists later made use of automatic writing, in different ways, to gain access to irrational or subconscious ideas; Gertrude Stein, significantly, took no interest in this aspect of it, but regarded it as a representational medium for depicting character. Her own style is not automatic writing, but the result of careful deliberation (without revision or deletion). The prose of *Three Lives* does not imitate the actual speech of the people portrayed, but instead seeks to project the quality of their minds and feelings about life through style. It is matter-of-fact, simple in vocabulary, syntactically naive, flowing, repetitive and monotonous in tone. As Gertrude Stein's method developed, all of these qualities were retained, as essential features of it, under the cover of different rationales.

Her famous prose style, as it appears in *The Making of Americans* and afterward, shares two general principles with Cubism; it rejects the technical conventions intended to gloss over the fictions involved in traditional methods of representation, and it offers itself as an embodiment of the new consciousness. Her writing does not tell a story, and tends to treat objects, events and characters as instances of her real subject, the general nature of reality. That reality, for Gertrude Stein, is strictly limited to immediate apprehension. It is the state of awareness present to the writer at the time he is writing, and no more. It corresponds, in the main, with Bergson's view that ultimate reality must be identified with the sense of constantly changing duration which is the most certain and most subjective of experiences. But it is more clearly linked with the 'stream of consciousness' defined by her favourite professor, William James. This concept first appeared in James's

Principles of Psychology (1890), where it was described as a flow of awareness continuous in itself, but containing separable segments of concentration as it moved from subject to subject. In the process of consciousness, the subjects of thought are distinct from each other, but thoughts themselves are toned by their contexts, and have a multiple identity that language cannot capture. Although we assign the name of the subject to our thought of it, the thought itself contains many elements which must go unnamed. 'Some of them are always things known a moment ago more clearly; others are things to be known more clearly a moment hence.'[15] Gertrude Stein attempted to cope with these difficulties of thought by moving from one moment of clear knowledge to the next, building up a unit out of ideas grasped separately as they come to consciousness, in a process that is quickly seen to correspond with the dissection of objects found in analytic Cubism, and with the modern principle of spatialization.

James felt that thoughts participated in the general medium of consciousness, and were bound together. But these ideas were far less important to Gertrude Stein than his perception that complete awareness is incompatible with the movement of thought. As she reported in 'The Gradual Making of the Making of Americans', she was disturbed by the fact that knowledge is gathered through time, but the feeling of knowing is momentary.[16] One of the primary constituents of her reality is a conception of time as a series of disconnected instants, each creating a new situation and requiring a new effort of the attention, each claiming equal importance with all others. To the strongly intellectual Cubist sensibility, the parts of the model visible at different times have an equal priority and are often depicted as superimposed upon each other, joined, or laid side by side. With Gertrude Stein, a comparable emphasis upon time as a series of equally important points took the form of following the movement of consciousness from moment to moment with the utmost fidelity, as her subjects did during her experiments in automatic writing. She found narrative, with its emphasis on sequence a problem, for in the modern consciousness, 'We really now do not really know that anything is progressively happening ... '[17] Subjective reality consists, not of succession, but of a sense of 'being something existing' whose movement is within itself, like the spinning or twisting of the object in a Cubist painting.

Gertrude Stein's term for the sense of reality that controlled her style was *the continuous present*. As a theoretical concept designed to engineer an encounter with what is indubitably actual, it represented one of the central aims of modernism. 'There is thus significant resemblance', observes Shiv K. Kumar, 'between Joyce's conception of the "continuous present tense", Gertrude Stein's "prolonged present", William James's "specious present", and Bergson's "real, concrete, live present".'[18] The continuous present is incompatible with memories, associations and other secondary actions of the mind, which simply confuse the awareness of what is actually before consciousness. 'For her', says B.L. Reid, 'what is real is what is now real.'[19] The continuous present is a self-sustaining actuality, the only thing of which the writer can be perfectly certain, and every extension of it in the way of re-collection, prior knowledge or causal reasoning creates an illusory impression, as perspective does in a picture. Like the plane of the canvas in a Cubist painting, the continuous present establishes a standard of immediacy which everything in the written work must observe.

In order to grasp the ultimate reality represented by the continu-ous present, perception and creation must be fused into a simul-taneous unity which excludes all consciousness that does not belong to the present. According to Bergson, this immediacy is attainable only in theory, for all perception enlists the aid of memory; we can perceive only in terms learned from the past, and the 'pure present' is nothing more than 'the invisible progress of the past gnawing into the future'.[20] Gertrude Stein thought she could overcome this difficulty, for she said that she possessed a gift she considered the mark of genius, the ability to listen and talk at the same time. What she seems to have had in mind is clarified by Bergson in a passage where he describes how reality would appear if time could be arrested and purely objective perception were possible:

If we were only to divide, ideally, this undivided depth of time, to distinguish in it the necessary multiplicity of moments, in a word to eliminate all memory, we should pass thereby from perception to matter, from the subject to the object. Then matter, becoming more and more homogeneous as our extended sensations spread themselves over a greater number of moments, would tend more and more towards that system of homogeneous vibrations of which realism tells us, although it would never coincide entirely with them. There would be no need to assume, on the one hand, space with unperceived movements, and, on the other, consciousness with unextended sensations. Subject and object would unite in an extended perception . . . [21]

The style of *The Making of Americans* seems to be the result of this pursuit of irreducible granules of reality isolated from the flow of time by the moment-by-moment awareness of the continu-ous present. Each perception appears as if it were totally in-dependent, without qualification or subordination, in the flatness of a world without the convenient fictions of time or space, where all that exists is fully present. Since the perceptions cannot move back and forth in time, or in and out in space, there can be no depth or complexity. These are replaced by an overlapping inherent in incomplete syntax, and by scarcely varied reiterations, each constituting a new approach from a slightly different point of view, and adding a new fragment of information until the subject is exhausted. The style makes a discursive rather than a narrative impression, not moving in any perceptible direction, but spreading out irregularly in a dense, continuous, repetitive medium, as if it were following Bergson's prescription and seeking the homogeneity of matter minutely perceived in an effort to unite with the objects it is representing.

There are many ways of making kinds of men and women. In each way of making kinds of them there is a different system of finding them resembling. Sometime there will be here every way there can be of seeing kinds of men and women. Sometime there will be then a complete history of each one. Every one always is repeating the whole of them and so sometime some one who sees them will have a complete history of every one. Sometime some one will know all the ways there are for people to be resembling, some one sometime then will have a completed history of every one.[22]

Repetition is very much like a force of nature at this stage of Gertrude Stein's work. 'Always from the beginning there was to me all living as repeating.'[23] The principle, if not the practice of her repetitions resembles that in Pound's 'make it new' and Joyce's 'the seim anew', for it is based on the view that renewal involves the use of what is past in a new way. Within the continuous present, she acutely argues, recurrence is not repetition, for each moment is an independent experience, not a remembered one. Remembering, whose purpose is to escape the continuous present, does simply recapitulate something from the past, thus sacrificing immediacy, and confusing two kinds of time, the actual with the recalled. But repetition is recollection purified by the continuous present; it is intended to achieve, not duplication, but what she called 'insistence'. If the record of ongoing consciousness calls for reiteration, it remains moving and alive, not a mere return to the past.

Tender Buttons was a more determined effort to achieve immediacy than had been possible in the character sketches of *The Making of Americans*, and a more direct use of Cubist principles. In it, Gertrude Stein imitates the Cubists by taking as her models familiar things that were at hand—'Objects Food Rooms'—as if to imply that her subjects were important only as themes for the activity of the expressive medium. By writing about inert material things rather than people, she could eliminate such threats to immediate perception as emotions, associations and recollections. She compared her work to that of the still-life painter; apparently she wrote while she was actually in the presence of her subjects in order to transcribe her experience directly, 'There they were and I was noticing.'

The prose of *Tender Buttons* is not intended to describe objects, or even to convey the feeling the observer experiences in their presence, but to find 'the words that made whatever I looked at look like itself'.[24] In an interview, Gertrude Stein explained that the work required severe concentration as she studied some object and tried 'to get the picture of it clear and separate in mind and create a word relationship between the word and the things seen'.[25] The method appears to be an extreme instance of Ortega y Gasset's principle of dehumanization, for it does not seem to matter whether the reader can enter into the relationship; all that counts, apparently, is that the text be an honest report of the author's encounter with the object. Some passages are reasonably representational, even banal, but many others have no perceptible connection with the subjects announced in the captions with which parts of the text are provided. Even more surprising, the language often descends to word-play, abandoning representation for the seductions of puns, ambiguities, non-sequiturs and syntactic or rhythmic patterns. One of the four renderings of 'Chicken', for example, reads: 'Alas, a dirty word, alas a dirty bird alas a dirty third, alas a dirty bird', a little design having less to do with meaning than with the accidents of language. There are also tricks like 'coach in china', 'blew west, carpet', and 'a rested development', and such patterned formations as 'One taste one tack, one taste one bottle, one taste one fish, one taste one barometer.'

Some critics feel that the prose of *Tender Buttons* is not as unstructured as it pretends to be, and find intricate relationships in its language. A favourite subject of analysis is the first section, 'A Carafe, that is a Blind Glass', which reads:

A kind in glass and a cousin, a spectacle and nothing strange a single hurt color and an arrangement in a system to pointing. All this and not ordinary, not unordered in not resembling. The difference is spreading.[26]

Michael Hoffman, points out the relationships among kind-blind, kind-cousin, spectacle-glass, but believes that they are inadvertent, and simply demonstrate the suggestiveness of words. Richard Bridgman translates the obscurity of the passage into a reasonable, but banal form of sense, declaring that the 'hurt' colour is the gray-green or purple of a bruise, and that the carafe is a 'spectacle' because it is something to look at. According to Allegra Stewart, the prose of *Tender Buttons* is intended to revive the reader's consciousness of the root meanings of words; the carafe is called 'a kind in glass and a cousin' because 'glass' and 'carafe' are both derived from the Indo-European root, *Ghar*. Further, 'glass' and 'spectacle' allude to sight, and the 'glass' is 'blind' because it is not the agency of sight itself, but only an aid to the eye.[27] Evaluations of this kind make it clear that *Tender Buttons* transcends the representational purposes on which it was based, and, like other experimental works, turns to the innate properties of language.

Gertrude Stein had replaced nouns with present participles whenever possible, because the latter were more expressive of the the continuous present. In the prose of *Tender Buttons*, nouns reappear, and the little book contains a wide variety of them. But the effects of the continuous present are apparent in many other special features; adjectives or verbal phrases often replace nouns, qualities are described as conditions, and verbs are replaced by present participles, or omitted altogether in favour of phrases reflecting a situation. These peculiarities reflect a Cubist sense that the object being described is only a cross-section of the 'process' with which Whitehead identified reality, and corresponds to Wittgenstein's conception that a thing is defined by the position it occupies in a 'Sachverhalt'—a state of affairs. Syntax is, in general, strictly observed, but without much subordination, and the logic of the grammar only serves to emphasize the absurd effects of the words themselves: 'A tiny seat that means meadows and a lapse of cuddles with cheese and nearly bats, all this went messed.' Abstract and concrete aspects of things are often confused, as if to bring together those aspects of the object that are sensory, and those accessible only to thought. 'A Box', for example, leads her to reflect that 'Out of kindness comes redness and out of rudeness comes rapid same question, out of an eye comes research, out of selection comes painful cattle.'[28] Incompatible or unrelated ideas and constructions are run together, achieving an effect of interruption or overlapping that prevents a sense of completion.

Gertrude Stein said that in *Tender Buttons* she was seeking language that was 'not the name of the thing but was in a way that actual thing', and that her avoidance of ordinary referential language was motivated by the intention to 'recreate the thing'. This effort at radical mimesis, at escaping from the mental world of the printed page into the physical one, at uniting mind and matter, is characteristic of the modern attempt to link art and life at some fundamental level. But it ignores the fact that language follows principles of selection and abstraction peculiar to itself, so that, even if it is real and does control our apprehension of the material world, it has an independent kind of reality. The limitation that Northrop Frye senses in purely intellectual rhetoric is also found in language in general; 'nothing built out of words can transcend the nature and conditions of words'.[29] Language—and, in fact, any other thing with symbolic potential—has the choice, with relation to a particular identity, of either meaning it or being it; it cannot do both. Hence, Gertrude Stein's notion that a word or group of words can, as far as consciousness is concerned, be 'that actual thing' is only her original version of the naive fallacy that believes words to be innately connected with their referents rather than arbitrary signs.

Gertrude Stein's misconstruction of the role of art in grasping reality seems related to a misconstruction of the nature of immediate perception. She regarded the continuous present, as we have seen, as a way of gaining access to reality by excluding all but immediate awareness. But Bergson denied that such a state of awareness was attainable.

Pure perception . . . however rapid we suppose it to be, occupies a certain depth of duration, so that our successive perceptions are never the real moments of things . . . but are moments of our consciousness. Theoretically, we said, the part played by consciousness in external perception would be to join together, by the continuous thread of memory, instantaneous visions of the real. But, in fact, there is for us nothing that is instantaneous. In all that goes by that name there is already some work of our memory, and consequently of our consciousness, which prolongs into each other, so as to grasp them in one relatively simple intuition, an endless number of moments of an endlessly divisible time. . . . Our perception presents us with a series of pictorial, but discontinuous, views of the universe . . . [30]

The writer is penned up in the mimetic character of his medium because perception itself is cut off from absolute contact with external actuality by such 'pictorial' qualities as memory, discrimination and sensory apprehension. Just as there is, in Bergson's analysis, a disparity between the neutrality of matter and the richly toned subjectivity of perception, there must be a radical difference between the object and the language that depicts it. One cannot depict a thing, only one's knowledge of it. Gertrude Stein's attempt to contradict Bergson's denial of the practical possibility of pure perception involves a confusion of consciousness with actuality, and of language with consciousness. In trying to escape knowledge and achieve contact with reality by slipping through the narrow aperture of the continuous present, she was sacrificing the instrumentalities that make perception possible. The thinning of perception that occurs when she tries to escape the conditions necessary to it is, of course, reflected in the enfeeblement of language resources apparent in her writing.

Writers have traditionally complained that language is inadequate for expressive purposes, and Gertrude Stein, instead of showing how this deficiency might be overcome, seems instead to confirm it. Her limited, narrow, repetitive idiom has an unmistakable resemblance to the dialogues in the work of Beckett, Ionesco and Pinter, which express the dwarfed consciousness of oppressed, isolated and impoverished minds. Gertrude Stein's prose anticipates the failure of the search for the self. As a record of that part of reality which the self grasps most firmly—immediate consciousness—it seems to succeed only in illustrating F.H. Bradley's gloomy view that the self is a seriously limited 'finite centre'. It shows that what can be possessed with absolute immediacy is hardly worth possessing, and that the mind must extend and multiply itself through its imaginative powers if it is to find a vision of life worth living. By ruling out recollection, reference, the expression of emotion, and, in fact, nearly all the functions language ordinarily performs, her work quarrels with the limits and potentialities of language instead of enlarging them. Her example is useful, however, because it shows that writers, unlike painters, cannot experiment without paying a certain tribute to the inherent requirements of their medium, which is primarily a medium that conveys meaning.

2 HULME AND POUND

Although it was soon to be competing with other purposes, the basic interest of the writers who met with T.E. Hulme and Pound to discuss poetry in various London restaurants between 1909 and 1914 appears to have been that of enabling poetry to achieve genuine contact with reality. Hulme advocated accurate, clear, dispassionate representation, and Pound made the first rule of Imagism 'Direct treatment of the "thing" ....' Two quite different motivations supported the urge for the faithful representation of external reality among modern writers. One was the familiar moral aspiration to tell truth, a deceptively simple aim which diverged under careful analysis, into two principles nearly opposed to the original one: Impressionism, and the aim of depicting, not what is, but what should be. Originally, it seemed possible to pursue both of these aims at once. Pound's declaration, in an early letter, that he intended 'To paint the thing as I see it' expresses faith in the process of perception.[31] But he could also say that the governing and general health of the state depend upon the clarification of the meaning of words, which gives the truth-telling faculty more than imitative power.

The other motive was aesthetic. Hulme's feeling that accuracy and directness generate pleasure, and Pound's principle that poetry ought to consist of concrete particulars because they evoke full response are parts of a range of opinion that saw an artistic, as well as a moral value in accurate representation. As we have seen, representation undertaken on aesthetic or moral grounds tends to shift into idealization, and even formalism, and to lose its imitative urgency. But whatever the principles of support for the imitative principle might be, there was general agreement that if it was to be followed in the new time that was at hand, innovation and experimentation in language would be required.

The London group knew nothing of Gertrude Stein, but they shared her view that language ought to be brought into more immediate relationship with actuality. Hulme, like her, was influenced by Bergson, having met him as early as 1907, and became an active interpreter of his ideas, though they did not correspond very well with his own. Hulme was a theorist of absolutist leanings whose emphasis on immediacy was only a part of a larger theory of art which led in an entirely different direction. He employed Wilhelm Worringer's principle that abstract, geometric art embodies a desire for spiritual stability to predict that an artistic period opposed to representation, and expressing itself through abstraction, was approaching. His interest in art of this kind led him to realize that innovation would be necessary if humanistic representationalism were to be superseded by an art of permanence and stability. For the next step in his rationale, Hulme turned to Bergson's ideas. He found an explanation for the limited, banal quality of ordinary perception and expression in Bergson's insight that the intellect, as a pragmatic function, distorts reality by packaging cognition in ways that make it a useful basis for action. In order to escape these modes of perception, the artist must 'disentangle' his perceptive capabilities from them, and confront reality in a state of emancipation from prior controls, a programme corresponding with Shklovsky's principle of defamiliarization.

It is at this point that Hulme's philosophy supports representation. He thinks of the artist as one who is free to contemplate things as they are, and to discover alternate ways of expressing common perceptions which have been conventionalized by the intellect and the functional purpose it serves. Hulme is interested in directness, accuracy, freshness, individualization and the other values of representation, and in the new modes of expression they will require. When we follow him further, we will encounter questions of aesthetic effect and the rendering of feelings, which are different parts of our subject. But his definition of art emphasizes the values associated with representation, and declares that departures from accepted language are essential to them, while implying that they are, in the final analysis, really aesthetic values.

You could define art, then, as a passionate desire for accuracy, and the essentially aesthetic emotion as the excitement which is generated by direct communication. Ordinary language communicates nothing of the individuality and freshness of things. As far as that quality goes we live separated from each other. . . . The particular kind of art we are concerned with here, at any rate, can be defined as an attempt to convey over something which ordinary language and ordinary expression lets slip through.[32]

But this persuasive statement in favour of experimentation is accompanied by practical suggestions of a disappointingly moderate kind. The writer, concludes Hulme, is 'compelled to invent new metaphors and new epithets', but not for genuinely representational purposes, for intuitive reality, as Bergson said, is not accessible in any sustained way, and Hulme offers no hope that it can be systematically decanted into language. Imitation generates aesthetic pleasure by moving closer to reality than ordinary language does, without necessarily gaining contact with it. It is the transcendence of present limits that counts. Only because language is usually impersonal and unpredictable is the effect of closer communion with actuality so satisfying, 'the one essentially aesthetic emotion it produces on us'.[33] Hulme's advocacy of precision reaches toward reality, then, primarily for the sake of resisting conventionalized expression. 'The idea is nothing', he says; 'it is the holding on to the idea, through the absolutely transforming influence of putting it into definiteness. The holding on through waves.'[34] Hulme's image vividly conveys the effort the writer must make to resist the corrupting effects with which language threatens his subject. This effort interested him because it was a way of 'holding on' against the shapeless flux of Bergsonian duration, of lodging a sharp wedge in the side of formlessness, and gaining a base for the abstract, geometrical art, not at all representational, which he really favoured.

While Hulme was resigned to the belief that language could never actually participate in reality, however closely it might approach it, so that the conveyer and the thing conveyed remained separate elements, Pound's Imagist poetic confidently eliminates this distance and asserts that language can possess, and import into the poem, the quality of reality itself. His ideal is that of a language which emulates reality both by dwelling on the concrete and particular, and by prompting the consciousness to relate it to universals, generalizing it into significance. Herbert N. Schneidau, who has persuasively demonstrated that Pound's passion for particulars was an aspect of his quest for universal meanings, nevertheless maintains that, as the Imagist and post-Imagist poems suggest, he regarded particulars as the source of universals, and pursued his quest through 'objective predication'.[35] In calling for 'Objectivity and again objectivity', saying that 'Language is made out of concrete things', arguing that the health of the state depends on 'the application of word to thing', and praising Hardy's poetry, as he did long after the Imagist period, because it was 'clamped to reality', Pound was motivated by the conviction that particulars alone can animate the potential relationships among universals. 'All knowledge', he said, 'is built up from a rain of factual atoms . . . '[36] He praised *Dubliners* and *A Portrait of the Artist as a Young Man* because they refined the factuality he admired in the prose of certain nineteenth-century French novelists into a medium of 'metallic exactitude'. Arguing that the work of Joyce and Eliot, though concerned with local scenes, nevertheless formulated general truths about the modern world, he said: 'Art does not avoid universals, it strikes at them all the harder in that it strikes through particulars.'[37] Confucius had counselled that knowledge must be based on 'concrete manifestations'; the reason, Pound explains, is that only primary experiences can fully engage the perceptions and generate real conviction.

From the Platonic point of view, the identification of particular with universal which Pound sought to bring about is contradictory, for particulars can only be transitory, while universals must have permanence, but the reconciliation of the two is a persistent theme of philosophy, religion and poetic theory. The name of Hegel's version of this reconciliation, 'concret Allgemeine' turns up in Canto VIII, where it shares a line with the name of a god, 'Poseidon'; Hegel's concrete possesses universality by virtue of its participation in the absolute, and the ultimate concrete universal is, of course, the absolute itself. These metaphysical associations are perfectly consistent with Pound's notion of reality as a mingling of the temporal and the eternal, the immediate and the ineffable. His own contribution to the traditional effort to unify particular and universal was his theory of the Image, a particular which radiates universal import through its association with emotions having a permanent status in human experience. Discussion of

Pound's theory must be deferred until a later chapter, but it is relevant to observe here that the Image calls for a vocabulary that is, in the first instance, referential, depending for its effect upon existential reality.

Donald Davie has observed that while Eliot and the Symbolists wrapped their perceptions in the envelope of their feelings, Pound adopted something resembling scientific objectivity by entering into the nature of externals in 'an attitude of reverent vigilance before the natural world'.[38]

> Light as the shadow of the fish
> That falls through the pale green water[39]

imprints itself upon the mind as a devoted tribute to the power of Confucius's 'concrete manifestations', displayed in one of its most fugitive instances, even if it involves no universals. For Pound felt that by immersing himself in the physical world, the poet acquires both knowledge and an asset opposed to it, a valuable innocence and neutrality. In his 1912 essay, 'The Wisdom of Poetry', he described the work of art and experience objectively perceived as parallel forces liberating the mind from preconceptions:

The function of an art is to free the intellect from the tyranny of the affects, or . . . to strengthen the perceptive faculties and free them from encumbrance, such encumbrances, for instance, as set moods, set ideas, conventions; from the results of experience which is common but unnecessary, experience induced by the stupidity of the experiencer and not by inevitable laws of nature.[40]

The statement discloses an unexpected subversive dimension in the first principle of Imagism: 'Direct treatment of the "thing", whether objective or subjective', and echoes Hulme's view that one of the purposes of accurate writing, 'holding on through waves' is the negative one of resisting subjective interferences. Pound praised Guido Cavalcanti's canzone, 'Donna mi prega', because it was 'dangerous' to the thirteenth-century intellectual system, exhibiting an independence of mind that relied upon experience rather than authority. The spirit of the poem, he said, is 'for experiment . . . against the tyranny of the syllogism', and it employs exact metaphors that contrast with ornamental Petrarchan imagery. Pound reported that Hulme registered astonishment on being told that Cavalcanti's language corresponded to particular sensations; but Hulme's surprise may have been due to his discovery that Cavalcanti had anticipated his own principle that the language of poetry ought to embody individual feelings. Pound's belief in the function of particulars in poetry was aptly expressed by a Russian who wrote to him about his poems, 'I see, you wish to give people new eyes, not to make them see some new particular thing.'[41]

The manuscript of Ernest Fenollosa which came into Pound's hands in 1913, and which he published in 1918 as *The Chinese Written Character as a Medium for Poetry* had much to do with his aim of bringing language into close relation with reality. Fenollosa described the ideograms of Chinese writing as 'a vivid shorthand picture of the operations of nature', [42] which imitate what they mean, preserving their links with the physical world even after their meanings have been rendered abstract or metaphoric. The ideogram must have presented itself to Pound as an undeniable instance of the 'application of word to thing', or rather, to the actions and processes of which, Fenollosa reminds us, things are mere phases. Fenollosa contended that Chinese words are basically verbal, embodying the interactions of reality, instead of freezing them, as the nominal words of phonetic languages do. He admits that Chinese speakers are not usually conscious of these elements, for the representational quality of the ideograms has become thoroughly conventionalized, and often lost altogether, and even those radicals which do have pictographic values are more often used for phonetic than for pictorial functions. But Fenollosa refuses to believe that the language as a whole was not originally pictographic, and in the simple examples that he chooses to illustrate his ideas, the naive Western eye can, if it chooses, find a pictorial immediacy that alphabetic writing lacks.

The ideogram had the advantage, said Pound, of a concreteness that guards against nonsense. Wittgenstein considered the 'hieroglyphic' as an analogue of his statement that 'A Proposition is a picture of reality', just as Fenollosa thought the ideogram 'close to nature', and Pound found in Chinese the integrity that Wittgenstein attributed to language generally—an inability to depart from reality without departing from the form of language itself. The subject is presented, not by direct imitation, but by capturing its essential features, as a recording or a musical score does, in accordance with consistent laws of transformation. Pound was particularly struck by Fenollosa's point that the Chinese convention does not leave particulars behind when it rises to non-concrete levels of communication, for it expresses abstractions by grouping signs into compounds, so that, for example, the character for clarity, 明月 (ming[2]), one of Pound's favourites, combines the radicals meaning the sun and the moon. In this way, particulars themselves articulate a context within which they acquire a general meaning. Pound showed how this method might be adapted to poetry, in accordance with Fenollosa's suggestions, by explaining the significance, within their cultural context, of the details in one of the Chinese poems he translated. The translation is probably based on a literal paraphrase found in the Fenollosa notebooks, which usually provided an English equivalent for each ideogram. Pound's task was to fit the units together in a way that would define the situation.

The Jewel Stairs' Grievance

The jewelled steps are already quite white with dew,
It is so late that the dew soaks my gauze stockings,
And I let down the crystal curtain
And watch the moon through the clear autumn

by Rihaku (p. 142)

Pound's note explains that the reader would know from its details that the poem tells how a court lady in a palace who arrived early waits in vain for a lover whose absence cannot be excused by the weather. The particulars project a general situation and beyond it, an even more general emotional of sorrow and disappointment. The theme is traditional in Chinese poetry, embodying one of the permanent states of emotion toward which Pound thought poetry should be directed, but the particularity of the details is not obscured by their general significance. What the detail is and what it suggests seem to form a unity, as Pound believed they did in the ideogram itself.

3 WILLIAMS AND CUMMINGS

In the poetry of William Carlos Williams, language and reality come together in a kind of inevitable miracle. This rightness is achieved by a series of steps that begins with a revolt against convention, in which, as Williams says, 'every common thing has been nailed down, stripped of freedom of action and taken away from use'.[43] If he is to escape this imprisonment, the poet must open himself to the direct experience of an unlabelled world, a world without signifiers, in order to regain a sense of 'the quality of independent existence, of reality which we feel in ourselves'. When he turns to writing, this sense serves as a touchstone for the authenticity of his words, filtering out those that are borrowed from convention, and admitting only those that share the 'independent existence' the other realities of the universe enjoy. Williams' image for this mutually energizing relationship is especially successful: 'The word is not liberated, therefore able to communicate release from the fixities which destroy it until it is accurately tuned to the fact which giving it reality, by its own reality establishes its own freedom from the necessity of a word, thus freeing it and dynamizing it at the same time.'[44] The word does not simply repeat the fact, it is 'tuned' to it, to acquire the quality which the imagination recognizes as authentic self-existence. That this is not an actual transfer, but something effected by the mind of the poet is made clear in an earlier passage from a different book, where Williams, has apparently worked out some of the other implications of this image: '. . . one does not attempt by the ingenuity of the joiner to blend the tones of the oboe with the violin . . . It is only the music of the instruments which is joined and that not by the woodworker but by the composer, by virtue of the imagination.'[45] The word's self-sufficiency is measured against that of the fact, just as the violin's A is measured against the oboe's and once their resemblance has been established, they are free of each other. Williams' view is the reverse of Bergson's. For Bergson, the object is a fiction abstracted from the torrent of intuitions; it is called into being by the word. But for Williams, the independence of the physical world is a support necessary to the authenticity of language.

Once its authenticity has been established in this way, the word is free to take part in a poem whose design has little to do with fact, just as a musical note whose pitch has been authenticated is free to take part in forming a melody. Hence, accurate representation paradoxically frees the word from the 'fixity' of mere representation. It is not stripped of its meaning, but when it participates in a poem, it is 'liberated from the usual quality of that meaning by transposition into another medium, the imagination'.[46] The object it represents is a prior necessity, for its serves as a kind of whetstone for sharpening the edges of meaning that enable the word to do its work. In describing the effect of Marianne Moore's poetry, Williams mentions a concept equally relevant to his own use of language, the 'clean' word, 'treated with acid to remove the smudges, washed, dried and placed right side up on a clean surface'. The bare, energetic syntax of Williams' poems helps to purify his words in this way, as J. Hillis Miller has shown, but another cleansing agent is the referent, which monopolizes the attention as a concrete object, dispelling secondary associations, so that 'Now one may say that this is a word. Now it may be used, and how?'[47] The poem which follows Williams's explanation of how words are 'tuned' by reality so that they are free to take part in the music of poetry is perhaps an example of what he means:

Black eyed susan
rich orange
round the purple core
the white daisy
is not
enough

Crowds are white
as farmers
who live poorly

But you
are rich
in savagery—

Arab
Indian
dark woman[48]

The words take part in designs developed within the poem which
have little to do with their meaning, yet the meaning is an essential
anchorage for each word. In the balance of colours and qualities
connected with the two flowers, the 'white' of the daisy and the
'white' of the poor farmers are two variants on a theme, as are the
'purple' of the black-eyed susan and the 'dark' of the Eastern
woman. On the other hand 'rich' and 'poor' have original shades
of meaning, but their referents within the poem do not shift.
('Poor' occurs only once, in any case.) Williams' exceptionally
acute investigations into the poetic use of words transform mere
reference into poetic function. Concrete, dispassionate observation
and reportage are, of course, essential; subjective feeling would
interfere with the thrusting, almost tactile effect of the reference.
The isolation of words and phrases in short lines is another aspect
of this. Nothing could be simpler than 'dark woman', yet placed
as it is, it provides a final surface for catching the meanings connected with the flower. The inconsistent modifiers, 'Arab/Indian'
increase the richness of the image and also diffuse the referential
effect of 'dark woman'.

There is a stage of consciousness for Williams which is silently
in touch with concrete reality:

The leaves embrace
in the trees

it is a wordless
world

without personality[49]

But it is clear that 'direct treatment' can be only relative, that physical actuality must be brought into the domain of the imagination if it is to be penetrated with feeling and significance. It is possible to gain access to authentic reality only by turning from the limitations of conventional reference to the particulars of actuality as they enter consciousness. This authenticity, however, is localized in the imagination, not in external reality.

The participation of the imagination in creating the effect, if not the fact of immediacy is especially clear in the poetry of E.E. Cummings. As an anarchic individualist, Cummings was undisturbed by the possible discrepancy between appearance and reality, and cared nothing for the fact that objects might illustrate essential truths of perception. For him, appearance was reality, and perception was truth. His immediacy had nothing to do with Pound's or Eliot's attempt to escape the interference of private emotion, or the disciplined attunement to externals of Williams. On the contrary, feelings and impressions are his real subjects; his ingenious innovations are directed, not toward a fuller perception of the object, but toward a more accurate egocentric transcription of his reaction to it. Thus, Cummings might be said to evade the trap inherent in objective representation by taking a different road entirely. But even if the new resources he devised are meant to express his impression of the object, not to engage in a futile struggle with objectivity, they do achieve a remarkable representational accuracy and vividness, and shake off the numbing effects of ordinary diction.

Like Gertrude Stein, Cummings wrote from present consciousness; each poem is the re-enactment, as if on tape or film, of some vivid moment cut free from past or future. He has a number of resources for freezing the moment, compressing a number of impressions into a single simultaneous glance in order to achieve the characteristic modern effect of spatialization. This is sometimes done by dividing phrases or individual words, and putting them in different parts of the poem, separated by other material. Unlike Gertrude Stein, however, Cummings did not limit himself to the actual present, or make himself the passive recorder of the moment of perception. His poems are obviously shaped and contrived, the products of an active ingenuity working toward a number of goals, one of which is the expression of immediate reactions. He works strenuously to augment the articulating, representational powers of language, increasing its verbal potential, and often adding a pictorial one, succeeding better than Gertrude Stein did in her aim of finding 'the words that made whatever I looked at look like itself'.

In the work of Cummings, as in that of Gertrude Stein and W.C. Williams the sense of sheer existence is a vitalizing force, never taken for granted, and constantly celebrated. Cummings is resourceful in devising word-combinations which are illogical and non-representational in the first instance, but nevertheless succeed in registering some neglected aspect of an experience, and bringing it sharply before the reader. In his first book of verse the famous 'Chansons Innocentes' speak of the world of childhood as 'mud-/luscious' and 'puddle-wonderful'; in an entirely different key, Cummings sees one of his favourite subjects, a whore, within a setting of 'moaned space'.[50] When he goes to help a woman lying in the street, he lifts her 'toylike/head'; it is one of the wonders of men in general that they have 'little derricks of gesture'. These ventures are not always successful; some strike us as shots in the dark that have gone astray, such as 'elaborate fingers' and 'women-coloured twilight' which certainly miss immediacy, whatever else they may accomplish. But it is notable that Cummings is even less successful in matching adjectives and nouns within conventional limits; a series of efforts with hands will illustrate. A drunken woman has 'one funny hand'; a gross man has 'forlorn piggish hands'; but a plain, stolid woman has 'mindless hands', the unconventional combination that is genuinely immediate.

Many of Cummings's poems of the 1920s are portraits or descriptions, done without much typographical innovation. These often have an almost baroque vividness and splendour (especially when the subject is a whore), but they do not convey a sense of immediate perception of the object. For example, in such a description as:

> the poem her belly marched through me as
> one army. From her nostrils to her feet
>
> she smelled of silence. The inspired cleat
>
> of her glad leg pulled into a sole mass
> my separate lusts
>
>   her hair was like a gas
> evil to feel.
>
>   (p. 107)

it is obvious that even the statements that are objective in form are no more than reports of feeling. There is no attempt to clear the words of connotation, to win their independence from emotion and base them firmly on referential meaning, as in the poetry of Williams. On the contrary, Cummings intends to compress as much feeling as possible into a series of dynamic, explosive points.

His notorious typographical innovations have a number of functions, and one of them is certainly that of imitating the subject through direct visual presentation. While his efforts in this direction differ somewhat from those of George Herbert and Apollinaire, since Cummings does not usually shape his lines to take the form of objects, they do often resemble the methods of Mallarmé, especially in *Un Coup de dés*, in employing the shapes of letters, punctuation marks and different typefaces to gain visual, rather than semantic effects. The practice is an attempt to 'transcend the nature and conditions of words' without quite abandoning words. It does not offer serious efforts at representation, but it does give the poem physical presence, and the combination of a discursive mode in its words with an existential one in its appearance is a serious challenge to our sense of how meaning operates. There is a striking example in a poem about melting snow, whose first word, 'SNO   ', suggests that the final W is still covered by unmelted snow. The device gives the white of the page where the letter belongs a striking physical immediacy. There is an analogous effect in the 'Ithaca' chapter of *Ulysses*, where the question 'Where?' that ends the chapter, an inquiry about Bloom, is answered by a black spot on the page. Joyce seems to say that his character exists specifically in the ink and paper of his book, and to deny that he has existence outside it. These interferences with the conventional action of language achieve a powerful representational effect, paradoxically carrying the comparatively pale words along with them. A Cummings poem describing a woman sitting on a café *terrasse* with morning sunlight shining through the trees has the line: 'ofpieces ofof sunligh tof fa l l in gof throughof treesOf'. 'Of' with its 'o' has been repeated to suggest the circles of sunlight coming through the leaves (one, we note, larger than the others), and the two 'l's of 'falling' have been isolated to suggest vertical beams of light. Something certainly seems to have been gained by sacrificing coherence to vividness. In a poem on the theme of separation, the subject is symbolically represented by a fly walking on a mirror, an image visually reinforced by a typographical device:

          . . . . a fly
          &

          her his Its image
          strutting (very
          jerkily) not toucH-

          ing because separated by an impregnable

                                                      (p. 241)

where the capitalized H pictures the fly with its reflection, the horizontal bar being the surface of the mirror.

Devices of this kind, which became more numerous and more ingenious in Cummings's poetry after 1930, certainly entail immediacy, creating direct visual impressions which parallel and support the fictional directness of the relation between the reader and the object being observed, such as the snow, the spots of sunlight and the fly. But what the reader is really in contact with is the poem itself, and with its subject only as it is represented through the poet's perceptions and the expanded resources of language. Hence, the innovations of the Cummings poem have something of the effect of the flattening of perspective in the Cubist painting; they draw attention to the worked surface of the poem, and effect an immediate encounter with the subject to the extent that it coincides with that surface. We have immediate experiences of the snow's capacity for blotting things out, of the round spots of sunlight, of the symmetry of the reflected fly; but these, it will be noticed, are only concrete clues to abstract meanings. They actually convey less of a sense of the object itself than the simple, direct, non-experimental line from the poem about the café: 'chairs wait under trees'.

4 SCIENCE AND FUTURISM

No writer of the early twentieth century who had the ambition of conveying a genuine perception of reality could entirely ignore the influence of science. Its discoveries cut the support from established ideas, and liberated thought by outstripping every other field in the imaginative, yet authoritative interpretation of the world. One consequence of this was a renewal of the traditional Romantic fear that science might be a threat to poetry. In the article which ultimately was extended into *Science and Poetry*, I.A. Richards declared that 'In its use of words poetry is just the reverse of science', a statement which he later modified, but which strikes the keynote of his early efforts to adjudicate what he took to be the rivalry between scientific and poetic cognition.[51]

Nevertheless, in a time that witnessed the disruption of familiar systems of thought through radically objective perception, experimentalists intolerant of every other form of control regarded science as a valuable source of standards and principles. Pound, for example, in his essay of 1913, 'The Serious Artist', stated that 'The arts, literature, poesy, are a science, just as chemistry is a science', and developed this parallel with a stream of science-inspired terms and analogues.[52] It was his idea that accuracy in reporting its findings ought to be the standard of art, as it was of

science, and that effectiveness in poetry could be defined as
efficiency of expression. Pound praised Joyce's early fiction because it depicted spiritual life with technological precision. 'He
deals with subjective things', he said in describing *Dubliners*, 'but
he presents them with such clarity of outline that he might be
dealing with locomotives or with builders' specifications.'[53] He
thought that the artist ought to approach his problems in the spirit
of a 'technician' bent on 'Honest Registration,' and to engage in the
'patient experiment' of testing various media and formulating
conclusions. Such experimentation might turn out to be poetry,
and in any case its 'data' would be useful either to the poet himself
or to his successors. The realistic and idealizing modes of art
could be understood as phases resembling diagnosis and cure
respectively. Pound was far from alone in adapting the vocabulary
and concepts of science to critical purposes. We have already noted
Eliot's famous analogy of the catalyst in 'Tradition and the Individual Talent', and as late as 1928 an essayist in the significantly
named Cambridge magazine, *Experiment*, declared that Valéry
and Hopkins, in spite of their differences, shared an 'almost
scientific precision without which it would be impossible to get
bodily across the physical quality of their experience'.[54]

As the modern period progressed, it became increasingly clear
that a prediction made by Wordsworth in the Preface to *Lyrical
Ballads* was being fulfilled:

> If the labours of men of science should ever create any material revolution, direct
> or indirect, in our condition, and in the impressions which we habitually receive,
> the poet will sleep then no more than at present; he will be ready to follow the
> steps of the man of science, not only in those general indirect effects, but he will
> be at his side, carrying sensation into the midst of the objects of the science itself.

In a 1922 article entitled 'The New Conditions of Literary Phenomena' Jean Epstein reported that the situation foreseen by
Wordsworth had come to exist. He pointed out that the devices
science offered for augmenting the senses, such as the telephone
and the microscope, were transforming as well as amplifying
perception. 'At certain moments these machines become part of
ourselves, interposing themselves between the world and us,
filtering reality as the screen filters radium emanations. Thanks to
them, we have no longer a simple, clear, continuous, constant
notion of an object.'[55] Richard Aldington, in an essay published
in the same year, argued that science had improved perception in
another sense; it compelled poets to confront the fact that nature
was full of contradictions.[56]

The full implications which science had for the arts were first perceived by the Italian Futurists and their gifted and flamboyant spokesman, Filippo Marinetti, who set out to define principles of literature and art appropriate to a technological age, and in doing so enunciated for the first time some of the fundamental impulses of the modern period. The aesthetic ideas they put before the English public between 1910 and 1914 in a series of lectures, exhibitions and performances were fanciful and advanced, but as some contemporary observers understood, their wild innovations sprang from a legitimate admiration for science's capacity to control reality. Convinced that art could condition and motivate society, they introduced the militancy of politics into the area of culture, actively challenging conventional ideas. They inaugurated an age of manifestoes. Maintaining that works of art should not be made to last, but should perform their missions, and then be forgotten or destroyed, they invented the concept of the permanent revolution, and what Harold Rosenberg has called 'the tradition of the new'.

The Futurists felt that such devices as the wireless, the engine, the airplane and new weapons of war were putting man in touch with fundamental sources of energy, while traditional values and attitudes cut him off from these new realities. Inherent in their philosophy was a heroic vision of man as a being who imitated his urban environment, setting aside respect, harmony, good taste and beauty for the sake of the values offered by violence, speed, boldness and destructiveness. He was to be admired because he rejected the traditional psychological processes and adopted the unthinking, hard, functional mode of being characteristic of the metals, pistons, vapours and electrical currents he encountered in his daily life.

The Futurists may have been both naive and hysterical in their enthusiasm for science and technology, but they made the scientific consciousness a permanent part of the modern aesthetic sensibility, and the effects of their adulation for the machine become apparent in the work of numerous artists outside the Futurist movement, such as Jacob Epstein and Fernand Léger. The imagery of science and its devices appeared in poetry, critics like Pound and Eliot used analogies drawn from scientific laws, and man was seen as a citizen of a technological civilization as well as a creature of nature.

Cubism as a movement was confined to the studio and art gallery, but Futurism set a new pattern for twentieth-century art movements by expressing itself through provocative public events, the remote ancestors of the 'happenings' that characterized a later period of experimentation. The new style was invented by Marinetti, who carried the Futurist gospel to a number of countries, including Russia, in a widely advertised series of public appearances. These ranged from comparatively peaceful lectures and art exhibits to violent political demonstrations and student revolts in Italy in 1914 and 1915 where Marinetti, seeking to force the country's entry into the war, was active as a speaker, and was imprisoned for a time. One of his methods for propagating Futurism was the *soirée futuriste*, a programme of unconventional speeches and performances intended to outrage the audience and, if possible, to create a disturbance. Such occasions became important parts of the Dada and Surrealist activities, and their emphasis on provocation and audience reaction anticipated the emergence of participatory theatre.[57]

Between 1910 and the outbreak of World War I, the British public had a generous exposure to Futurism, thanks to Marinetti, whose activities directly influenced the literary and artistic stirrings of the time. In a sort of preliminary appearance, a 'Discours futuriste' delivered at the Lyceum Club in April, 1910, he said little about Futurism itself, but undertook a Futurist analysis of the English character. Apparently without irony, he praised the belligerent national pride, individualism, the passion for sports, especially boxing, and the interest in armaments he took to be typical of England, and was critical of traditionalism, the respect for aristocracy, the tendency to fall into habitual routines, and most emphatically of '*snobisme*'.[58] When the audience applauded instead of displaying anger, Marinetti advised it to ignore the English custom of hospitality, and to show its real feelings by hooting at him.

In March 1912 a showing of Italian Futurist paintings at the Sackville Gallery and another London lecture by Marinetti gained considerable notoriety and acceptance for the movement. When Marinetti made another visit to England in November 1913, he was the guest of honour at a dinner and attended by 'sixty of the intelligentsia', many of them painters, and the occasion was widely reported in the press. Later in the month he gave readings of his poetry to a number of literary and artistic groups. Richard Aldington, who attended one of these sessions, reported in *The Egoist* of 1 December 1913 that Marinetti had had an alarming, but attractive effect and advised his readers to read the recently published anthology of Italian Futurist poetry. By the time Marinetti returned, in 1914, to give a series of lectures and to perform a concert of noises at a London music hall, Futurism had become a topic of the day, widely discussed, reported on, misunderstood, and loosely linked with anything novel or daring in the area of clothing and design.

In spite of the clamour raised by Futurism in England, at least one writer understood that it was a serious attempt to arrive at a general philosophy. R.F. Smalley, writing in the conservative *British Review* in August, 1914, identified with the Futurists the motivation later critics were to see in the experiments of the Cubists, that of achieving a rendering of reality that would be valid in the modern period. They were making the point that 'the mind sees more than the eye', and that vision alone, uninformed by scientific truth, could only yield illusions. 'They are legitimate products of the age we live in,' wrote Smalley, 'and they have thrown a quite intelligible challenge to the ideas they find dominating that age . . . '[59]

Futurism acquired few English adherents. The only painter who seems to have sympathized with it fully was C.W.R. Nevinson, and there were no English Futurist writers. Hulme, Pound, Wyndham Lewis and their contemporaries were actively hostile, but it is apparent that they were nevertheless strongly influenced by Marinetti, for they formed a counter-movement, Vorticism, which seemed designed to block the Futurist threat by a new synthesis which incorporated many of its characteristics, such as the admiration for machines and geometric forms, impatience with human weaknesses, and an overbearing manner of approaching the public. The remarkable series of Futurist manifestoes formulated many of the innovations which came to be central to modern literature. This was only partly due to direct influence. As the century progressed, English and American writers who had had no direct link with the movement itself turned to its ideas, often re-inventing them, because they were, as the Futurists proclaimed, unavoidable parts of the modern consciousness. The Futurists touched literary experimentation at many points, but for the present I should like to focus on the linguistic innovations they proposed for solving the problem of imitation in a technological age.

Their doctrines began with the view that reality itself had been radically transformed by technology. The nineteenth-century critics of urban life from Disraeli and Friedrich Engels to Charles Booth and Beatrice Webb had regarded the development of industrialism as a threat to traditional human values. But the Futurists, through a combination of impatience with the backwardness of Italy, and a naive delight in mechanical miracles, saw in technology moral and spiritual potentialities which would render the old values obsolete. Machines were free of human weaknesses. They were powerful, mindless, enduring, and through their shapes and rhythms produced an entirely new kind of beauty. In painting, this admiration manifested itself in mechanical and geometrical forms, in attempts to convey movement by depicting the subject in various positions, as in a photographic double exposure, and in the use of 'lignes-forces', non-representational lines supposed to express the rhythmic movements the form makes in its intuitionally apprehended movements into infinity. Like the Cubists, the Futurist painters regarded the model as a point of departure for capturing a philosophic version of reality that transcended mere vision, and there are numerous technical resemblances between the two schools. The Futurist principles of literary style, outlined in detail by Marinetti in 'Manifesto Tecnico della Letterature Futurista' (1912), amount to a belligerent assertion that language must enjoy complete freedom if it is to express the new ideas. Marinetti's catchword for his literary doctrine was 'le parole in libertà.'

He maintained, in accordance with the Futurist doctrine that machines are superior to human beings, that language must not express personality; verbs should have neither person nor tense, but should be used only in the infinitive, because this form is 'round as a wheel', and capable of accommodating numerous relationships. Adjectives and adverbs must be suppressed (presumably because they convey subjective ideas), the first person should be dropped, and images should be based, not on anthropomorphic assumptions, but on an appreciation of objects and physical matter, 'l'ossessione lirica della materia'. Since coherence is a specifically human concept, such evidences of it as syntax, connectives, and logical imagery should be eliminated. Compound nouns are encouraged because they express the multiple knowledge of reality given by such experiences as flying in an airplane and because they juxtapose objects significantly without limiting their significance through overt connective links. Punctuation is to be replaced by mathematical and musical signs indicating physical, rather than merely conceptual realities. Using these principles, Marinetti wrote texts like the following description of Messina:

fumo del vulcano appello lanciato ai vesuvi stromboli   perfidia delle vegetazioni = travestimenti del terremoto minaccia di un giardino troppo profumato odore pepato del pericolo   polveriera + volonta + lavoro + comfort + spensieratezza della fecondazione notturna = Messina[60]

Marinetti also proposed a 'Rivoluzione Tipografica' involving the use of printing to give words movement (in opposition to the static devices of Mallarmé), and type of different sizes and ink of different colours to distinguish themes within a single text. In his own poems, he broke up the hitherto irreducible unit of the word, partly as a way of expressing subjective feelings. Under the

heading 'Ortografia Libera Espressiva' he declared that the
Futurists would no longer accept their words from tradition,
but would, under the influence of 'ebrietà lyrica', or lyric intoxication, deform and remould them, cutting them short or elongating
them, strengthening their centres or extremities, increasing or
diminishing the numbers of letters. Such transformations, described as 'onomatopeico psichico', are intended to achieve 'espressione
sonora ma astratta di una emozione o di un pensiero puro'.[61]
What Marinetti had in mind is illustrated in this description of a
train:

> treno   treno   treno   treno   **tren   tron**
> **tron   tron**   (ponte di ferro: **tatatluuuuntlin**) **sssssssiii**
> **ssiissii   ssiisssssiiiii**[62]

The passage alternates between words with ordinary meanings
to imitations of the changes in sound as the train goes from an
overland track to one that crosses a bridge and then sounds its
whistle. Marinetti acknowledged that writing of this kind would
not be comprehensible at first, but maintained that the public
would eventually become accustomed to it.

The Futurists had a strong sense of the arbitrary limitations that
had become fixed in language, and were seeking ways to escape
its lineal, temporal and conventional quality. Their critique of
practices made sacred by mere habit is nearly always valid and
damaging, and their innovations, hare-brained and impracticable
as many of them were, often expressed authentic aspects of the
modern sensibility. With the Futurists, as with Gertrude Stein, the
rejection of conventional language practices is an attempt to
achieve a closer imitation of reality, through technological consciousness in the case of the Futurists, through the continuous
present in the case of Gertrude Stein. But Gertrude Stein's
attenuated, flat, repetitive idiom is more limited than conventional
language, while the inventiveness the Futurists brought to the
task of imitation introduced valuable new expressive resources.
It is obvious that their attacks upon conventions of spelling,
punctuation, typography and syntax have had a lasting effect.
Practices that were novel in the poetry of Pound and
E.E. Cummings became commonplace after the middle of the
twentieth century, especially among American poets. To them,
the conventions of spelling, punctuation and typography are
archaisms no longer strong enough to be worth attacking, and the
field of language is perfectly open and plastic, so that the writer
is free to be as radical as his sensibility demands in improvising
methods appropriate to his purpose and his moment in history.

This condition is one the Futurists would have approved, and one which they did more than any other group to bring about.

5 COLLAGE IN LITERATURE

In book 3 of *Gulliver's Travels*, Swift describes a group of projectors who anticipate the modern technique of *objet-trouvé* by using objects instead of words in conversation, carrying whatever is needed about with them in large bags. He is mocking the belief that this 'artificial converse' would be an improvement on language in terms of health, convenience and brevity. Whatever its follies, a medium of this kind would fulfill the demand for immediacy so urgently felt in modern art by circumventing the symbolic function altogether.

There is, of course, a crucial difference between an actual object and a symbolic form. Words and symbols have referential meanings which operate between two easily-distinguished things, the sign and the thing signified, and their purpose is that of enabling the observer's mind to move from something present to something absent. But the meaning of an object is intrinsic; it does not refer to anything else, and is in itself a direct stimulus to action or decision. In the process of symbolization, this immediacy is normally lost. It cannot penetrate the frame of a painting or become attached to the letters of a word. The lines, colours and forms seen in a picture can, of course, be regarded simply as markings having a certain degree of interest in themselves, but if they join to form a work of art, even a non-representational one, they cannot have the authenticity of an ordinary object. Susanne K. Langer has said:

> Every real work of art has a tendency to appear . . . dissociated from its mundane environment. The most immediate impression it creates is one of 'otherness' from reality—the impression of an illusion enfolding the thing, action, statement, or flow of sound that constitutes the work.[63]

Verbal works of art suffer a second separation from objective reality, for, as Whorf showed, words can be used meaningfully only within the framework of the language as a whole, and within the conception of reality it embodies. These indispensable mediating elements naturally interfere with strict objectivity. In discussing the flexible and contingent qualities of diction, Winifred Nowottny observes:

> It is inevitable from the very nature of language that choice of words implies choice of attitude, the choice of a certain kind of mental structure within which

the object is seen, or to which it is assimilated, or by reference to which it is explained. The nature of language is such that there can be no such thing as a neutral transcription of an object into words.[64]

A literary work, then, is doubly insulated from reality because it is symbolic and because it uses a medium that is itself tainted with subjective elements.

The technique of *collage* was originally devised as a way of closing the gap between art and reality by following the example of Swift's projectors, and enlisting objects from the real world in the cause of art. It came into use about 1912 when Braque and Picasso, as one of their new Cubist methods, began inserting such materials as newspaper clippings, Métro tickets and concert programs into their paintings. Some saw the new technique as an effort to eliminate the arcane, symbolic aura of art by appropriating parts of the real world and putting them physically into the painting. According to Louis Aragon, the Cubists used it to assert the reality of the picture, to establish an element of authenticity around which the relationships of the painting could be organized. However, it acquired many complex and contradictory implications, and seemed to emphasize the contrast between art and reality instead of abolishing it. Aragon reported that, while it was first used to create effects of design, it soon became a quasi-literary resource, for the external object affixed to the painting became an expressive unit, with independent significance, like a word.[65] Max Ernst treated his *collage* elements as metaphors, using objects in such a way that they had the appearance of other things. According to Picasso, this was, in fact, one of the original motivations of the technique.

The sheet of newspaper was never used in order to make a newspaper. It was used to become a bottle or something like that. . . . If a piece of newspaper can become a bottle, that gives us something to think about in connection with both newspapers and bottles, too. This displaced object has entered a universe for which it was not made and where it retains, in a measure, its strangeness. And this strangeness was what we wanted to make people think about because we were quite aware that our world was becoming very strange and not exactly reassuring.[66]

Far from merging two different kinds of reality, then, *collage* testified instead to the disjointedness and incongruity of experience. The meeting between actuality and the imagination sponsored by *collage* demonstrates a sharp demarcation between the two, but it also engages the real world in an aesthetic venture. It may emphasize the authenticity of the inserted element, its immunity from the control of the imagination; or it may withdraw it from immediate experience, and magically transform it into a symbol.

The logical conclusion of *collage* is the form called 'ready-made' or *objet-trouvé* invented by Marcel Duchamp, which consists simply of identifying found objects as works of art and exhibiting them accordingly. This new art form, though originally regarded as a hoax, raised troubling questions about the distinction between art and actuality, demonstrating, among other things, that the artist could dispense with the symbolic elements that intervened between himself and reality, and that real objects could acquire the 'otherness' that characterizes illusionary art. In a recent essay obviously influenced by political interests, Aragon has pointed out some of the more radical implications of *collage*. He thinks of it as a way of opposing bourgeois values, such as the expression of individuality, and the uniqueness of the work; it is poor and easily reproducible, and its materials come from common life and express a naive view of reality, offering nothing capable of glorifying the artist or his civilization. These qualities make *collage* an anti-technique with the potential power of revolutionizing purely aesthetic values as well as political ones.

Aragon adapted *collage* to writing, inserting a telephone conversation he had overheard into his novel, *Les Beaux Quartiers*. Against the objection that this is really quotation rather than *collage*, he argues, 'Mais c'est que toute citation peut, au contraire, être tenue pour un collage. . . .'[67] This claim is perhaps too sweeping, for quotations and allusions can be integrated into literary texts in ways that neutralize the *collage* effect. But something that is clearly a counterpart of *collage*, the unintegrated intrusion of reality in the form of quotations and interpolations into the imaginary sphere of the story or poem is a characteristic resource of modern literature.

None of the experimentalists felt the claims of the existent more strongly than William Carlos Williams. As we have seen, the depiction of objects in his poems is based on the conviction that the poet must establish a firm contact with actuality, guarding against such evasions as private emotion, associations and metaphors. Actuality was a crucial, if by no means a final value in the poetic transaction for Williams, and he felt that the poem should achieve a status in actuality co-eval with that of any non-symbolic object. 'I mean a progress downward to the beast', he wrote, explaining his opposition to employing externals for allegory or symbolism, 'To the actual. To the devil with silks.'[68] He followed the efforts of the Cubist painters to grasp the truth of what is seen, and to amplify the role of the imagination in perception. Bram Dijkstra has shown that Williams considered the painters the true pioneers of the modern consciousness, and undertook to emulate their methods in his poetry.[69] The literary version of *collage* is one of his poetic techniques, and it might be seen as a natural culmination of his efforts to attune imagination to reality. 'Della Primavera Trasportata al Morale' proceeds by listing the mundane realities that are the basis of the poet's faith in the existent world, prefacing them by 'I believe'. Appropriately, many of these are *collage* insertions, not described, but borrowed as directly as possible from the non-symbolic world, pictorial as well as verbal. Describing the precious nondescript actualities of a vacant lot, Williams does not fail to quote the sign on it, 'BUY THIS PROPERTY.' Other appropriations are the banalities of a political speaker, quoted, in effect, verbatim, and a listing of the dishes on the menu of an ice-cream parlor, complete with prices. 'One could catalogue', said Williams in *A Novelette*, 'but only if it were a catalogue to be a catalogue'.

> I believe
> Spumoni $1.00
> French Vanilla .70
> Chocolate .70
> etc.
>
> (p.62)

So inclusive is this faith in actuality that it embraces a poison label reproduced complete with skull and crossbones, and signs, apparently from hospital walls, with their pointing arrows. The visual reproduction of these non-verbal signs is true, graphic *collage* which lends its status to the verbal borrowings; both acquire an immediacy that by-passes symbolism, becoming particularly effective expressions of the devotion to actuality with which the poem is occupied.

This commitment to reality through *collage* is an important element in *Paterson*, much of which consists of letters, excerpts from documents relating to the history of Paterson, an interview with a reporter, and similar intrusions. Near the beginning of Book V, Williams, referring to his interest in Dada, Surrealism and *Last Nights of Paris*, the novel by Philippe Soupault which he translated in 1929, asks what has become of the art of the time. He answers that it has survived and merged with actuality:

> —the museum became real
>
> The Cloisters—
>
> on its rock
>
> casting its shadow—

Thus using the replica of medieval architecture constructed in a park in upper Manhattan as a symbol of the way in which the constructions of art have impressed themselves upon our way of grasping reality. There follows a misquotation from Aragon's poem from *Le Paysan de Paris* :

> la réalité! la réalité!
> la réa, la réa, la réalité![70]

whose insistence on dealing with nothing but reality is one of the controlling principles of *Paterson*, expressed most obviously through its *collage* elements. One page of the poem reprints a statement about government financing by a citizen who bought space for it in a newspaper, another a list of the geological specimens found at various depths during an attempt to bore an artesian well in the vicinity of Paterson in the late nineteenth century. Although these exhibits have some connection with the themes of the poem, no attempt is made to work them into the text, or to soften the line of division between them and the imagined parts of the poem. They lie embedded in the poetry like blocks of raw material, sharply differentiated from the rest, yet sharing with it the quality of sheer existence, of 'réalité'.

Ulysses is famous as a book which combines a mythic framework with a high degree of realism, but Robert M. Adams has shown, in his study, *Surface and Symbol*, that it contains a great deal of reality in addition to its realism. Adams's painstaking investigations have revealed that *Ulysses* is full of perfectly accurate dates, names, addresses and other minor facts whose authenticity adds nothing to the novel's effect, and is bound to be missed, in any case, even by the best-informed reader. Among these are: the names and addresses of the cabman who takes Boylan to his rendezvous with Molly, and of the family which employs the servant girl Bloom encounters at the butcher's; the list of those participating in the bicycle race in Phoenix park; the valuation of certain houses that catch Bloom's eye; and the religion of the man named Boyd who is mentioned in a conversation about Paddy Dignam's children. These and dozens of other facts of a similar order of triviality are drawn either from Joyce's knowledge of Dublin or from such sources as the newspapers and *Thom's Directory*. Why did Joyce imitate—or rather, appropriate—when it would have been easier, and equally effective, to invent? He said in one of his letters that he had no imagination, a mind like a grocer's assistant, and the firm actualities of Dublin life were essential points of departure for him. But Adams relates Joyce's practice to the experimental mood of the modern period:

Just about the time of *Ulysses'* appearance, the arts of collage, *trompe-l'oeil*, and *objet-trouvé* experienced a second or first birth at the hands of the plastic artists. . . . Artist and audience stood in a new, unmediated relation to an object which might be categorized as either 'life' or 'art'.[71]

Ulysses is full of parody or invention that creates an impression of *collage*. But there is also much true *collage* in it. Adams discovered an inexplicable paragraph in the 'Wandering Rocks' chapter, beginning 'An elderly female, no more young . . . ' which is simply excerpted verbatim from a newspaper. The newspaper is also the source of the list of births and deaths read by the Citizen in 'Cyclops'. The books in Bloom's bedroom, the music for the ballad of Harry Hughes and the Jew's daughter, and the numerous actual persons, addresses, names, dates and events that punctuate the novel may well have been introduced as aids to Joyce's creative energies, but they also have the effect of *collage*, taking their place side by side with the products of pure imagination.

Pound generally tried to achieve precision by the improvement, rather than the evasion of language, but it is not surprising to find that the poet who said, 'Knowledge resides in particulars' and 'All knowledge is built up from a rain of factual atoms . . . '[72] should experiment with the authenticity of his medium. There is little sign of *collage* techniques in his earliest poems, though 'To a Friend Writing on a Cabaret Dancer' contains some lines from Gautier's 'Carmen est maigre'. But in *Mauberley*, as John Espey has shown, borrowing became a vital part of his poetic method. The situation is complicated somewhat by the presence of passages that only appear to be quotations—a device also used in the *Cantos*—and by a passage cited from a fictional author. Much of this is unlike *collage*, for it is integrated grammatically into the poem, but the practice does show that Pound, like Joyce, Eliot, William Carlos Williams and others, was ready to regard borrowing as a legitimate part of poetic creation.

The *Cantos* is a work which has been marked and deformed by reality in an exceptional way. The ellipsis marks and black bars found in Cantos XIV, XV and LII represent names that Pound used in uncomplimentary fashion, and which have been deleted from the text. Cantos LXXII and LXXIII were written in Italian and never published because they expressed an admiration for Mussolini and Fascism which was unacceptable to the public. These unplanned interventions of social and political reality have a *collage* effect, for they are literal invasions of the work by external facts. From a purely aesthetic point of view, they contribute to the textural differentiation of the poem's surface, and, somewhat like damaged classical statuary, reflect the struggle between the imagination and the intractable forces of the real world.

True *collage*, with its characteristic effect of creating an intersection between actuality and art, is an important element in the *Cantos*. Large parts of the poem consist of excerpts from letters, diaries, official documents and the like, which are offered as instances of 'life' rather than 'art', and represent intrusions into the poem by external, usually historical reality. Many of these are translations rather than originals; and even when the original language is used, Pound nearly always introduces minor changes, unobtrusively shaping his *objet-trouvé* to his own purposes in a small way. These changes are often intended to promote an effect of immediacy and authenticity. In quoting or translating, Pound uses archaisms and dialect, repeats a translated phrase in the original language, and introduces abbreviations such as 'shd' and 'wd' when they do not appear in his printed source to suggest the presence of a manuscript; mathematical and secretarial signs seldom found in poetry convey the atmosphere of the account-book. A defective signature is reproduced exactly as it was found, with some of the letters missing.

Pound's use of *collage* elements in the *Cantos* is exemplified in Canto XXXIV, which is made up largely of quotations (few of them exact) from the diary of John Quincy Adams. Pound has selected some of Adams's observations which correspond with his themes of economic exploitation, the decline of cultural values, the vulgarity of society and the corruption of government. As a general rule, it is impossible to appreciate them fully without knowing their context in Adams's diary and in history. The conversation with President Monroe dated January 18th, 1820, for example, is about a figure comparable to Baldy Bacon in Canto XII or the Giddings of Canto XVIII, a buccaneering business-man intent on making money in foreign parts. In the passage dated Christmas, 1820, Adams is sadly observing that the members of his family, like Pound's contemporaries, are losing their appreciation of literature. He also complains that a monument displays bad taste and that American life lacks culture. His own interests are displayed by his remark (quoted almost *verbatim*) that Shakespeare expressed common thoughts in uncommon words, an observation made after he had compared *Antony and Cleopatra* with Plutarch. The enigmatic 'Mrs. Eaton . . . ' is an allusion to the wife of President Jackson's Secretary of War, who attracts some attention in Adams's diary because of the scandal occasioned by the fact that she had lived with her husband openly for a period before they were married.

Pound's quotations from Adams are, in spite of minor changes, genuine and essentially accurate, but he does not hesitate to omit, and also to embroider them for the sake of improving the impression of immediacy. Some phrases from Adams concerning the poor showing made at the inauguration of William Henry Harrison and the exploitation of the Indians by state governments, especially Georgia, are accompanied by the phrase, *haec sunt infamiae*, 'these are the infamies.'[73] Though it appears to be another quotation from Adams, it is nothing of the kind, but an addition made by Pound himself. On the same page, the triangle representing the pyramid set up by Mordecai Noah is similarly Pound's contribution. Adams did not quote the inscription or draw the pyramid, but simply gave an account of seeing it during a visit to Grand Island *en route* to Buffalo. During this trip, the ex-President visited a number of cities in upper New York State where he was surprised by lively demonstrations in his honour, each featuring a 'fireman's torchlight procession'. Pound's repetition of the phrase is a witty rendering of Adams's record. In the same way, the extensive excerpts from Jefferson, John Adams, documents from the history of Siena, letters from and to Sigismundo di Malatesta, and so on are nearly always touched slightly by Pound's shaping hand, and they are certainly chosen to support his themes, but they are true *collage*, for they introduce the physical presence of facts into the poem.

Substantial portions of the Chinese cantos (LII-LXXI) are summary-translations from Joseph-Anne de Mailla's *Histoire Générale de la Chine* and other sources of information about China. Much of this is perfectly accurate but some is fictional, and since it is marked by paraphrase, selection and interpolation, it does not amount to *collage*, but creates a somewhat lesser impression of authenticity. This impression is strengthened, however, by the ideograms, which are striking visual presences, creating a valuable effect of immediacy, even if they are not understood. Pound is said to have inserted Chinese words into the *Cantos* while he was confined in the D.T.C. by cutting the characters from his dictionary and pasting them on the page, a reversion to the original method of *collage*.

Eliot's use of borrowed material is not exactly like either Pound's or Joyce's and offers an interesting instance of the different use of a similar technique. In his earlier poems echoes and quotations are assimilated into the texts, in a method resembling that of *Mauberley;* lines from Laforgue are dovetailed into 'Rhapsody on a Windy Night' and 'Conversation Galante', poems expressing a Laforguian consciousness. In 'Gerontion', short passages borrowed from Edward FitzGerald, Lancelot Andrewes and *The Education of Henry Adams* match the general tone perfectly, thus emphasizing Eliot's preference for integrating such materials into the texture of his poems instead of letting them obtrude.[74] For Eliot, the possibility of communicating the immediate is a nebulous conception; experience can rise to meaning only through the mediation of a sensitive individual consciousness. He says for example;

> ... what we experience as readers is never exactly what the poet experienced, nor would there be any point in its being. ... What the poet experienced is not poetry but poetic material; the writing of the poetry is a fresh 'experience' for him, and the reading of it ... is another thing still.[75]

Hence, when a quotation appears in one of Eliot's poems, it is likely to lose its original identity, and become something else within the new context. He did not feel the desire for an escape from language to extensional reality we have been perceiving in other modern writers, or object to the tendency of language to impose its patterns on experience; he asked only that these patterns be appropriate.

It is in this spirit that the borrowings of *The Waste Land* and *Four Quartets* are brought into their poems, not to survive as inert chunks of reality, but as participating expressive elements. They are not factual, as those in *Paterson* are, but represent other literatures or forms of expression. Rather than objects, they are 'objective correlatives', external reflections of subjective ideas. Eliot is not concerned with preserving their original meanings and condition, but appropriates the borrowed material, sometimes by no more than a few deft changes which shift its meaning into the key of his poem. Though drawn from widely scattered sources, they seem, in the final analysis, to be saying, as a friend of Tennyson's once declared, 'The world is one great thought and I am thinking it.'

Yet the *collage* method used in *The Waste Land* cannot be entirely ruled out of a discussion of the convergence of art and actuality. At the beginning of the poem, to be sure, the echoes and allusions are under firm control, and play their part as reliably as the other elements. The borrowings from the reminiscences of Countess Marie Larisch in the first verse paragraph, the elements from Ezekiel, *Tristan und Isolde*, Dante, Baudelaire and numerous other sources fit smoothly into the ongoing sense. But this is a view of the poem we have gained only through years of study with the help of such analysts as Cleanth Brooks, and it is significant that some of these allusions have only recently been discovered. The reader of 1922 who most fully understood Eliot's purposes knew only that he was in the presence of an impersonal idiom which spoke for 'the mind of Europe' rather than for the poet himself, and was capable of deploying whole cultural formulations as if they were single words or expressions. Even if the many voices and many sources of consciousness in the poem contribute to a fairly consistent mood, their assimilation is not complete. The discontinuities between the language of the poem itself and such interpolations as the helmsman's song and the pub conversation are essential to the effect of confirming the feelings being expressed. Only because they are 'found' rather than invented and emerge from other sources than the poet's imagination can they serve as evidence for his case.

In fact, as *The Waste Land* progresses, the borrowings seem to escape to some extent from the poet's control, and to speak with voices of their own—not without the poet's collusion. With the heaping of unassimilated quotations at the end—'These fragments I have shored against my ruins'—Eliot gives up his careful stitchery and acknowledges that the attempt to subdue his materials to the purposes of a single formulation has reached its limit. The 'fragments' are piled against the 'ruins' of the poet's consciousness as if their physical presence mattered more than the particular ways in which they might be interpreted. Thus, the poem ends as if it were reaching out into a dark room. What it touches is not so important as the fact that it touches something. The technique of *collage* itself has little to do with the quest for permanent values that is the theme of *The Waste Land*, and this particular use of *collage* is, it seems to me, an acknowledgement of despair. The group of quotations, many of them apparently unconnected with the problems of the poem, is only a bleak substitute for the spiritual renewal Eliot is seeking. They offer a contact with reality, but it is not a victory, merely, as the poem says, a brace improvised to prevent collapse.

Collage, like all the experimental efforts to link language with extensional reality, paradoxically destroyed the notion that art is an imitation of life, and showed that the aesthetic experience depends on a sense of the crucial distinction between them. We have noted Robert M. Adams' observation that Joyce's details in *Ulysses* might be interpreted as either 'art' or 'life', and Roger Shattuck has described *collage* in particular as a 'deliberate *cross* of art and life'.[76] What these critics have identified is not a blending, but a confrontation between incompatible alternatives, whose meeting, like Bergson's 'reciprocal interference of series' sets up a startling and energizing conjunction that depends, for its effects, on art remaining art and life remaining life.

The effect of this conjunction is not reconciliation, but Shklovsky's 'defamiliarization', which brings about an awareness that approaches, if it does not achieve, a sense of immediacy. The modern devices for achieving contact with reality are, I think, perceived in the same way. Picasso, we recall, reported that the first *collages* generated a feeling of strangeness appropriate to the modern world. A related feeling seems involved in one of the young Stephen Dedalus's adventures with words in *A Portrait of the Artist as a Young Man*. The boy tries the water-cocks in a hotel lavatory. 'There were two cocks that you turned and water came out: cold and hot. He felt cold and then a little hot: and he could see the names printed on the cocks. That was a very queer thing.'[77] The queerness might well be a sense of the discrepancy between his direct experience of the water and the verbal symbols attached to it. The reader feels the same incongruity in Williams's 'Della Primavera' when he moves from the poet's words 'I believe' to the transcription from the ice-cream parlour menu, and in the line from Cummings where the 'o's' picture the spots of sunlight in the scene the words are describing. The notion implied in these passages, that non-symbolic elements may share the functions of symbolic ones, is a kind of aesthetic witticism. The juxtapositions create a sense of incongruity, not harmony. They generate an irony which depends for its effectiveness, not on a successful disguising of the real as imaginary, or vice-versa, but on a sharp awareness of the two separate realms of being they represent. Adams, after exhibiting the numerous factual details in *Ulysses*, reports that they do not form subtle underlying patterns, as might be expected. They do not, in short, enter into the art of the book, but remain actualities. The effect of this is to increase the sense of the ironic interplay between art and actuality which even the comparatively uninformed reader of *Ulysses* experiences in some measure.

This brings us to the point mentioned at the end of chapter I, that *collage* epitomizes the newly invented imitative techniques by cultivating a sophisticated sense of the comedy that art and life, reality and imagination, human and non-human, enact in their relationships with each other, exploiting both their superficial resemblances and their fundamental divergences. The found object insolently staring at us from its pedestal in the gallery and the scraps of newspaper incongruously forming a representational design in a painting sharpen our sense of the medium itself, rather than what it represents. Cummings's poem about the grass-hopper, which hops about the page in imitation of its subject, does not create a sense of the grasshopper's presence, but makes us aware, as perhaps no other poem does, of the actuality of letters and the dimensions of the page. It does not demonstrate at all that language can enter the extensional world, but rather renews our sense of its autonomous power to embody our perceptions of it.

III ACTS OF MIND

IT SEEMS then, that the most brutal thrusts toward physical immediacy, such as literary *collage* and unconventional typography only show that it is impossible to possess external reality through words. The central modern statements on this subject are perhaps those made by Bergson in *Matter and Memory*. As we have seen, he felt that language and other conceptualizing media translate a non-spatial process made up of inseparably interpenetrating elements into spatial terms, introducing ideas of separation and extension into it in order to create intelligible objects of reference. While this objectification is a necessity of practical life, it is also a fertile source of error. But the substitution of words for objects interferes with perception in an even more radical way. It divides what Bergson described as the integral phenomenon of perception into internal and external parts, each following its own order. All words but proper nouns are generic, while all objects are particulars; the grammatical and other relationships of language do not follow those of the physical world. To overcome this disjunction, an artificial system of reference and description is devised in which the experience of immediacy is 'disarticulated'.[1] This system is conventional language. This sacrifice of immediacy has been described by Cassirer:

> The more richly and energetically the human spirit engages in its formative activity, the farther this very activity seems to remove it from the primal source of its own being. More and more, it appears to be imprisoned in its own creations—in the words of language, in the images of myth or art, in the intellectual symbols of cognition, which cover it like a delicate and transparent, but unbreachable veil.[2]

Although it might seem desirable to rip this veil aside in order to enter 'the paradise of pure immediacy', Cassirer argues that to the philosopher at least, this path is closed, and that his road to knowledge lies through a study of the forms that shape intuition. When the bride of Ozymandias strips herself in Stevens's 'Notes Toward a Supreme Fiction', Ozymandias says:

> the bride
> Is never naked. A fictive covering
> Weaves always glistening from the heart and mind.

74

In fact, these secondary reactions to the primary stimuli make up most of what is meant by culture, science and aesthetic experience, and a world without them would be naked indeed, perhaps consisting of nothing more than the homogeneous vibrations Bergson saw as the common property of mind and matter.

Interpreters of reality therefore tend to accept the conformations the mind imposes on the raw data of experience. In an early statement, Pound accounted for the Greek myths and poetic awareness generally as expressions of a kind of mind which, instead of merely reflecting externals, draws its ideas from inner sources: 'Their thoughts are in them as the thought of the tree is in the seed . . . '3 Eliot admired the metaphysical poets and such nineteenth-century French figures as Laforgue and Corbiére because they had found accurate 'verbal equivalents' for exceptional states of mind relevant to the modern situation. With Pound and Hulme, as we have seen, the concern with precision was only a phase of a more general interest in the working of the mind and the possibilities of embodying it in language. They regarded precision in the treatment of physical particulars as a model for precision in the treatment of feelings, sensations, emotions and ideas. The interaction between fact and the observing mind, the processes through which perception, thought and intuition grasp and manipulate experience, and the discrepancies between matter and consciousness are overt themes in twentieth-century thought. 'Picasso', said E. E. Cummings, only half complaining, 'you gave us Things/which/bulge: grunting lungs pumped full of sharp thick mind'.4

The interest in psychology converged on the experimental period from many sources. Browning's renderings of specific casts of mind in dramatic monologues were widely imitated, especially by Pound and Eliot. The psychological novelists exerted an influence. Pound described *Mauberley* as 'an attempt to condense the James novel', and *The Waste Land* originally had as its epigraph a passage from Conrad's *Heart of Darkness*. Joyce learned the interior monologue technique from the French novelist, Edouard Dujardin, and was familiar with the ideas of Bergson. Gertrude Stein had been influenced by William James, Hulme had met Bergson, and Freud, though hardly known to most English and American writers at the time, was beginning to penetrate the atmosphere, and to confirm the current interest in irrational processes of thought. The French Symbolists, especially through the medium of Arthur Symons's *Symbolist Movement in Literature*, exposed the possibilities of states of mind not known to conventional thinking. The effect of machine civilization on psychology was one of the major themes of the Futurists, and the disruptions of language undertaken by the Dadas and Surrealists were efforts to achieve a closer correspondence with thought. The conviction that the arts shared affinities with each other implied a point of meeting in inward experience, and aroused curiosity about the processes which translated effects from one sense into another.

This interest manifested itself in the emergence of many new forms and techniques. Whole styles, such as the dramatic monologue, the interior monologue, the stream of consciousness, and automatic writing surrendered deliberate creation to the direct imitation of thought, replacing the traditional relationships of grammar by the subtler connections of association, memory, and similar linkages, so that free syntax became common. Other styles were deliberately invented to reflect states of mind through peculiarities of rhetoric, vocabulary and allusion, a technique that often verged on, and ended in, actual parody. Poetic imagery was influenced by images drawn from subconscious thought and dreams. Techniques following particular activities of the mind came into use. The Futurist emphasis on analogies, particularly disconnected ones, acquired considerable influence. Irrational forms of thought, such as hallucination, obsession and paranoia gave rise to novel literary devices.

The usual view is that conventional language itself is an adequate counterpart of mental reality. Descartes and his followers practically identified linguistic and mental processes. Whorf's idea that language exercises a kind of dictatorship over perception, and Wittgenstein's statement that we cannot say what we cannot think approach the same identification, from different directions. Chomsky believes that there is an affinity between the essential structure of language and an inborn 'linguistic competence'. But the introspective obsessions of the modern period found that ordinary language cannot record the complexities of mental life. Conventional language, though itself no doubt a creation of mind, is no better adapted to capture the authenticity of mental than of material reality. According to Bergson, we recall, it invariably omits most of the concrete experience of intuitive thought, and can only provide markers to indicate its direction, for '(verbal) images can never be anything but things, and thought is a movement'.[5] Bergson illustrates the divergence that can exist between words and subjective experience by observing that an adult may grow to dislike the flavour or odour he liked as a child, but continues to use the same name for it. He follows this with a description of the phenomenon familiar from advertising and propaganda, the imposition by language of its own patterns, with the effect of persuading us that we like things we do not like, and in general, disrupting our relations with the reality of our own minds. Such distortions, Bergson feels, are inherent in language, not mere abuses of it, for 'there is no common measure between mind and language'.[6]

One of the great currents of modern literary experiment combined the conviction of Bergson and Cassirer that conventional language cannot do justice to thought with the belief that important sources of meaning are to be found in those kinds of thought which had been neglected because they were considered disordered and irrational. The perception that dreams, hallucinations, phobias, obsessions and subconscious thoughts might give new insights into the human condition was not limited to Freud, Jung and other pioneers in psychology. Writers and painters were also feeling the power of these newly-acknowledged manifestations of the imagination. It was a time for what Wallace Stevens has called the nobility of the imagination, 'a violence from within that protects us from a violence without'.[7] Winifred Nowottny has pointed out that language that is not true in a recognizable sense simply compels the reader to find some sense in which it *can* be true. 'The peculiarity and violence of the language forces us to look for or imagine a situation capable of calling such language into being.'[8] Deranged forms of expression imply that there is some framework within which they possess power and relevance, a suggestion corresponding to the experimental tenet that the modern age needed a new universe of discourse.

The modern artists most conscious of these needs were those belonging to such quasi-organized movements as Futurism, Dada and Surrealism, for each of these groups claimed that its literary and aesthetic idioms embodied the spirit of a general revolution. The writers among them felt that linguistic experimentation had profound implications, that, as Wittgenstein put it, 'to imagine a language means to imagine a form of life',[9] and that new forms of expression were capable of transforming civilization by bringing forward neglected mental energies. The psychological themes they pursued were also conspicuous in Anglo-American experimentation. Since it is a tradition of English romanticism that poetry is a record of the kind of subliminal thought that sets itself against physical reality,—'emotion recollected in tranquillity', 'the interpenetration of a diviner nature than our own' or 'reflections on the acts of the mind itself'—modernists writing in English may not have felt the need to carry the exploration of irrational states of mind as far as the Europeans did. But in their emphasis on mental reality, as in other respects, they were a part of the same distinctive modernism, and they can be better understood if they are seen against the background of the more extreme psychological experimentation of Continental writers.

1 NEW VIEWS OF THE MIND: FUTURISM, DADA, SURREALISM

In spite of their enthusiasm for machines, the Futurists were not indifferent to the spiritual potentialities of human beings. They expected the subjection of man by his machines to create a new type of human being with new intellectual capacities. The 'Manifesto dei Pittori Futuristi' of 1910 declares that science has transformed humanity, and that the 'psicologia nuovissima del nottambulismo', which seems to owe something to Freud, has demonstrated the importance of unusual character-types such as the *apache* and the *cocotte*. Marinetti, in a statement called 'L'uomo moltiplicato e il regno della macchina', declared that the man of the machine age would identify with the mechanical contrivances he lived with, adopting their rhythms and sharing their intuitive mysteries.[10] The new man would be cruel, omniscient, and aggressive, free of such weaknesses as kindness, love and moral suffering. Since machines will enable him to move about quickly, to fly, and to extend his will through space, he will become multiple, capable of adopting many perspectives.

The innovations demanded by Marinetti in his 'Manifesto Tecnico della Letteratura Futurista' in May, 1912, are proposed in the name of a machine-age consciousness.[11] Literature must pursue a programme of dehumanization, reversing conventional personification, and coining metaphors for human situations from physical and chemical reactions, and from motors and mechanical objects. In accordance with the drive to embrace reality discussed in chapter 2, language must be freed from traditional habits, and must aim at expressing the immaculate non-humanity of material things. This liberation can be achieved only by an asyntactical, non-logical poetry which is free to penetrate the essence of matter, destroy the barriers separating it from the psyche, and create *'una psicologia intuitiva della materia'*.[12] In addition to the compound nouns, elimination of punctuation and various perversions of grammar and typography mentioned in the last chapter, this effort involved the important new method of 'lo stile analogico'. Analogy, properly used, is no less intellectual a device than the syllogism, which Marinetti denounced; but by treating analogical

relationships as definitive instead of merely probable, he transformed it into one of the irrational mental processes that corresponded with the modern concept of the imagination as 'a violence
from within'.

The Dada assault on language, though similar in many ways
to that of the Futurists, was based on a different intention, the
destruction of communicative and expressive resources. The
Dadas tried to empty language of meaning by using it in fragmented
and incoherent forms in order to regain the innocence of a world
in which things have no names and can therefore escape the
categories set up by the intellect. They were seeking the wood in
Alice in Wonderland in which Alice and the fawn, having forgotten
what they are called, also forget that they are enemies. The
perversions of literary forms which appeared in the performances
at the Cabaret Voltaire in Zürich in 1916, and in later Dada
publications and activities, exhibited the ironies of chance and the
absurd vitality of irrational thought. There were *poèmes simultanés*,
in which several poems were read aloud at one time so that nothing
could be understood, and the recitals of Kurt Schwitters, which
consisted of nonsense-syllables or single letters organized into
quasi-musical sequences, allowing the human voice to be heard
without the interference of intellectual meaning.[13] The Dada
insistence on spontaneity, incoherence, contradiction, obscenity
and other expressions of anarchic psychological energies is
perfectly ambiguous; it can be interpreted both as a militant form
of humanism, a defence of every manifestation of the psyche,
or as an ironic attack upon all values and distinctions. Tristan
Tzara, in his famous instruction for writing a Dada poem by
cutting words out of a newspaper, shaking them up in a bag and
so on, assures the reader that 'The poem will be like you.' The
method that has come to be called 'found poetry', the repetition of
clichés and trite phrases borrowed from newspapers and casual
conversations, and automatic writing, the process of pouring out
the contents of the mind in writing without forethought or
controls in order to show that it participates in the inconsequence
of reality in general, are perfectly double-edged. It is perhaps not
surprising that *Ulysses* should have been mistaken for a Dada work,
for it makes ample use of both spontaneous thought and the
banalities of language.

Dada continued the tradition of absurdity founded by Alfred
Jarry through his 'science' of 'Pataphysics, which he described
as the method of imaginary solutions, and many of its techniques
for reducing language to nonsense parallel those used by Jarry in
his poems and plays. In his play, *La Première Aventure Céleste*

de Mr. Antipyrine, for example, Tzara used one of Jarry's main devices, echolalia, as in 'synthetise amertume sur l'église isisise les rideaux dodododo'. One of the characters, Mr. Cricri, declares: 'il n'y a pas d'humanité il y a les réverbères et les chiens', and the play ends as Mr. Antipyrine announces, 'nous sommes devenus des réverbères', repeating the word nine nerve-racking times before the final 'puis ils s'en allèrent'.[14] Tzara resorts to another method of levelling language in his 'Manifesto on feeble love and bitter love', which begins with a series of verbal equivalents, such as 'preamble = sardanapalus, one = valise, woman = women, pants = water'. absurd equations resisting any systematic understanding.[15] His observation that conventional language, in spite of its usefulness, is not needed 'for our solitude, for our intimate games, and our literature' anticipated the rejections of language to be found in future, more anguished contexts. Beckett's 'Unnamable', for example, declares that 'all these strangers, this dust of words' is useful only for creating mildly amusing patterns, that 'there is no great difference here between one expression and the next, when you've grasped one you've grasped all', and the Professor in Ionesco's *The Lesson* teaches his pupil that words are merely collections of sounds, without meaning.

Paradoxically, however, the ingenious wrecking techniques the Dadas devised for dismembering language turned out to have positive values, for they showed that even the most fragmentary and formless elements of language harbour an unmistakable capacity for signification. In *The Order of Things*, Foucault observes that the modern period is distinguished by its awareness of a persistent, enigmatic meaningfulness inherent in language itself that refuses to be silenced, attributing this inescapable articulateness to the feeling that linguistic roots have some resemblance to what they signify.[16] This notion sheds a suggestive light on the strange fortunes of the Dada monosyllable in modern literature. The Dadas chose the name of their movement by chance from a dictionary because the word had a trivial and irrelevant meaning ('hobby-horse'), but 'da' is an Indo-European root which is found in words meaning 'give' in various languages, and might be thought of as one of the most universal of all words. It might claim to be the central word of *The Waste Land*, where it appears as the voice of the thunder promising rain, and the linguistic root of the Sanskrit words 'give, sympathize, control', which define the virtues the poem looks to for relieving the spiritual sterility of modern life. Hence, it means almost nothing in the one context, almost everything in the other. The Dada irony could hardly be balanced on a finer point.

Jacques Rivière, in an unsympathetic but important survey of Dada ideas appearing in 1920, emphasized some of the positive motives behind the Dada distortions of language. He explained that they sought to escape logical and aesthetic controls in order to grasp absolute psychological reality, to project the human spirit as an integrated whole. Hence, they took the view that anything that is said or done makes as much sense as the loftiest effort of the spirit, and that the repression of spontaneity is the only possible mistake. The primary Dada assumption about language, says Rivière, is that it has no fixed value, that words are meaningful only as the accidental consequences of spiritual activity, and that the expression of spontaneous thought has more reality than anything resulting from logic or taste. The Dadas follow the Symbolists in detaching words, not only from their referents, but even from their prescribed meanings, so that they no longer act as signs, but as agencies of original meaning. 'Le langage pour les Dadas n'est plus un moyen; il est un être.' In the Dada use of language,

Tout mot, du moment qu'il est proféré, ou seulement envisagé par l'esprit dans un éclair, a une relation avec lui. Tout mot, puisqu'il est venu à la penseé, l'exprime. . . . Tout mot donc est justifiable, est expressif, arrivant après n'importe quel autre, présenté sous n'importe quel jour, revelant n'importe quoi.[17]

Hence, the Dadas may have driven specific meanings out of language, but they also confirmed that inherent meaningfulness which Foucault describes. Tzara, writing some time after the movement had ceased to function, acknowledged that its apparent nihilism was rooted in a fundamental humanism:

Dénonçons au plus vite un malentendu qui prétendait classer la poésie sous la rubrique des moyens d'expression. La poésie qui ne se distingue des romans que par sa forme extérieure, la poésie qui exprime soit des idées, soit des sentiments, n' intéresse plus personne. Je lui oppose la poésie activité de l'esprit. . . . [18]

Such poetry was not confined to language, but language was certainly one form in which it could manifest itself.

The Surrealists, like the Dadas, valued language less for its own sake than for its usefulness in carrying out a spiritual revolution: poetry, like the other arts, was to be a means of overcoming the polarities and categories of rational thought, and enabling the imagination to establish a partnership with material reality. The Surrealist ambition, often compared with that of the alchemists, was the achievement of a psychological condition in which all contradictions are reconciled, especially those between human

wishes and external necessity, and all experience is transformed
into the gold of fulfilled desire. Literature and painting were the
main channels for this effort; the indifference of Surrealism to
aesthetic considerations had the advantage of permitting complete
freedom of form, but did not by any means rule out the survival
of banal techniques, as the paintings of Chirico and Dali show.

Initially Surrealism, as it was interpreted by its leading theoreti-
cian, André Breton, regarded language as important only because
it was an ideal medium for merging the psychological and material
realms. Breton, who was remarkably conservative for a revolutionary, faced the need for technical innovation in language
grudgingly. But since Surrealism aspired to revolutionize reality,
and since Breton was one of the leading exponents of the idea
that language is a crucial force in the creation of thought and the
definition of reality, linguistic experimentation was inevitable
as a part of the Surrealist program. In the *Manifeste du surréalisme*
(1924), this meant no more than the recording of thought through
automatic writing, the technique invented by the Dadas which
Breton put to new uses, exposing the world of subconscious ideas,
and capturing the creative potentialities of chance.

The automatic texts which Breton wrote in collaboration with
Philippe Soupault display great originality in their association of
ideas and use of imagery, but, as Breton later pointed out, they
did not interfere with syntax, as the experiments of Joyce and
others did. However, it soon became apparent to Breton that
language had contributions to make beyond its ability to record
subconscious or pre-conscious thoughts. In an essay, 'Les mots
sans rides', which was written at a time when he was occupied
with working out the ideas of the *Manifeste*, he wrote: 'On com-
mençait à se défier des mots, on venait tout à coup de s'apercevoir
qu'ils demandaient à être traités autrement que ces petits auxilia-
ires pour lesquels on les avait toujours pris. . . . ' He proposed to
enable language to reach its full power by detaching words from
their dictionary meanings through the study of their sound,
structure and effect, and by attending to their interaction with
each other. He dated the appreciation of words as concrete things
with rights of their own from the time when vowels were first
associated with colours (an observation apparently made with
Rimbaud's sonnet, '*Voyelles*' in mind). It is wrong, he now sees,
to take the word for granted:

C'est un petit monde intraitable sur lequel nous ne pouvons faire planer qu'une
surveillance très insuffisante. . . . Il est des mots qui travaillent contre l'idée
qu'ils prétendent exprimer. Enfin même le sens des mots ne va pas sans mélange
et l'on n'est pas près de déterminer dans quelle mesure le sens figuré agit pro-

gressivement sur le sens propre, à chaque variation de celui-ci devant corres-
pondre une variation de celui-là. [19]

In the *Manifeste du surréalisme* itself, Breton protests that the
referential style of the ordinary novel is irrelevant to the inner
life, and declares that 'Le langage a été donné à l'homme pour
qu'il en fasse un usage surréaliste.'[20]

While doctrinaire Surrealism addressed itself to a general
revolution of thought rather than a mere reform of language, some
of its poets found that words themselves opened unexpected
paths to imaginative freedom. These new possibilities take two
forms among the Surrealists. The first is the use of context to
detach the word from its ordinary meaning, making it the vehicle
of a radical re-ordering of ordinary reality, in accordance with
Paul Eluard's lines:

> The earth is blue like an orange
> Never a mistake words do not lie

which claims for the verbalizations of the irrational mind the
infallibility that Wittgenstein claimed for statements made in
conventional language. The second is a manipulation of language
allied to punning, the mechanical transposition of sounds, and the
exploitation of similar sounds to generate meanings that have the
virtues of being irrational, the results of chance and often immensely suggestive. Before the first *Manifeste* of Surrealism, Robert
Desnos published in the journal *Littèrature* a number of witty
aphorisms purporting to be the work of a personage called Rrose
Sélavy. These followed the simple formula of taking a phrase and
making a sentence of it by scrambling the phonic elements to
form a new and usually entirely irrelevant meaning. For example,
'Les lois de nos désirs sont des dés sans loisir', toys with 'lois' and
'désirs' to make 'dés' or 'dice', and 'loisir' or 'leisure', and to
arrive at the statement, "The laws of our desires are dice without
leisure." In his next work Desnos exploited the irrational resemblances involved in puns and homonyms. Roger Vitrac undertook
re-arrangements of sound less methodical, but more elaborate
than those of Desnos:

> La bouche vidée, biche dévouée, des sons, des dons
> glanés par les paroles . . .
> (Mouth emptied, devoted darling of sounds, of the gifts
> gleaned by words . . .)

One of Vitrac's methods was the creative re-writing of notices,
so that 'Défense de fumer' or 'No smoking' became 'Défense

de fumer les fusées des femmes', in which 'fusées' means a grouping of some kind, with possibilities ranging from 'fistulas', and 'rockets' to a 'run' of musical notes. Michel Leiris, regarding words as a kind of explosive powder to be detonated by the spark of imagination, seized upon personal associations suggested by their sounds, and redefined them accordingly, without reference to their original meanings. Thus, 'crime' becomes 'une mine de cris', or 'a mine of cries', and 'cadavre' becomes 'Le cadenas s'ouvre', 'the padlock opens'.[21] These arbitrary perversions of words may seem frivolous, but they demonstrated that language offers the poetic mind an entry into fantastic, irrational alternatives to reference, a resource most fully exploited, of course, in *Finnegans Wake*.

Looking back at the origins of Surrealism a generation afterward, André Breton acknowledged that automatic writing had not fulfilled the hopes attached to it, and maintained, rather surprisingly, that language had been the central concern of Surrealism, that its main theme had been

nothing less than the rediscovery of the secret of a language whose elements would then cease to float like jetsam on the surface of a dead sea. To do this it was essential to wrest these elements away from their increasingly narrow utilitarian usage, this being the only way to emancipate them and restore all their power.[22]

As evidence of the need that had been felt at the time for resisting the 'depreciation of language', he cited the parallel efforts of a number of experimental groups, including the Futurists, the Dadas, the French 'phonetic cabal', and the exponents of a 'revolution of the word' as he called it, typified by Joyce and Cummings, among others. Breton disapproved of these on theoretical grounds. He felt that Joyce, for example, was merely following naturalist principles in trying to imitate the flow of thought in the interior monologue, while the Surrealists were making an effort to grasp the 'prime matter' of language in their use of automatic writing. But he conceded that all of the linguistic experimenters shared with the Surrealists the belief that the true value of language for literature lay in its innate expressive capacities rather than in its referential ones.

2 HULME AND POUND

Marinetti's belief that language must reflect the psychological effects of a machine age, Tzara's view that it must resort to almost any means to escape the impositions of reason and tradition, and Breton's idea that it contains deep autonomous meanings corres-

ponding to subconscious thought all have their counterparts in
the theory and practice of their Anglo-American contemporaries.
It was generally acknowledged that, if language is to do justice to
mental reality, it would have to set aside such obligations as
reference, intelligibility and traditional usage. T.E. Hulme, who
was perhaps the least willing of the English writers to concede
this, was nevertheless compelled by his investigation of the
relation between thought and language to take a position favourable
to experimentation. Hulme follows Bergson in maintaining that
the intellectual functioning of language prevents the mind from
gaining contact with the vital, radically interpenetrative nature of
reality. Bergson's observation that if intuition could be sustained,
it would achieve all the objects of philosophy is stated in another
form by Hulme when he says, 'Could reality come into direct
contact with sense and consciousness, art would be useless, or
rather we should all be artists.'[23]

Behind Hulme's approval of innovation is a deep suspicion of
language, a conviction that the arbitrary symbols are always
threatening to lapse into meaninglessness. Ordinary language
strikes him as a retreat from the expansiveness of nature to the
thin utterance of a 'conjuror who does tricks with that curious
rope of letters, which is quite different from real passion and
sight'.[24] In order to perform its communal function, language
must attach its words to meanings that people are supposed to
share. In actuality, however, they do not refer to anything that is
actually experienced, but to vague classes of ideas, concepts and
feelings. Instead of bearing meaning born out of genuine thought,
they hang in the mindless air between speakers as inert symbols of
the hollow convention that private feelings have some sort of
common existence. 'Each of us', says Hulme, rephrasing one of
Bergson's ideas about language, 'has his own way of feeling, liking
and disliking. But language denotes these states by the same word
in every case, so that it is only able to fix the objective and impersonal aspect of the emotions which we feel.'[25] He maintains that
words lose their referential capacity unless they are linked to the
specific private thoughts of the speaker or writer.

Hulme was impressed by Bergson's view of the universe as a
mutually interpenetrating phenomenon with no separable elementary entities, an 'intensive manifold' where any change that
takes place must be a radical one, which contrasted with the
traditional atomistic idea of a mechanical universe, a grouping
of units like checkers or billiard balls where change is only superficial, for each situation is only a transposition of an earlier one.
Hulme thinks ordinary language is comparable with the mechanical

universe, a system in which words with fixed meanings are moved about uncritically over the plane of external reality. Since they are merely counters, merely conventional symbols for references based on agreement rather than actual experience, they can no more generate meaning than the pieces in a game of chess can decide the moves to be played.

In genuinely poetic language, according to Hulme, the word bears the writer's individual experience as its meaning, and carries this with it, contributing a novel quality to its context. His happy image for writing that functions in this way is a cater-pillar with its hairs. The caterpillar's segments are words, the hairs their particular meanings as they arise in the mind of the writer. On the one hand, the hairs stick fast to the segment they grow from, the original, private meaning adheres to the word; on the other, they are its means of moving along to another position, the meaning imparts something genuinely new.[26]

Hulme's recommendation for producing language that would convey the writer's particular, private meaning and that would avoid the deadening communal meaning assigned to words by ordinary usage is expressed in his image of the architect's curve. Ordinary language, like the wooden French curves used by draughtsmen, provides a way of expressing feelings that is standard, but only approximate. To gain accuracy, one has to bend the curve out of its original shape; in the same way, the writer has to take the conventions provided by language, and exert pressure on them to make them correspond with the individual meaning he has in mind. The originality that results is not in itself an advantage. 'It is only the defects of language that make originality necessary', says Hulme, rediscovering Mallarmé's perception that poetry exists to compensate for the inadequacies of language.[27]

The earliest modern English poems that attempted to bend language to fit the particularities of thought were the dramatic lyrics written by Pound and Eliot about the period 1908–20. The effort to create idioms faithful to elusive inward passages of consciousness generated some of the most significant of the new linguistic resources. Because Pound and Eliot set out to grasp feelings firmly, instead of merely exploiting suggestion as the Symbolists did, the pressures they exerted on words and images raised their connotative and associative potential to new levels. In their structure, these poems anticipate the psychological principles behind *Ulysses*, *To the Lighthouse* and other major works of the experimental period. They follow the associative movements of uncontrolled thought, circling about a few points of consciousness, turning upon themselves in apparently disconnected ways, without links or joints, through relationships arising from the interior of the thoughts themselves. All of this moves them away from conventional ideas of poetic language, syntax, structure and imagery.

The representation of mental activity is only a part, though a vital part, of Pound's poetic. At its head stands the non-psychological conviction that absolutes are an indispensable part of human experience. 'Without gods, no culture. Without gods, something is lacking.'[28] Men make their closest approach to these absolutes through the feelings and emotions whose persistence throughout history shows them to be universal aspects of the human condition. Poetry articulates these primary experiences in stable and definitive form through a series of precise linkages, first between the emotions and certain externals, then between the externals and language whose concreteness and immediacy make it capable of evoking the emotions independently. When these relationships are successfully established, the result is great literature, 'language charged with meaning to the utmost possible degree'.

The analogues Pound chose to define the relationship between the work of art and the feeling it reflects or evokes show that he thought it could be very exact; poetry, he said, gives 'equations for the human emotions',[29] it is like the magic spell which produces a particular effect, the mathematical formula representing a circle or a curve, the Chinese ideogram that uses concrete objects to refer to such an idea as 'red'. The relation is not an imitation, but an evocation, by means of external form, of a thought or emotion having a permanent status in human experience. In distinguishing between poetry and prose, Pound made the independent existence of the poetic experience the point of difference, speaking exactly as if the poem were the record of an encounter with something scientifically verifiable. 'In the verse something has come upon the intelligence. In the prose the intelligence has found a subject for its observations. The poetic fact pre-exists.'[30]

Pound shared with Eliot the concept of a literary tradition consisting of works from various times and languages which exert mutual influences upon each other through the minds of readers and authors. The poetic fact pre-exists, not only in the poet's intuition, but also in earlier literature, so that the question of recording an individual psychological experience shades off into that of responding to a tradition, the accumulation of many psychological experiences. The poet feels both the control of the past and the invigorating effect of a first-hand confrontation with the 'poetic fact', which gives him the resources for evoking it anew, out of his own convictions. But while Eliot's tradition is centred upon 'the mind of Europe', Pound's is far less exclusive, embracing not only China, America and Egypt, but patterns of thought outside literature. The comparative studies that attracted him, such as mythology, translation, the syncretism of the arts, and the parallel movements of political, economic and artistic developments are premised upon the supposition that the totality of minds we call tradition generates forms that can be observed in entirely different fields of behaviour and expression, a concept that operates vigorously in the *Cantos*. Eliot feels only that the poet must be generally aware of his tradition; but Pound shows, both in his verse and criticism, that he thought a poem must be written with reference to a model or group of models which anticipated it in evoking its effect. Cultural history, in Pound's view, consists of the migration of specific sensibilities through various times, places, languages and forms of expression. Each work of art is a segment in a process of transformation and metamorphosis, a member of a definable historical sequence concerned with permanent, primary emotions. Because these emotions are inevitably deadened by repetition and the forms expressing them become obsolete, the artist who enters the arena of history has the responsibility of finding new particulars through which they can be made accessible to his contemporaries.

Pound's views on this subject seem to be descended from some of the ideas about art set forth by Browning in Book I of *The Ring and the Book*. In explaining why he chose an old murder trial recorded in a collection of forgotten documents as the subject for his poem, Browning argued that the poet cannot create, but can only revitalize something that once had a life of its own. The poet's task is to seek out moribund or rejected forms, to perceive the truths they enclose, and bring them to life again through imagination. Pound, like Browning, seems to believe that sheer invention, rising out of nothing, can only be trivial, and that the poet's creative powers depend upon some *donnée* that has its own vitality. The weakness of this view, of course, is that there is no way of knowing whether the effect a modern mind receives from a canzone of Cavalcanti or an apothegm of Confucius is, in fact, connected with its original 'life'. It is even harder to be sure that the modern re-creation will evoke the same impression, instead of substituting an entirely different one. The fact that all of this is buried irrecoverably in the subjective responses of readers and authors divided from each other by time, language and custom may invalidate Browning's claim to 'truth' and Pound's dogmatic views of art, but it does substantiate the position, in which both, almost in spite of themselves, concur, that what poetry seeks to imitate is not things, but thought.

While this may seem to contradict the impression that Pound is a poet of concrete actuality, the contradiction—if there is one—lies in his view of the poetic function of language. Pound does not accept the notion that the poem exists in the counterpart reality of the 'virtual', an aesthetic realm reserved for art, but regards it as a portion of the primary subjective reality of mental life. The identification of the artifact of the poem with what is, after all, an aspect of nature, mental process, violates the boundary between the man-made and the natural. It is an extension of the effort to transcend the limits of personal perception by uniting external and subjective facts which Roy Harvey Pearce has observed in Whitman and in W.C. Williams's dictum, 'No ideas but in things.'[31] Just as writers like Williams and Gertrude Stein seek to gain a superior validity for their perceptions by entering into the 'essential reality' of objects, Pound seeks to attach to the poem the validity of thought. Poetic language becomes, as it does in Mallarmé, a self-sustaining absolute, 'a logos that has the essentiality of the object as a referent; as the expression of radical perception it is itself radical',[32] though we should say that in Pound's quasi-dramatic poems, it acquires the essentiality of thought and sensation.

Pound was often forced to protest that his interest in tradition was not mere antiquarianism, that he did not intend simply to imitate the classics. That was Mauberley's foible, the attempt 'to maintain "the sublime"/In the old sense'. What Pound envisioned was a collaboration between the central, definitive emotions found in traditional works and contemporary images capable of re-formulating them, a conjunction which would vitalize both. On the one hand, the traditional element is renewed as its continuity with the present is established, and it is given a part in contemporary consciousness; on the other, being 'new' to the present, it demands something more than the conventional use of current idiom. The immediacy discussed in the last chapter is essential, as a way of preventing renewal from becoming mere recollection. The fragmentation of syntax asserts the independence of an image or idea from the network of conventional linguistic relationships. Quotations, ideograms, hieroglyphics and the like offer immediate, concrete experiences of fully achieved forms, benchmarks to be used for measuring the accuracy of Pound's translations into his own idiom. Slang, abbreviations and contemporary printing conventions move in the opposite direction; they point to equivalents that once existed, and created parallel impressions in the past.

Pound's linguistic originality began with attempts to convey character or states of mind through style in poems written through fictional or historical characters. He described these poems, which he called 'personae', as steps in a search for his own identity which he carried on by first creating and then casting off 'complete masks of the self in each poem'.[33] Since the poem is a verbal mask, its expressive features are represented by its traits of style. It is severed from the self, so that the poet is free to improvise a style different from his own, and when the speaker is a historical figure, the formation of the style involves the imaginative re-creation of a feeling from the past. Taken as a group, the many poems of this kind Pound wrote, with backgrounds as different as Imperial China, medieval Provence and Anglo-Saxon England, represent an experiment in diversity of style resembling the procession of parodies in Joyce's 'Oxen of the Sun' chapter. Motivated by the purpose of bringing dead souls to life, Pound felt justified in penetrating linguistic and historical barriers, and moving about freely among the rules of language and the limits of time to evoke scattered contexts and assemble them into meaningful designs. This method, the method of the *Cantos*, can be seen at work in the two 'Villonauds' published in Pound's first volume *A Lume Spento*, and if the poems themselves are weak, they do at least illustrate a resource that Pound continued to use—the re-shaping of language to fit psychological states.

The state in question, one Pound obviously felt worth renewing and making accessible to his contemporaries, was the striking combination of despair, wit, irony, rakishness and self-pity displayed in Villon's verse. Pound asserted its existence as a distinct complex of attitudes by inventing the sub-genre of the 'Villonaud' to express it. The poems reproduce some of Villon's characteristics, including the ballade form, occasional borrowed or translated phrases, and perhaps the tendency toward linguistic innovation found in his poems written in *argot*; but it is more significant that they also employ new resources to achieve their Villonesque effect. The first stanza of 'Villonaud for this Yule' will illustrate:

> Towards the Noel that morte saison
> (*Christ make the shepherds' homage dear!*)
> Then when the grey wolves everychone
> Drink of the winds their chill small-beer

And lap o' the snows food's gueredon
Then makyth my heart his yule-tide cheer
(Skoal! with the dregs if the clear be gone!)
Wining the ghosts of yester-year.

(p. 24)

This is not a translation of any specific original, but an effort to capture what had better be called Pound's intuition of Villon's consciousness. An uncharitable reader might conclude that Pound has simply thrown together some archaisms and French words in order to achieve a vaguely historical flavour. But the mixed diction follows the principle Pound was to use on a much larger scale in the *Cantos*, the blending of resources from all times and places into a single conformation. The Chaucerian 'every-chone' and 'makyth' establish the general historical period, the French words suggest a sense of place, the 'chill small-beer' and 'Skoal!' contribute the madcap irony of gallows humour. 'Yester-year' is, of course, borrowed from 'Where are the snows of yester-year?' Rossetti's masterly rendering of Villon's refrain, 'Mais où sont les neiges d'antan?' But it would be a mistake to see it as a weak concession to a rival translator; it is, instead, a way of marking a spot in the past where the emotion Pound wishes to recreate has been successfully recreated before, and of acknowledging the tradition to which he is contributing.

Instead of directly imitating the speech of his subjects in these poems, Pound devised equivalent locutions intended to achieve a similar effect in a contemporary context. In 'Cino' the character's devil-may-care attitude is expressed in asyntactical sequences, 'Lips words and you snare them', and 'Eyes, dreams, lips and the night goes', in such careless neologisms as 'wind-runeing' (which seems to mean the whispering of the wind) and 'us-toward', in slangy clippings, 'Pollo Phoibee' and 'fulgence', and in the unsolemn use of 'wander-lied'. These deviations are not specific to the historical period, or even to the character being projected, but rather to the mood expressed in the poem.

Much of Pound's originality can be traced to this motivation. Intent upon catching the exact vibration of the mood of some earlier work, he follows the method, in his 'personae', near-translations, and poems on historical subjects, of patching together a miscellany of vocabulary, allusions, and tones and levels of language. The anachronisms, distortions and what K. K. Ruthven calls 'creative mistranslations' found in such poems as 'The Ballad of the Goodly Fere', 'The Seafarer' and 'Homage to Sextus Propertius' reflect Pound's intention not to imitate, but to recreate.

The result is a distinctly experimental, even improvisational poetic medium which comes under much firmer control in *Mauberley*, and is expanded in the *Cantos*. If these poems are understood as efforts to give new life to permanent, though elusive emotions in a style devised for the purpose, their peculiarities become much more intelligible.

3 ELIOT

T.S. Eliot's three early monologues, 'The Love Song of J. Alfred Prufrock', 'Portrait of a Lady'—which is equally the self-portrait of a man—and 'Gerontion' are written in a remarkable poetic idiom inspired by the poems of Jules Laforgue, in which the speaker expresses the nearly incompatible feelings of personal despair and a wider, ironic consciousness of his inadequacy. The spiritual incapacity exposed in these poems emerges in faded gentilities of speech, courteous hesitations, exaggerated punctilio and hollow-sounding aphorisms—'Think/Neither fear nor courage saves us',[34]—and also in flat, toneless statements which, regardless of their actual content, are really admissions of defeat—'In the room the women come and go/Talking of Michelangelo' (p. 4). The impression of unendurable self-knowledge from which Eliot's people suffer, composed of self-pity on the one hand and self-judgment on the other, rests, to a great extent, on purely linguistic resources. Two of these are especially prominent: echoes of past uses of language, ranging from overt allusions or paraphrases, to the more general reverberations aroused by such words as 'universe' or 'history': and the imagery. Both of these ways of exposing thought appear in 'Preludes' and 'Rhapsody on a Windy Night', which are dramatic lyrics expressing the feelings of particular minds, though without the ironic modulations found in the monologues.

Eliot's practice of sowing his poems with quotations and paraphrases, fragments of language bearing the marks of earlier use, gives them an archaeological dimension reflecting a basic agreement with Pound about the relationship of the poet to his forerunners. This agreement is clearly expressed in 'Tradition and the Individual Talent', where Eliot speaks of 'definite emotions' passing from one work to another, which make it logical to regard the whole literary tradition as a 'simultaneous order'. Pound's statement that universals are best expressed through particulars turns out, on examination, to be a shorter confirmation of Eliot's view that 'we shall often find that not only the best, but the most individual parts of his (the poet's) work may be those in which the dead poets, his ancestors, assert their immortality most vigorously'.[35] But Eliot sees contrast in this relation where Pound sees resemblance; where Pound pressed for renewal, Eliot spoke of 'transmutation'; where Pound is interested in the permanence of emotions, Eliot is concerned with loss and emptiness. There is a corresponding difference in their dramatic lyrics. Pound's reflect his conviction that the poetic imagination can enter into the feelings of historical figures far removed in time and place, and use them, if only temporarily, as masks of the self. But Eliot's speakers are fictional contemporaries marooned in the *ennui*, futility and rootlessness of modern life, and they display an utter inability to escape their identities. They are illustrations of the passage from F.H. Bradley's *Appearance and Reality* used in one of the footnotes to *The Waste Land* which describes the self as a closed circle that limits the individual's knowledge to his own experience. Hence, when the speakers of Eliot's dramatic poems merge the language of other contexts with their own, they express an anguished awareness of the gulf between their empty lives and the irrecoverable vitality of the past, not a sense of union with it. Even allusions to dark patches of history and literature perform this function. Prufrock's references, in one section of his poem, to Hamlet, Chaucer's clerk, and royal fools like the one in *Lear*, the reference of the 'lady's' friend to Juliet's tomb, and Gerontion's quotation from Matthew recall episodes of evil and violence, but they also involve people who were acting to fulfill their desires or follow their convictions, thus displaying precisely the kind of personal worth lacking in the speakers themselves.

Neither poet seemed concerned with delineating full-fledged characters, in Browning's manner, because for both the monologue was, paradoxically, a form of depersonalization. Pound, we recall, described his monologues as devices for rejecting false notions of the self, and this withdrawal is even more obvious with Eliot, who thought the poet did not need to undergo the experiences he used in his poems. His tendency to deal with states of mind rather than fully conceived personalities, and his technique of conveying these through external images seem indebted to F.H. Bradley's reduction of individual identities to 'zones of consciousness'. According to Bradley, the concept of personal identity is difficult to sustain, because it means that thoughts must be continuous and consistent throughout a lifetime. The only force that links our varying states of mind to each other is memory, which is obviously too defective to insure unity. If there is some essence of mind which never changes, the contents of the mind passes back and forth between it and the parts of the psyche which are borrowed or changeable, so that the line of demarcation between the essential self and the contributions of the outside world is blurred. What we usually take to be an individual self, therefore, Bradley describes as a 'zone of consciousness', a phenomenon not sharply marked off from its material context. Experience consists, not of a mind reacting to externals, but, as Eliot says, of 'non-relational, immediately felt unity' in which internal and external are blended together, exactly as they are in Bergson's account of perception in *Matter and Memory*.

If Eliot owed his concept of the self to Bradley, it is natural that his monologues should embody vague moods, and that each speaker should be immersed in his environment, rather than able to deal with it on equal terms. Perception, instead of being a dialectic transaction between the two poles of internal and external reality, tends to be a merging of the two into a continuum in which distinct ideas of subject and object are lost. Eliot's objective correlative is not merely a concrete image that speaks for itself but an external that has been taken into the mind and wrapped in an envelope of signification, so that it becomes a feature of the mind, cooperating with it, and requiring no interpretation, for it is an 'immediately felt unity', establishing a continuity between the perceiving mind and the externals it perceives.

These images are the most important 'psychological' innovations of Eliot's early monologues, and became, like the literary allusions, a permanent feature of his style. 'A pair of ragged claws/Scuttling across the floors of silent seas', and 'Hakagawa, bowing among the Titians' have no other function than that of striking some exact, but elusive modulation of feeling in the character who is speaking. Pound's images are related, through feelings, to external absolutes; Eliot's, though they are more strictly psychological, having no aspirations beyond the embodiment of moods or feelings, nevertheless have absolute implications of their own. They are points where the mind and the external world meet and support each other at the limits of personal certainty, becoming a series of points marking the outward boundary of the 'finite centre'. The images that succeed each other in Gerontion's mind—'Rocks, moss, stonecrop, iron, merds'—are linked by association. By tracing them, the reader learns what Gerontion's world means to him, and discovers the shape and shaping power of his identity.

Language imitative of the associative, impressionistic activity of mental life survived in the styles of Pound and Eliot, even when they were not writing monologues. The general loosening of structure, freedom of syntax, and unconventionality of diction and imagery involved in the close portrayal of a mind at work offered positive stylistic values of their own. The end of 'Gerontion' has the loose, asyntactic form of the old man's uncontrolled musing:

> Gull against the wind, in the windy straits
> Of Belle Isle, or running on the Horn,
> White feathers in the snow, the Gulf claims,
> And an old man driven by the Trades
> To a sleepy corner.
> Tenants of the house,
> Thoughts of a dry brain in a dry season.
>
> (p. 23)

Such images, allusions and juxtapositions appear in *The Waste Land* without the pretext that they are expressions of a particular consciousness. The point that the poem as a whole simulates the thought of Tiresias appears only as a kind of rationalization in one of the footnotes. Similarly, *Mauberley* and the *Cantos* are not monologues, nor even the expression of any one fictional mind, but they take full advantage of the linguistic freedom found in the stream of consciousness.

4 JOYCE

This freedom is the premise of Joyce's interior monologue, where the relationships that ordinarily control language are replaced by such psychological mechanisms as memory, association and analogy. In Joyce's work these are all controlled, as has often been pointed out, by his thoroughly rational structural purposes. For Joyce, the mental processes were sources of new techniques, not quasi-mystical ways of approaching ultimate reality. His method, the imposition of firm patterns on processes modelled after the free activity of the mind, first appears in *A Portrait of the Artist as a Young Man*, although only a few parts of the novel are actually true interior monologue.

As Dorothy Van Ghent has shown, the boy who is its hero regards language and its relationships as a key to the puzzling world he lives in.[36] Since Stephen's strongest emotional responses are evoked by words, he regards them as his final reality. His inhospitable environment is useful to him mainly as a way of illuminating the meaning of language. His artistic visions and his attempt to write are little more than narcissistic surrenders to the sensuous verbal heterocosm that blots out the real world around him. This, it should be clear, is not the same sensibility that Joyce himself exhibits, and their different relationships to language mark an important distinction, in this autobiographical novel, between the 'young man' who is its protagonist and the 'artist' who is the author.

When Stephen's mother says, 'O, Stephen will apologize', and Dante answers, 'O, if not, the eagles will come and pull out his eyes', the accidental rhymes enable the boy to reshape the two remarks into a clearly patterned little poem. He places himself in the centre of the cosmos through a series of concentric words beginning with 'Stephen Dedalus', and ending with 'The Universe.' He thinks that he has grasped things when he has learned what they are called, and is certain that 'God's real name was God'. The feeling of Eileen's cold white hands over his eyes is significant because it explains how 'Tower of Ivory' can be used to mean the Blessed Virgin. Language is an indispensable metaphoric equivalent for the child's feelings and experiences; as he grows into a young man, he persists in seeing the world as something that exists through and for language. The kiss of a prostitute affects him like 'the vehicle of a vague speech'. He brings the comforting plainness of a lane home to himself through vigorous words, 'That is horse piss and rotted straw.' When he is disgusted with himself for gormandizing on heavy food, the feeling presents itself in the form of an image of the word 'Dublin' with its letters slowly jostling one another out of position, a first anticipation on Joyce's part of one of the devices of *Finnegans Wake*. His name exercises a mysterious verbal magic that controls his destiny. When he is urged to consider the priesthood, the thought of the name, 'The Reverend Stephen Dedalus, S.J.' calls forth an unpleasant image of priests, and makes him realize that he does not want to be one of them. On the other hand, his decision to become an artist springs from the moment when his schoolmates jokingly call out his name in Greek forms, 'Stephanos Dedalos! Bous Stephanoumenous! Bous Stephaneforos!' so that he identifies himself with the 'fabulous artificer' and is ready for his quasi-mystical vision of the girl wading in the sea.

Stephen's moments of spiritual turmoil are accompanied by a sense that language has lost its meaning, the same feeling that Hulme recorded when he noted that it might become a mere 'rope of words'. During the visit to Cork, remorse at his shameful thoughts renders him nearly faint, so that the signs on the shops lose their meaning. He can recall himself to reality only by reaching for it through language, by recalling his own name and the names of the things around him. When he explains his aesthetic theories, his strongest arguments take the form of definitions, and the words 'tundish' and '*jupes*' disturb him because they unsettle strands of the verbal network around which his life is organized.

After his conversion, every detail of life and the universe as a whole seems to exist for the sake of exhibiting the benign power of God; but we realize, before long, that this state of mind is only a temporary variant of his real conviction that it exists to manifest the power of language.

When it is organized into literary form, language serves Stephen as a register or counterpart of feelings, and is as capable of evoking emotive responses as any sensuous experience. The rhythm of a line from Newman suggests the dignity of priesthood, and a chance phrase from a work on geology, 'A day of dappled seaborne clouds' delights him as if it were a chord of music. In his analysis of his response to words, he decides that he cares, not so much for their meanings and associations, as for 'an inner world of individual emotions mirrored perfectly in a lucid supple periodic prose'. As he walks to his College, each sight seen on the way is transposed into a literary experience:

The rainladen trees of the avenue evoked in him, as always, memories of the girls and women in the plays of Gerhart Hauptmann... His morning walk across the city had begun, and he foreknew that as he passed the sloblands of Fairview he would think of the cloistral silverveined prose of Newman, that as he walked along the North Strand Road, glancing idly at the windows of the provision shops, he would recall the dark humour of Guido Cavalcanti and smile, that as he went by Baird's stonecutting works in Talbot Place the spirit of Ibsen would blow through him like a keen wind. . . . [37]

There are, of course, no direct connections between these places and the passages of literature they recall; Stephen associates them with each other through obscure synaesthetic processes. The historical context of this exceptional sensitivity to the evocative power of language is the suggestive, incantatory verse of the decadence and the early Yeats. Stephen's infatuation with the echoes and colourings of words and with 'liquid letters of mystery' naturally leads to the effete, if accomplished villanelle of chapter V. But its importance is not to be underestimated, for it is the germ of Joyce's own mastery of language. Stephen's vision of 'Europe of strange tongues and valleyed and woodbegirt and citadelled and of entrenched and marshalled races' embodies a romanticism that is the root of Joyce's art. But while Stephen can use his passion for language only to write his villanelle, his author can turn it to the purposes of A Portrait of the Artist, and ultimately to those of Ulysses and Finnegans Wake.

This control manifests itself in A Portrait through the way in which language is used to reflect Stephen's development. The style is skilfully modulated to correspond to his changing spiritual condition, from the lisping childhood speech and flat schoolboy prose of the first chapter to the distrustful irony and romantic aspiration of the diary entries at the end. At the beginning of chapter III, for example, the boy, newly disillusioned by his encounters with prostitutes, has cynical and ruthless thoughts about food: 'The swift December dusk had come tumbling clownishly after its dull day and, as he stared through the dull square of the window of the schoolroom, he felt his belly crave for its food. He hoped there would be stew for dinner, turnips and carrots and bruised potatoes and fat mutton pieces to be ladled out in thick peppered flourfattened sauce. Stuff it into you, his belly counselled him.' (p. 102) After the first day of the retreat, he devours a greasy dinner, but is later repelled by his doltish surrender to appetite, and when the retreat is over, and Father Arnall's sermon has done its work, the narrative tone, as Stephen thinks of food again, reflects the simple passivity of the newly penitent mind: 'On the dresser was a plate of sausages and white pudding and on the shelf there were eggs. They would be for the breakfast in the morning after the communion in the college chapel. White pudding and eggs and sausages and cups of tea. How simple and beautiful was life after all! And life lay all before him.' (p. 146) Much of the art of the *Portrait* rests on this deliberate shaping of styles into the embodiments of Stephen's feelings, so that the prose speaks to us through its rhetorical elements as much as through its content.

Joyce's fluid prose medium also marks the periodic returns of Stephen's mind to certain themes and images. 'The dance of feelings', says Hugh Kenner, of this aspect of the novel's style, 'has its objective correlative in the dance of words.'[38] When the priest divides the class into teams represented by the red rose of Lancaster and the white rose of York, Stephen recalls the mistake he made as a baby in singing of a green rose; but he also speculates that the green rose may be less a mistake than an imaginative creation, surely the thought of a boy who is destined to be an experimental writer. Another vivid detail of childhood, the green and maroon brushes belonging to Dante, recurs like a Wagnerian leitmotif; Stephen notes that his schoolmate, Fleming, has coloured the picture of the earth in his geography book green and maroon; the colours appear in the holly and ivy of the Christmas decorations at home, and in Stephen's vision of Dante at Parnell's funeral, dressed in the velvet fabrics from the backs of her brushes.

The incident of the hot and cold water-cocks at the hotel is part of a design that runs throughout the account of Stephen's childhood. Hot and cold make up the experience of wetting the bed on the first page, the memory of being shouldered into the

cold water of the ditch is juxtaposed with that of his mother and
Dante sitting by the fire, the cold of the bedsheets is followed by
a warm glow; the two polar sensations dominate the boy's experience of school. The earth in his geography book looks like a ball.
Years later, an observation of the professor during a college lecture
leads one of the boys to joke, 'What price ellipsoidal balls!' The
two occurrences of the word become associated in Stephen's
mind during the composition of the villanelle, as he thinks of the
earth as 'a ball of incense, an ellipsoidal ball'. Naturally, the
phrase kills his inspiration. 'The rhythm died out at once; the
cry of his heart was broken.' (p. 218) His recollection of an evening
spent with Emma Clery is narrated in a couple of sentences that
repeat *verbatim* the description of the event that took place ten
years before: 'It was the last tram; the lank brown horses knew
it . . . .' (p. 69 and 222) The recurrence of a thought is embodied
in an exact repetition of words.

These verbal imitations of mental processes are, of course,
only anticipations of the method that was to be more fully
developed in *Ulysses*. While the major form of *Ulysses* springs
from the consciousness of Joyce himself, large parts of it are
composed in styles that imitate or reflect the thought processes
of other minds. There are three easily-distinguished principles
of stylistic imitation in *Ulysses*: first, the interior monologue,
which purports to reproduce the uncontrolled flow of ordinary
thought; second, the dramatization of irrational thought found in
the 'Circe' chapter; and third, the numerous parodies, occurring
principally in the 'Cyclops', 'Nausicaa' and 'Oxen of the Sun'
chapters which embody particular habits of mind.

Because it represents language in its post-Einsteinian, post-
Bergsonian phase, free of the restrictions imposed by such notions
as time and place, objective and subjective, presence and absence,
the interior monologue may be regarded as the archetypal modern
style. While it follows the conviction of Freud and Jung that the
major significance of life is to be found in the operation of the
mind, it has little or nothing to do with the subconscious. Its
material is thought which is somewhat above the level of minimal
consciousness, clear enough to the mind to be verbalized, but
too vague to be deliberately expressed. This mental activity is
neither James's stream of consciousness nor Bergson's *durée*, but
material which has been organized and spatialized by the filter
of language, though to a lesser degree than most verbal records
of thought.[39]

If we were to ask language to do full justice to the multiple flow
of the mind, with its interpolations of memory and expectation

and its subtle shadings of feeling, we should find James's or Proust's style more appropriate, for these have such resources as subordination, balance, an abstract vocabulary, and transitional devices capable of making numerous intricate connections among the data of thought. What distinguishes the interior monologue is not what it has, but what it lacks; its freedom from the requirements of sentence syntax and ordinary logical discourse opens to it the wider—or, at least, different—possibilities of uncontrolled thinking, a new and freer syntax of fantasy, association and recall, and puts all experience upon the same plane.

The form reaches a kind of impoverished perfection in this respect in Faulkner's *The Sound and the Fury*, where the idiot Benjy's perfect recall of persons and events, and his indifference to time and place produce a mental arena in which things can be moved freely from their original positions to be juxtaposed according to the associations they have for him. It is possible to make conventional sense of Benjy's monologue by linking his recollections to the indications of time that occur; but after doing this, we are likely to prefer his version, in which events twenty-five years apart gain a poetic significance when they are set side by side. The freshness of these new narrative shapes, freed of the forms imposed by chronology, testifies to the value of the method of juxtaposition. Nothing could demonstrate the verbal commitment of the modern period more conclusively than the fact that even Benjy's world is shaped by words. The ambiguous words, 'Caddy', 'ball', and 'Quentin' are knots that tie the crucial associations of his life together; one of the great sources of his anguish is the fact that no one else understands these verbal connections.

The monologue style, as Joyce used it, is an asyntactic recital, full of concrete images, that moves in widely-varying expressive rhythms. It is enriched by memories of past events and verbal materials that have been read or heard, but is restricted, in its reporting of external events, to the narrow aperture of the character's perceptions and reactions. Joyce varies his use of these formal features to express the intense individuality of his people with remarkable vividness and intimacy. The idiom of each monologue is so thoroughly characteristic of the person thinking it that it is impossible to confuse a line from one of them with any of the others. Early critics thought that Joyce had achieved a faithful imitation of the stream of consciousness in the monologue, but it is now clear that it is a convention, like any other literary style, without special claims to psychological accuracy. But because he did take ordinary mental processes as material, Joyce made the point, a sufficiently novel one for the 1920s, that the mind, even in its most common manifestations, possesses extraordinary vitality.

Perhaps the single most conclusive demonstration of the literary potentialities of interior monologue is the 'Proteus' chapter of *Ulysses*. Stephen's informed and critical consciousness pillages every aspect of his experience as it shapes what he sees and recalls into meaningful conformations. In this exclusively mental world, the usual distinctions between past and present, legend and reality, theory and fact are eliminated, so that the record of his thought processes involves identifications characteristic of myth and poetry. The sights Stephen encounters on the beach become embodiments of his memories and desires, the events of his life become instances of traditional historical patterns, and passages of verse and prose that seem to formulate his own situation occur to him. He thinks of his own conception as a part of the current of generation beginning with God, so that his father and the ghostly image of his dead mother are seen as agents of the eternal will, and he wonders whether he shares the divine substance. A moment of thought about the history of the beach he is walking on produces a vivid montage of the Norse invaders who once landed there, whales gone aground, and people coming out to salvage their blubber.

Stephen's mind also moves rapidly through details of his own recent activities, so that the narrative of his residence in Paris is told in a compressed string of images toned with associations typical of his cynical and self-distrustful attitude. He recalls his fantasies of being suspected of murder in Paris, but proving his innocence through punched Métro tickets ('You seem to have enjoyed yourself'), then an attempt to cash a money order just as the post office is closing, then the motives that took him to Paris, the pornographic magazines in his luggage when he returned, and finally the words of the telegram that brought him home: 'Mother dying come home father.'[40] The passage is like a dramatic lyric by Eliot or Pound; it is not a narrative, but a record of the mind grasping images in accordance with its own motives, a transmutation of external experience in the alchemist's oven of memory and emotion. The final line is the exact wording of the telegram Joyce received from his father when he was in Stephen's situation; for the reader who knows this fact, it raises all the questions associated with *collage*, questions of the mysterious links and disjunctions between art and reality.

The Stephen of the 'Proteus' chapter is manifestly the same as the one in *A Portrait*, for words continue to mediate the entry of reality into his consciousness, and his own verbal creations are vital elements in the rhythm and structure of the chapter. A boat stranded on the shore strikes him as a near approximation of the metaphor used by a critic to describe the prose of Gautier, '*Un coche ensablé*', and this leads him to the characteristic insight that physical reality amounts to no more than its semantic value: 'These heavy sands are language tide and wind have silted here' (p. 44). Bloom attempts to write his name on the sand in the 'Nausicaa' chapter, but Stephen has no need to do this, for to him physical appearances have a spontaneous verbal import. He takes the sights on the beach at the beginning of the chapter, both as a text that 'I am here to read', and as Boehme's 'signatures of all things'. The words *nacheinander* and *nebeneinander* that occur during his test of walking blind are from Lessing's *Laokoon*, where a distinction is made between arts that unfold themselves in time, whose elements appear sequentially (*nacheinander*) and those that are simultaneous, whose elements are spread out in space adjoining each other (*nebeneinander*). In the first two paragraphs of his monologue, Stephen organizes reality according to Lessing's division, for the first paragraph is limited to visual appeals, the second to auditory ones.

In each of these paragraphs, Stephen turns to testimony from literature to clarify the meaning of the physical experiences he is analysing. In the first, he recalls some comments about objects from Aristotle's *De Anima*: in the second, he explains the solidity of the ground he is walking on as the creation of Blake's mythical figure, Los (p. 37). His practice of unfolding his experiences in ideas, phrases and images from other writers produces a world haunted by feelings generated in literature, as it does on his walk to the College in *A Portrait*. Far from being a mere game of allusions, the device is a way of calling upon sensibilities already formulated in particular verbal contexts, and mingling or juxtaposing them with others, to produce effects of special depth and strength.

In Stephen's monologue allusions are likely to be most effective when they involve ironies reflecting his own division of mind. Recalling (or imagining) a reproach for reading old books by the heretical Joachim de Floris, whom he calls Joachim Abbas, he thinks of another figure who was alienated from humanity, Swift. Asking why the multitude should be so hostile, he thinks, 'Abbas father, furious dean, what offence laid fire to their brains?' combining Joachim, Swift and Jesus during his agony into a single formulation of the sort of martyrdom he identifies himself with.

Though it dispenses with conventional syntax, Joyce's interior monologue uses grammatical elements for its own purposes. Short, fragmentary locutions often suggest intense emotion which breaks the stream of consciousness, while the unpunctuated, flowing style of 'Penelope' creates the uninterrupted, low-level consciousness of daydreaming. In 'Proteus', Stephen's sensitivity to the different styles in which people express themselves leads to numerous short parodies or borrowings of rhetorical effects that suit the subject. Kevin Egan's scandalized reaction to the female bath attendant in the Swedish bath-house is given in his own rhythms, 'Most licentious custom. Bath a most private thing,' and the story of the Fenian leader who escaped from prison disguised as a bride is punctuated with the characteristic 'Did, faith' of the Irish story-teller. 'In gay Paree' and the 'nicey comfy' with which his wife is described also seem to be reflections of Egan's speech. (p. 43) Since the cocklepickers he sees look like gipsies to Stephen, he thinks of them in the passage of gipsies' cant which, he decides, is as good as the language of Aquinas. Their dog strikes him as looking like a heraldic device as he runs across the beach, or so the language suggests: 'On a field tenney a buck, trippant, proper, unattired.' (p. 46)

If the innovations in sentence structure in 'Proteus' reflect movements of thought, the neologisms and other verbal distortions are due to Stephen's interest in words and their power. His resistance to convention is brilliantly embodied in his inventive attacks upon language. The younger Stephen of *A Portrait* was perhaps more openly rebellious, but he had not yet learned how to deviate productively from the rules of language. However, the Stephen of 'Proteus' does modify words in the privacy of his own thoughts, thus taking a first step toward becoming the great verbal alchemist of *Finnegans Wake*. By far the most interesting of the verbal departures in this chapter is the superb nonce-word 'contransmagnificandjewbangtiality'. It expresses Stephen's ironic view that both theories of the Mass, consubstantiation and transubstantiation, were extravagant inventions of Jewish mysticism intended to create astonishment. But it also shows that Joyce has perceived that the normally indivisible unit of the word can, like the atom, yield unexpected outpourings of energy when it is divided. It is, of course, a remote ancestor of the thunder-words in *Finnegans Wake*; like them, it treats comically the notion that a supernatural event can release far-reaching consequences.

Bloom's monologues are much less interesting from a strictly verbal point of view than Stephen's. Bloom has considerable practical knowledge, he is more observant than Stephen, and his monologue is more evenly balanced between external perceptions and inner reactions, often segregating these from each other into separate sentences. His monologue, like Stephen's, displays the mind's ability to live in several worlds at once, for he can be flippant and serious, sentimental and practical, frightened and curious at nearly the same moment. Bloom's attempts at organized thought are among the great sources of comedy in *Ulysses*. They include efforts to deal with abstract matters: 'Because the weight of the water, no, the weight of the body in the water is equal to the weight of the. Or is it the volume is equal of the weight? It's a law something like that' (p. 72); to possess simple truths: 'Broken heart. A pump after all, pumping thousands of gallons of blood every day. One fine day it gets bunged up and there you are' (p. 105); and to gain insight into the past: 'Those old popes were keen on music, on art and statues and pictures of all kinds. . . . They had a gay old time while it lasted.' (p. 82). He seldom thinks of words, as distinct from their meanings, and his ideas about them are feeble: 'Father Coffey. I knew his name was like a coffin.' (p. 103); 'Rip van Winkle we played. Rip: tear in Henry Doyle's overcoat. Van: breadvan delivering. Winkle: cockles and peri-winkles' (p. 377). Sometimes, through Bloom's confusions, words take an active part in the comedy of his thoughts. He thinks of the Dead Sea as a 'Vulcanic lake', (p. 61), and matches his remembrance that one must not joke about the dead with the motto: '*De mortuis nil nisi prius.*' (p. 109)

Still, Bloom is sensitive enough to words to see from time to time that they can be transformed into one another, though these shifts are never more than trivial. When he hears (or recalls) the schoolchildren saying the alphabet in 'Calypso', their recital approaches a sentence of nonsense words, and their way of saying 'geography' becomes a totally different word, 'joggerfry' (p. 58). At his first glance at the Rev. Elijah Dowie's throwaway, with its comment on 'the blood of the lamb', he thinks he sees his own name (p. 151). He is puzzled by 'parallax', and thinks it may have something to do with 'parallel', and agrees with Molly's opinion that such words as 'metempsychosis' are 'only big words for ordinary things on account of the sound'. Like Stephen, he sometimes thinks of literature in connection with his experiences, but most of these are recollections of songs, limericks, comic poems and the like, and while he does occasionally recall such works as *Hamlet* or Gray's 'Eulogy', his ideas about them can be comically inaccurate or banal. He thinks, for example, that the joking of the gravediggers in *Hamlet* displays a profound knowledge of the human heart. Bloom shares Stephen's view that the physical world is articulate, but while this is a profound unconscious conviction with Stephen, which controls his understanding of all experience, it occupies Bloom's mind only in a trivial way, as a superficial conceit. When he hears the noise made by the flyboard of the printing press at the newspaper office, he thinks, 'Doing its level best to speak. . . . Everything speaks in its own way' (p. 121). But all the machine has to say to him is 'sllt', and the church bells he hears at the end of the 'Calypso' chapter say no more than 'Heigho! Heigho' (p. 70).

The verbal interest of 'Penelope' arises from two sources—its imitation of the movements of Molly's thoughts, and the arbitrary patterns Joyce has imposed upon them. The language itself is very close to what we must take to be Molly's ordinary speech, but the omission of punctuation and the occasionally merged grammatical constructions convey the sense of an unbroken flow of pre-verbal thought. This continuity supports the content, which consists of linked, blended and interpenetrating memories from all parts of Molly's life. Connective tissue is eliminated, and the concrete data of recollection—and, to a small extent, of present events—are crowded together into a dense, resistant fabric. The suppression of time and the selectivity of Molly's feelings transform whatever the reality of her experiences may have been into her version of it, a world of memories available to her consciousness, and structured according to her own fears and desires. Whatever the circumstances of her first meeting with Boylan in the D.B.C. may actually have been, the occasion be-comes, in her memory, a string of events consisting of Boylan's awareness of her feet, her visit to the lavatory, her troublesome underclothing, the lost gloves, Bloom's suggestion that she advertise for them, and her return to the restaurant in the hope of meeting Boylan again.

In spite of appearances, however, her consciousness is not the final determinant of form in 'Penelope'. In a letter to Budgen of August 16, 1921, Joyce said that the slow movement of the eight sentences of the chapter was intended to imitate the spinning of the earth, and that the four cardinal points of the female body were indicated by the recurring words, *because, bottom, woman, yes*. Joyce's characters organize their thoughts in the way events associate themselves in their minds; but this in turn is subjected to the abstract verbal control decreed by Joyce himself. S.L. Goldberg has described this situation as one in which the character exercises what Coleridge called the primary imagination, shaping the raw data of sensation into definable objects and experiences that become material for Joyce's secondary imagina-tion, the power of inventing forms that satisfy the requirements of art. In thinking of the soul as a 'form of forms', Stephen is recalling a passage from Aristotle's *De Anima* which Goldberg cites: ' . . . the soul is analogous to the hand; for as the hand is a tool of tools, so the mind is the form of forms. . . . '⁴¹ The interior monologue embodies in words this power of ideas to generate other ideas.

Interior monologue is only one of a wide range of objective styles characteristic of experimental literature which oppose the conventional expectation that a work is 'self-expression' by speaking in a voice that is obviously not that of the author. Another of these is parody, a device that is used in several ways in *Ulysses*. Its status as a psychological form is less evident in the literary imitations of the 'Oxen of the Sun' chapter than in the part of 'Nausicaa' that deals with Gerty MacDowell. Working within a tradition as old as *Don Quixote*, Joyce identifies Gerty's mind with the sensibility displayed in the girls' stories she has read, and conveys its qualities by imitating their style. Her state of mind is exhibited by the vocabulary, sentence structure, tone, imagery, allusions and other technical features of the text. Gerty's thoughts of an ideal lover are expressed with an archaic, chivalric formality: 'he who would woo and win Gerty MacDowell must be a man among men', (p. 351). Inversion, stock phrasing and exaggeration convey her shallow romanticism: 'No prince charming is her beau ideal to lay a rare and wondrous love at her feet but rather a manly man . . . ' (p. 351). The simile she uses to describe his kiss is totally banal: 'It would be like heaven' (p. 352). And her version of the words of the marriage service displays her inability to attend to anything outside her daydreams: ' . . . for riches for poor, in sickness in health, till death us two part, from this to this day forward' (p. 352). This is a use of language far removed from the referential function, for it conveys its message through stylistic features, with very little dependence on content. The 'Oxen of the Sun' parodies are less pointed psychologically, for they count on evoking a sense of their originals to gain their effect. Still the description of the tin of sardines in the style of Mandeville (p. 387) exhibits credulousness, the Pepys section (pp. 396 ff.) independently expresses a clear, crisp practicality, the Huxley one (pp. 417 ff.) has an unmistakable no-nonsense aggressive air, and the Dickens passage (pp. 420 ff.) displays its sentimentality eloquently enough.

While interior monologue adequately reflects the lower levels of conscious thought, Joyce found that if he wanted to take advantage of the vast creative energies of the subconscious, he would have to resort to a new form, the quasi-Expressionist drama of the 'Circe' chapter. This chapter gives unquestionable evidence of Joyce's remarkable appreciation of the irrational mental processes.

Like Freud's 'dream-work' it dramatizes subconscious thoughts, but for the purpose of articulating, rather than disguising them. Eliot uses a similar device in *Murder in the Cathedral*, where the four Tempters are objectifications of ideas that are occurring to Thomas, and there is the additional similarity that each of them speaks in a different style and metre. In 'Circe', the former lives of the people and innumerable details of the day they have just lived through return in distorted or exaggerated form, and fall into new relationships with one another. The chapter is obviously a dramatization of thought, yet it is not easy to say whose thoughts these are, for the speeches of the characters do not always correspond with their previous actions and knowledge. Some parts of the drama are apparently not thoughts at all, but new events occurring in Nighttown, and while they too are passed through the screen of irrational perception, they cannot be identified with the minds of any of the characters. Arnold Goldman has suggested that 'Circe' represents 'Joyce's fantasia on his own novel',[42] which would mean that it is the one part of *Ulysses* where the author speaks most directly, in spite of its dramatic form. Unlike the interior monologues, the chapter is not attached to any specific personality; it has the indefiniteness of a Bradleyan 'zone of consciousness' like the early monologues of Pound and Eliot, and appears to dramatize unconscious rather than conscious processes. It also seems possible to think of the chapter as the product of a mind enclosing those of the characters themselves, one which includes and merges with all of them, so that the transpositions can be explained as the migrations of ideas within a single consciousness, and the new characters and ideas as activities of this quasi-omniscient, fantasizing mentality.

The vitality of 'Circe' is due primarily to its action rather than its language, but language acquires special privileges and powers in this hallucinatory world. The stage-directions, microscopically exact, always specific, exhibit a range and vigour of vocabulary that achieves a unique, burly texture. Even when they present the grotesque, violent and incongruous, they never change their measured, objective tone.

On a step gnome a totting among a rubbishtip crouches to shoulder a sack of rags and bones. A crone standing by with a smoky oil lamp rams the last bottle in the maw of his sack. He heaves his booty, tugs askew his peaked cap and hobbles off mutely.   (pp. 429–30)

This idiom is not outside the scope of conventional language, but it has the effect of creating rather than describing, partly because its style is the one normally used for a stage-setting, but also because the images it details so scrupulously are clearly improvised. The dialogue, in contrast to the cold efficiency of the stage-directions, changes its tone according to circumstances, so that Elijah speaks in an American idiom, J.J. O'Molloy, defending Bloom at his trial, uses legal terms, and Bloom himself shifts from a kind of abrupt telegraphese to the political bombast of the 'stump speech' and the shy feminine language of Bello's sexual partners. Objects become even more articulate than they are in the interior monologues, and the bells, the gong, the quoits of Molly's bed, Lynch's cap and the kisses that fly out of Bella's house to greet Bloom all contribute remarks to the conversation.

Since it is thought which is being dramatized in this scene, words, whose power is normally restricted to the recording of ideas, are able to generate new scenes and actions. When Bloom mentions some Negro entertainers, two black dancers appear on the stage. Zoe's 'Go on. Make a stump speech out of it' is followed by the appearance of Bloom as the Lord Mayor of Dublin delivering a long political address. Bloom's transformation into a female is caused by Mulligan's declaration that he is 'bisexual'. After Simon Dedalus's cry, 'Think of your mother's people!' a rapid sequence of the day's events flashes through Stephen's mind, culminating in the image of his dead mother, who appears to reproach him and drive him to the climactic action of the scene, the smashing of the lampshade. A number of figures, such as Philip Beaufoy, Henry Flower, and Philip Drunk and Philip Sober, who have had no existence except as verbal expressions, appear as characters. In this context, words are not distinguished from things, and have the power to cause events, as if they were actualities themselves. Joyce has returned to the emphasis Stephen Dedalus placed on words in *A Portrait*, but this time for the purpose of dramatizing subconscious thought.

The idiom of *Finnegans Wake* begins to take shape in this chapter. The handful of neologisms in 'Proteus' are only Stephen's witty word-plays, but in 'Circe' we see how words can be split open and grafted to each other to articulate modulations of feeling.

Most, thought not all of the verbal distortions affect names. When Bloom sees himself in a concave mirror, he is 'longlost lugubru Booloohoom' (p. 434); on the other hand, a convex mirror shows him, more cheerfully, as 'Jollypoldy the rixdix doldy' (p. 434). He calls the train that nearly ran over him at the Westland Row Station a 'mangongwheeltracktrolleyglarejuggernaut' (p. 452), multiplying its identities, and explains a temporary discomfort as 'Brainfogfag' (p. 436). The promised land that

Lord Mayor Bloom promises the citizens of Dublin is a new 'Bloomusalem', (p. 484) but when Elijah says the name of the sacred city he is interrupted by the phonograph which sardonically turns it into 'Whorusalaminyourhighhohhhh' (p. 508). The head of Shakespeare which appears in the mirror when Stephen and Bloom look into it rages at his cuckoldom and Bloom's in syllables torn from a speech of the player queen in *Hamlet*, so that 'None wed the second but who killed the first!' becomes 'Weda seca whokilla farst.' (p. 568) He describes the action of one of his plays as 'How my Oldfellow chokit his Thursdaymomun', (p. 567) which identifies Stephen, who has just told Zoe that he was born on a Thursday, with Desdemona. These are fruitful collisions between a word or name developed through the usual long process-es of history and an individual, even eccentric impulse, which show that the word can be detached from its conventional meaning and used for a new purpose and that its semantic properties can be maintained and exploited, even while its original form and meaning are being reshaped. Joyce solved Hulme's problem of expressing individual perception with the communal instrument of language, not by bending the curve of meaning, but by re-inventing Lewis Carroll's portmanteau-word.

A general discussion of *Finnegans Wake* must be postponed until chapter 7, but some observations about its psychological aspects are appropriate here. Although it purports to embody the activity of a dreaming mind, its noisy and intensely verbal idiom is not a record of dreaming, but rather a form of language stylized according to the principles of thought characteristic of dreams. *Finnegans Wake* and Joyce's experiments generally remind us that all knowledge except the most immediate is either buried in memory or scattered about in extensional space beyond the limits of present perception, and that language exists to gather all this material into a single interconnecting network. It has resources capable of relating the past to the present, and the absent to that which is at hand, yet it also acts to block perceptions off from each other, for the assumptions that Whorf showed to be inherent in language are, from Bergson's point of view, conventions preventing a true grasp of reality. Joyce's psychologically-oriented styles attempt to overcome these limitations by unlocking the assimilative and integrating power of language. Because 'the mind is wider than the sky', language that has access to the full energies of thought can ransack space and time, bringing the most incompat-ible elements together, and creating forms and relationships that have no models in physical reality. The interior monologue, the drama of 'Circe', and *Finnegans Wake* are progressively more radical efforts to free language from the patterns of conscious thought; through the convention that his book was the recital of a sleeping mind, Joyce was able to exploit this freedom fully, and paradoxically to achieve a result that is perhaps more intricately organized, more deliberately controlled, more 'conscious' than any other work of literature.

The merging or blending of words that is the central point of its style imitates the way the subconscious manifests itself in dreams or slips of the tongue. When the Jarl, in the story of the prankquean, becomes a 'tristian', the word bridges religion and the Tristan legend. At one point, Earwicker is told that but for his wife there would be neither 'breed and washer givers' nor 'a vestal flouting in the dock', puns combining two relevant meanings.[43] Freud's dream-mechanism of condensation or over-determination is often represented verbally. When the prankquean addresses the Jarl in 'the arkway of trihump', three figures connected with Earwicker are recalled, Noah, Napoleon and Humpty Dumpty, so that he acquires a multiple identity. Obsession, the persistence of ideas, is represented by such devices as the interweaving of the names of rivers and words relating to water into the language of 'Anna Livia Plurabelle' in the form of puns: 'Yssel that the limmat?' (p. 198), and locally by distortions reflecting the presence of a determining preoccupation, 'bedoueen the jebel and the jpysian sea'. (p. 5) This last effect can be used to make a single short sentence or passage echo many of the book's recurrent themes, braiding them together into a unified strand. A minor example is the sentence in the story of the prankquean Grace O'Malley, describing the kidnapping of one of the twins: 'So her grace o'malice kidsnapped up the jiminy Tristopher and into the shandy westerness she rain, rain, rain' (p. 21). Two of the key books of *Finnegans Wake*, *Alice in Wonderland* and *Tristram Shandy* are referred to, and Grace is said to 'rain' because she is a prototype of Anna Livia, who is associated with the Liffey and water in general. Joyce's dream-idiom speaks in the context of multiple existences so successfully that, as David Hayman has shown, the meanings in a given sentence can be analysed and extended nearly indefinitely, and Clive Hart has speculated that 'ultimately, there is . . . no such thing as an incorrect reading' of a passage in *Finnegans Wake*.[44]

Because language is itself a mental function, the psychological styles come much closer to imitating thinking than referential styles come to imitating external reality. But the veil that divides language from the physical world also divides it from the mental one, and Wittgenstein's 'copy theory' is equally invalid when it is thought, rather than material reality that is to be copied. The Surrealists believed they were grasping the true nature of the mind through automatic writing, and *Finnegans Wake* reworks the elementary principles of language in order to capture the flow and multiplicity characteristic of inner life; but neither impresses us as a successful imitation of thought itself. The efforts made to embody pure thought in language seem to prove only that there is an impassable barrier between the articulate and the inarticulate, but modern literature profited immensely from them nevertheless. A number of the modern theorists illuminate this situation, showing both why language remains distinct from thought, and why psychological styles nevertheless convey vital insights into it, and extend the expressive possibilities of language itself.

5 THE PSYCHOLOGICAL STYLES

Cassirer's view that immediate experience must be radically transformed if it is to be expressed symbolically applies to the immediate experience of mental reality, and sharply divides it from language. Every means of fixing thoughts into symbols is indirect, involving the interplay of private and external impressions. 'Art can no more be defined as the mere expression of inward life than as a reflection of the forms of outward reality. . . . ' Language, like any other medium, moves some distance away from the feelings it deals with in endowing them with meaning: ' . . . all linguistic expression, far from being a mere copy of the given world of sensation or intuition, possesses a definite independent character of "signification"'.[45] While the signifying techniques of conceptualization cannot convey thinking accurately, they are nevertheless vital processes in which the spirit defines itself by gaining control over its experiences. It is these processes, rather than the experience of thought itself that art in general and the psychological styles in particular, reflect. Bergson anticipated the interior monologue in speculating on the possibility that a novelist might try to report the flow of thought in all its fullness by identifying the manifold, fleeting impressions of which mental states are composed. He said that such an attempt was bound to fail because words and 'homogeneous time' could not reflect more than the shadow of actual thought. His discussion suggests that language imitating thought can be no more than one of the 'veridical hallucinations' to which pure realism and pure idealism reduce perceptions. But the effort to record it would be valuable, because it would call attention to the irrationality and complexity of thought, and bring us for a moment, as Bergson puts it, into our own presence.[46]

Language is inescapably hybrid. It can express private feelings only through conventions drawn from common sources, and it is always encumbered as Hulme strongly felt, by the weight of its traditions. Further, even the purest expression of inwardness is impossible without the mediation of forms of expression based on externals. Even if, as Cassirer formulates it, the mind, in communicating, 'apprehends the object and at the same time apprehends itself and its own formative law',[47] that formative law cannot be detached from those governing the physical world. As has often been observed, terms referring to movements of the mind nearly always resort to roots describing physical activities: 'conceive' is from a Latin root meaning to take or seize, 'attention' is from the Latin root meaning to stretch, and even the Anglo-Saxon 'understand' acquires an unexpected pictorial quality when it is considered etymologically. Thoughts themselves can perhaps dispense with metaphors from external life, but expression cannot. Fenollosa convincingly pointed out that the mind, in describing relationships, has no choice but to follow the examples provided by nature: 'Had the world not been full of homologies, sympathies, and identities, thought would have been starved and language chained to the obvious. There would have been no bridge whereby to cross from the minor truth of the seen to the major truth of the unseen.'[48]

Winifred Nowottny, considering language in its poetic function, sees similar limitations and potentialities in it. 'For the purpose of ordinary discourse this discrepancy between what we abstract (and think of as "the meaning") and what we abstract it from (the particulars and relations which mean) is scandalous, and better not thought of at all. . . .'[49] What the poet does in representing his meaning is not imitation, but a kind of dramatic enactment of what is in his mind. While verbal art cannot grasp the immediacy of mental reality, it nevertheless gains vital resources by modelling itself on the activities of the mind. The explanation of this paradox lies in an understanding of the relation between the work of art and its model which no one has done more to elucidate than Susanne K. Langer, who has shown why attempts to close the gap with thought, like Surrealist automatic writing, should be comparatively ineffective, while language that uses thought as a principle of stylization, like Joyce's, can be vital and meaningful.

According to Langer, art works separate themselves from the rest of reality because they alone exist for the sole function of evoking feelings. The artist works more or less representationally, using models found in the real world (for what others would there be?), but he is not motivated by the ambition of rivalling reality, and in borrowing from it he excludes those parts of it which are not related to his purpose. What he produces is neither an object nor the imitation of an object, but what Langer calls a 'non-discursive symbolic form'. The environment of the work of art is therefore not ordinary life, but an illusion of it which has the advantage of liberating the imagination from the constraints of actuality, and enabling it to perceive things more clearly than in the uncontrolled confusion of real life. The perceptions and the feelings involved match the work of art in being illusory, no more than shadows of actual experiences: '. . . what art expresses is *not* actual feeling, but ideas of feeling; as language does not express actual things and events but ideas of them'.[50] These counterpart feelings are not inadequate substitutes for real ones, but experiences in their own right within the arena of the imagination. They are obviously different from the feelings stimulated by actuality. Suffering and joy do not move us in art as they do in life, though they do move us. They do not affect us directly, but in cooperation with other parts of the work. The feelings of art are differentiated from actual feelings by their distance, coolness, flexibility, and accessibility to imaginative participation, inducing what Stephen Dedalus calls a psychological condition of 'stasis'.

The modern psychological styles do not duplicate mental reality then, but enable us to experience a fictional version of it which imitates it at the distance imposed by the necessities of imitation, borrowing those parts of it appropriate for art, and dispensing with others. Through these borrowings new modes and forms of expression entered modern literature. The associative energies of the mind encouraged the development of styles based on juxtaposition. Dreams and hallucinations called attention to imagery, and to the significance of its exaggerated and grotesque forms. Memory provided a model for the statement and recurrence of a theme, as in the Wagnerian *leitmotif*. The dramatic lyrics of Eliot and Pound used the sort of scattered materials that enter the current of undirected thought. Admiration for the machine and a desire to specify a psychological counterpart of its power and impersonality motivated the Futurists and writers influenced by them. The newly-discovered interpenetrating, subconscious and multi-dimensional qualities of thought suggested the interior monologue, automatic writing and the dream-style of *Finnegans Wake*. These offer, not an experience of thought—which we can have, for better or for worse, without reading—but of the activities, relationships, and formulations characteristic of thought as they have been captured in words. What we experience in such a line as 'I have measured out my life with coffee spoons' is not so much Prufrock's feelings of futility—though they are, of course, involved—as the marvellous aptness of the image for expressing these feelings. We re-live Prufrock's hopelessness only as an illusion; but we encounter the success of the words in formulating it as a direct, primary experience. The psychological episode of modern literature as a whole played its part in deepening our sense of the nature and quality of the mind; but it could not do this without inventing forms of expression appropriate to new modulations of consciousnes.

IV FORM AND LANGUAGE

THE HOLISTIC views of Chomsky and other theoreticians suggest that languages have structures which provide places, however moveable they may be, for each of their words. However, when a word is used for literary purposes, it is also put within a second framework which intervenes between it and the larger conformation of the language as a whole, displacing it to some extent from its position in the dictionary, the grammar and the etymological filiation. There is a difference between the word that occurs in a literary work and the word used in ordinary language that corresponds to the difference between objects in works of art and objects in the real world which is underlined by *collage* and the 'ready-made'. 'Literature exists', observes George Steiner, 'only because there can be realized . . . a membrane to divide it from the common flow of discourse. . . . The membrane may be exceedingly thin and permeable. . . . But there must be a separation, a voluntary sifting according to observable criteria, for the novel, poem, or play to achieve actual being.'[1]

The enclosure that separates the word in a literary work from the rest of the domain of verbal expression is the form of the work. The word must be imagined as suspended within this space by invisible strings which connect it to a circumference made up of all the other words that constitute the work and its form. In the first sentence of *Pride and Prejudice*, 'It is a truth universally acknowledged, that a single man in possession of a good fortune, must be in want of a wife', the context that follows specializes the meaning of nearly every word in varying degrees. The single man with his fortune is specifically Bingley, the wife is, somewhat less specifically, one of the Bennet girls, and the truth universally acknowledged is no truth at all. The relations between the novel as a whole and its words operate openly and familiarly, little special analysis is necessary, and the strings controlling the meaning remain invisible.

But in experimental works, with their emphasis on the autonomy of language, the control exercised by the form becomes more pronounced and self-conscious. When Frank Budgen objected that he had never heard the spars of a ship called 'crosstrees' as they are in *Ulysses*, Joyce said that the word could not be changed because it was connected with one of his themes and occurred again elsewhere.[2] When the young Stephen Dedalus sees the word 'Foetus' carved on a desk in his father's old schoolroom in Cork, the incident picks up at least three resonances that have been circulating as themes through the echo-chamber of *A Portrait of the Artist*: Stephen's erotic obsessions, the process of his development, and the suggestive power of words. These connections with the larger dimensions of the novel could not have been established by any other word, nor even by this word if it had been brought forward in a different way.

1 THE FORMAL EMPHASIS

It had been the nineteenth-century view that style is no more than an envelope or container that is at its best when it is least conspicuous. The demotion of content and the ascendancy of form began with the realization that content cannot be unaffected by style. This was modulated, in turn, to the perception that aesthetic and expressive values are matters of style, technique and form rather than content. In contrast to previous usage, 'form' now became whatever individualized a work, content whatever it shared with other things. It was no experimentalist, but W.P. Ker, Professor of English at University College, London, who, in a 1912 Cambridge lecture offered as an alternate sense of the word form, 'that in virtue of which the poem differs from every other creature in the world'. 'Thus', said Ker, 'poetical form turns out to mean simply the poem itself; the poem as an individual thing is all form; what is not form in it is not poetry.'[3]

One of the major modern principles maintained that perceptions can be made genuine objects of experience only if they are embodied in the formal properties of the work. In the artificial division between content and form, content is derivative, and offers only a vicarious experience. Keats's nightingale is only a shade, a faint echo in the reader's mind. But the harmonies of the stanza Keats invented, his words and images, and the curve of the poem's movement between dream and reality are primary perceptions. Contrary to the traditional opinion, a significant work of art achieves immediacy, not by vivid imitation, but through its formal properties. They have to be detected intellectually, but when they do enter perception, they operate on the intuitive level. Every line, shape and colour of a painting, and every element of verbal organization in a literary work is felt as an expression of the state of mind that produced it.

It is possible to compile an impressive anthology of statements supporting this view from the works of modern writers. Pound, arguing that only a precise artist left an adequate impress of his personality and private thoughts in his work, said: 'We find these not so much in the words—which anyone may read—but in the subtle joints of the craft, in the crannies perceptible only to the craftsman.'[4] Wyndham Lewis, who was particularly conscious of the relation between feeling and the actual shape of a work, observed that literature is really speech, and added 'There is an organic norm to which every form of speech is related. A human individual, living a certain kind of life, to whom the words and style would be appropriate, is implied in all utterance.'[5] Distinguishing between poetry and prose, William Carlos Williams defined poetry as: 'new form dealt with as a reality in itself'; while the form of prose depended on its subject, 'the form of poetry is related to the movements of the imagination revealed in words— or whatever it may be—the cleavage is complete'.[6] And he predicted, writing in 1923, that the 'next great leap of the intelligence' would be from imitation to 'the facts of the imagination'.[7]

Many of the convictions about these matters that the Anglo-American experimenters were coming upon more or less casually were being developed, at about the same time, into the critical doctrine called Formalism by a group of Russian theorists. There is no adequate explanation for this parallel. It is true that Marinetti and the Italian Futurist movement played a germinal role both in Russia and in England, for the Russian Formalists had been motivated by the radical poetics of Russian Futurist poets, and the English, as we have seen, were impressed enough by Marinetti to form a movement of their own. But Italian Futurism had little to do with the specific direction taken by these theoretical developments. The Russian Formalists looked upon the literary work, as the experimentalists did, as an aesthetic fact, rather than an effort at communication. Like them, they tended to dismiss content, or to regard it as an aspect of the aesthetic effect, and to consider the work as a self-contained, autonomous form. This involved divorcing words from their referential functions, and emphasizing the value they acquired as arrangements of sounds and significations. After World War II, the contest between content and form took a new turn, as pop art and 'naked poetry', documentary dramas and other media tried to find direct paths to reality by eliminating 'treatment' as far as possible. Many of these ventures have roots in the Dada rejection of the basic conception of form. This was, however, only a phase of the efforts made by artists of the early modern period to demonstrate the neutrality of content and the decisive power of technique. Such exercises as Monet's series of paintings of Rouen Cathedral and Wallace Stevens's 'Thirteen Ways of Looking at a Blackbird' show that a single subject can serve as the basis for very different effects.

Literary forms and techniques are moulds registering the impress of thought, and they must change when modes of thought change. 'The poem comes before the form', said Eliot, 'in the sense that a form grows out of the attempt of somebody to say something. . . . Forms have to be broken and remade.'[8] When familiar concepts like sequential time, the self, and the unitary meanings of words fall into disrepute, such literary resources as plot, climax, character-analysis and parallelism lose their virtue. When there are neither gods nor heroes, epics cease to appear. After profound changes of consciousness, it becomes necessary to find expressive resources compatible with new beliefs, to make the universe intelligible again. New convictions about the nature of reality cannot be expressed as the content of works that follow traditional forms; they can be felt as living beliefs only if they become the principles of artistic behaviour, and can be read intuitively from the body of the work itself. 'Revolution', said Wyndham Lewis, 'is *first* a technical process . . .'[9] E.E. Cummings, praising T.S. Eliot's *Poems* (1920) for 'their overwhelming sense of technique', emphasized the vitality inherent in genuinely new resources of expression. 'By technique', he wrote, 'we do not mean a great many things, including: anything static, a school, a noun, a slogan, a formula. . . . By technique, we do mean one thing: the alert hatred of normality which, through the lips of a tactile and cohesive adventure, asserts that nobody in general and some one in particular is incorrigibly and actually alive.'[10]

The depth of the modern literary revolution is attested by the fact that it witnessed, not only new forms and techniques, but changes in the premises upon which they are based. The rise of such forms as the ballade, rondeau and villanelle in the nineteenth century did not signal any serious advance in poetry, since rhyme, metre and refrains persisted as the constituents of form, but the dramatic monologue and Hopkins's innovations in verse were significant, for they introduced new methods of organization. The twentieth-century poets sought not only freedom from the old forms, but the discipline of new ones. Some of the early poems of Eliot and Pound were efforts to reproduce severe old forms in the new idiom, imitations of Gautier's precise quatrains. The comparatively free medium found in 'Prufrock' and 'Portrait of a Lady', lines of variable length with rhymes occurring in an unpatterned way, is found in Matthew Arnold's 'Dover Beach' and 'A Summer Night'. Marianne Moore admirably represents this aspect of the modern encounter with form, for she invented an entirely new prosodic discipline. Her poems characteristically consist of stanzas that match each other syllable by syllable, with a limited number of rhymes to signal their formality. The language itself, loose, casual, nearly colloquial, weaves flexibly in and out among the rigidly-demarcated lines, over-running their ends and avoiding any marked rhythm. The effect is that of a due observation of form at its most demanding, together with freedom from its constraints.

The experimentalists regarded the rise of free verse with scepticism. It was a part of the Imagist doctrine to avoid the regularity of the metronome, and Pound wished to break the pentameter, but these moves toward freedom were usually accompanied by a sense of responsibility toward some other conception of rhythm. Eliot, denying that verse could be free, nevertheless acknowledged that in the absence of rhyme, the words of a poem had to succeed on their merits, and were, in this sense, liberated.[11] Hulme saw that old metres gave the poet artificial support, and had a hypnotic effect on the reader, while the new versification had to create a definite form.[12] What was true of verse was felt to be true of the larger literary forms; it was not merely a question of inventing new ones, but of finding entirely new principles of organization. It had always been legitimate to ask, when examining form, whether it was coherent, consistent, proportional, appropriate to content, and so on. But the experimentalists thought of form as an independent expressive resource, capable of speaking directly to the reader's feelings.

It is a notorious fact of the modern period that writers with very different motivations can be found sharing similar ideas of form and using the same techniques. The styles of Gertrude Stein's *Melanctha* and the Gerty MacDowell passage of Joyce's *Ulysses* are imitations of the thoughts of naive young women, and while their immediate effects may be roughly comparable, their ultimate meanings within the works in which they appear are entirely different. Marinetti was politically reactionary, yet in the hands of the Russian poet, Mayakovsky, a Futurist poetic idiom performed excellent service in expressing the aspirations of the early Soviet state. The 'telegraphic' style advocated by Marinetti and the asyntactical prose of Bloom's interior monologue have different intentions and effects, yet there are undeniable technical similarities between them. The imagery of dreams and irrational thought appears both in the works of the Marxist-oriented Surrealists and in *The Waste Land*, whose author once described himself as a royalist. Molly Bloom's soliloquy and

Guillaume Apollinaire's book of poems. *Alcools*, share a militant opposition to punctuation; yet this does not mean that Joyce and Apollinaire had much in common. (Though it does seem that *Molly* and Apollinaire, both pleasure-loving, hearty, and fond of hoaxes, might have got along very well together.)

The modern period therefore abundantly illustrates the point made by Georg Lukács in his criticism of the tendency of bourgeois critics to emphasize stylistic matters, that similar techniques can spring from contrasting intentions; Lukács concludes that the analysis of technique alone is not enough to determine the motives in which it originates.[13] But if we accept the modernist principle that the message is embedded in the form of the work, and see it against the background of Cassirer's view that literature does not record preconceived ideas, but provides an arena in which the spirit achieves self-realization, it seems fair to infer that writers who invent comparable techniques must share similar feelings, even if these are only about things so fundamental as time, space, memory, the self, and the interaction of external and subjective worlds. The divergences arise only when these basic intuitions are elaborated into political and philosophical opinions. The convergences of differing sensibilities upon remarkably similar conceptions of form is evidence of a kind of consensus among modern writers of varying and even incompatible views. 'My brother artist', wrote Pound in 1916 'may, and probably does, disagree with me violently on all questions of morals, philosophy, religion, politics, economics; we are indissolubly united against all non-artists and half-artists by our sense of this fundamental community, this unending adventure towards "arrangement", this search for the equations of eternity.'[14]

2 FRAGMENTATION

Experimental works often seem to have no form at all, but to consist of dissociated fragments. Marinetti said that the style appropriate to the modern age was one that expressed 'l'immaginazione senza fili', a telegraphic style that used the stripped, essentialized language of a telegram, or 'parole in libertà'. 'By wireless imagination', he wrote, 'I mean an entire freedom of images and analogies, expressed by disjointed words and without the connecting wires of syntax.'[15] He recommended analogy as a poetic method, but thought Futurist poets might strip their analogies to bare essentials 'Giungeremo un giorno ad un'arte ancora più essenziale, quando oseremo sopprimere tutti i primi termini delle nostre analogie per non dare più altro che il seguito ininterroto dei secondi termini.' Such a style would, of course, sacrifice intelligibility. 'Essere compresi', wrote Marinetti, 'non è necessario.'[16]

Marinetti's telegraphic principle is an aspect of the modern art of juxtaposition, a mode that respects the concrete, avoids the discursive and transitional and exploits the clash of enigmatic and contradictory encounters. Effects of distinctness, separateness and clear focus were among the prominent technical motives of the time. These were connected with naturalism, and also with scruples against imposing arbitrary relations on subject-matter; but each of the experimentalists found different values in modes of discontinuity and contrast.

Yvor Winters dubbed this effect 'qualitative progression', and objected to it because it ignores the rational aspects of language, emphasizing connotative elements, and because works in which it is employed, such as Eliot's poems and the *Cantos*, depend so heavily on the independent vitality of isolated passages that they create a disintegrative impression. T.S. Eliot, in his introduction to St. John Perse's *Anabase*, contended that images have a logic of their own; Winters considers this an example of the way in which qualitative progression is unsatisfactorily rationalized, but Graham Hough finds in Eliot's view the germs of the two kinds of discontinuity typical of modern literature: 'The first is that any appearance of obscurity is merely due to the suppression of connecting matter: the logic of the poem is like the logic of any other kind of discourse. . . . The second . . . is that the poem is constructed according to a "logic of the imagination" which is different from ordinary logic.'[17] We recognize in these Roger Shattuck's homogeneous and heterogeneous varieties of juxtaposition.[18] The first can be translated into familiar ideas if the connectives between the fragments are filled in. But the second exploits the incongruity of the juxtaposed elements to suggest new and undetermined relationships; or, alternatively, as in Surrealist writing, it may leave gaps no feat of the imagination can fill, leading to the doors of the unknown.

One of the important effects of *The Waste Land* arises from the diversification of voices from part to part, each character speaking in his own idiom, and testifying to the universality of spiritual loss from his own point of view. The publication of the manuscripts has shown that this inconsistency was not the result of Pound's elimination of transitions, but was inherent in Eliot's original conception of the poem. Its quoted fragments propose an aesthetic of ruins, for it is possible to regard the destruction time brings to stone or language as a creative re-shaping. Eliot, for whom poetry

was in part a process of ransacking the ruins of history for worth-
while remains, said that he reproduced the quotation from Hera-
clitus at the beginning of 'East Coker' in Greek because modern
language cannot express the meanings of the key words in Greek
philosophy. To the modern reader, these will be 'wild' meanings,
not controlled by any context he knows, and powerfully suggestive.
Pound exploited this aspect of the fragment very directly in
'Papyrus' which reads:

> Spring . . .
> Too long . . .
> Gongula . . .

(p. 122)

This poem, as Hugh Kenner has explained, is based on a few
Greek letters plus the name 'Gongula' (thought to be the name of
one of Sappho's lovers) that survive on a rag of ancient parch-
ment. It is not a translation, but an inventive inference suggested
by the fragment.[19] The quotations gathered at the end of *The
Waste Land*, the 'fragments shored', call upon the reader to work
out relationships among them through a similar process of
invention.

Discontinuity is a vital structural principle in Joyce's work.
It appears on the minute scale of the paratactic phrases of the
interior monologue, and in the largest dimensions of his books.
A Portrait consists of five narratives separated from each other in
time and diversified in style, and most of the chapters of *Ulysses*
obey determinants of their own which separate them in style from
the rest of the novel. They are, to be sure, connected by the *schema*,
which holds them in a rigidly ordered unity, but what we feel
in reading the chapters themselves is a vigorous incohesiveness.

Valéry Larbaud was apparently the first to note that Joyce
worked from lists of phrases which he underlined (or crossed out)
in coloured pencil, according to the episodes they belonged in,
and the first of many critics to compare this method to mosaic.[20]
In his more recent study, A. Walton Litz has found that Joyce
began *Ulysses* with his general plan in mind, and accumulated
on sheets of separate paper annotations of newspaper phrases,
people's mannerisms, stray facts and similar materials. He inserted
these into the early drafts of his chapters, gradually thickening
their texture and strengthening the style in this way. This
procedure has several implications, but it shows that much of
Ulysses was composed from separate bits of experience, entirely
discontinuous, which Joyce undertook to fit into a predetermined
design.[21]

The staccato, inexplicit quality that entered Pound's poetry after 1912 came from a number of sources. Pound reported that Ford Madox Ford expressed his view of some of his early poems by rolling on the floor in agony and that this taught him the value of the direct, conversational, clipped style of verse that Ford favoured. Ford was an early advocate of what came to be considered Imagist doctrines, the clear treatment of objects, omission of connectives and exploitation of a natural interest in externals. He once pointed out that a list of the brief descriptions of things to be sold at auction made tolerable reading, and was saying in 1913 that 'the business of the poet today' was 'the putting of the one thing in juxtaposition with the other'.[22] Ford's advice, the poems of H.D. and Eliot, and his own convictions about concreteness led Pound to the sort of poem that depends upon a succession of cleanly-sculptured, pregnant images put before the imagination without a shred of excess verbiage:

> An image of Lethe,
>   and the fields
> Full of faint light
>   but golden,
> Gray cliffs,
>   and beneath them
> A sea
> Harsher than granite,
>   unstill, never ceasing . . . .
>
>   (p. 117)

The discovery of the Chinese ideogram moved him in the other direction at first, for the poems of *Cathay* (1915) were written by providing connectives to join the isolated words in Fenollosa's transcriptions of Chinese poems. But Fenollosa's essay on the Chinese character as a medium for poetry described the ideogram as a non-discursive reflection of concrete reality, and Pound learned that it was better to let the words form their own connections. The ideogram, as Fenollosa saw it, is a representation of something from nature, compressing in itself all the meanings relevant to that thing, not a concept or abstraction which isolates meaning. It establishes relations with its context, not through the artificial linkages of grammar, but by sending forth meanings, like radiations, to join with similar radiations from other words. In poetry, 'a word is like a sun, with its corona and chromosphere; words crowd upon words, and enwrap each other in their luminous envelopes until sentences become clear, continuous light-bands'.[23]

The speaker of the ode on Pound's tomb at the beginning of

Mauberley calls him, among other things 'Capaneus; trout for factitious bait'. There is a very long distance between the Greek hero who was struck by Zeus with a thunderbolt for boasting, and the credulous fish, and the path we are to take in joining them is not entirely clear. Perhaps the element the two have in common is folly. As Joyce said in describing his own creative processes, the particulars fuse only after they have been together for a long time; but this fusion, when it does occur, is bound to be something new. The idiom of juxtaposed particulars is fundamental to the *Cantos* at every level of organization.

> Then Actaeon: Vidal,
> Vidal. It is old Vidal speaking,
> stumbling along in the wood,
> Not a patch, not a lost shimmer of sunlight,
> the pale hair of the goddess.
>
>   Canto IV (p. 14)

Actaeon, a youth who saw Diana in her bath, and Vidal, the Provençal trouvére, were both torn apart by hounds at a time when they had the outer appearance of animals. Pound has included in the passage the deep shade Ovid describes at the pool where the goddess bathed. The effect of this juxtaposition is that of Hopkins's principle of rhyme, difference with similarity, as the young Actaeon and the old Vidal, one in the guise of a stag, the other as a wolf, are linked through their identical deaths.

The same method is followed in each Canto as a whole; each might be regarded as an ideogram juxtaposing diverse materials as a way of stimulating the mind to participate in the poem by moving between them. Canto II, the first one organized in this way, consists of: an invocation to Browning about his poem, *Sordello*; an allusion to a description of moonlight shining on water by the Chinese poet, Li Po (or So-shu); three lines describing a seal in the water, comparing it to the daughter of the Celtic sea-god, Lir; a passage condemning Helen for bringing doom to Troy; a glimpse of the sea-god Poseidon capturing the mortal maiden named Tyro; a long narrative freely adapted from the *Metamorphoses* about Bacchus transforming sailors into animals during a voyage to Naxos because they did not believe that he was a god; then brief returns to So-shu, Poseidon and Tyro, and a generalized description of Hellenic seascape and landscape. Disparate as these may seem, there are some common themes among them, such as the sea, troublesome women associated with it, metamorphosis, divinities and human faith in them, and poets. The surface discords forestall any easy connections. Instead, the abundant meanings of each of the elements strike deep roots into some general substratum of meaning, to establish multiple oppositions and relationships with each other there. As the reader turns each fragment over in his mind, he finds some aspect of it that fits another, through similarity, contrast, parallel or some other relationship. When all the fragments have been lined up in this way, the result is not a paraphrasable statement, but a sequence in which obscurity has been eliminated, Fenollosa's 'clear, continuous light-bands'.

A recent critic has objected to the different styles of *The Waste Land* by saying: 'It is as though a painter were to employ a pointilliste technique in one part of a picture, and the glazes of the high renaissance in another.'[24] The comment is meant as a fundamental, even a fatal objection to the common experimental method of ranging different styles in apparently discordant formations as a way of forcing appreciation out of its conventional framework. The problem, as Robert M. Adams has formulated it in discussing the even more jarring discontinuity created by Joyce's use of factual details in the design of *Ulysses*, is that 'we lose control of a standard of relevance' unless we can think of the work as a unit to which all of its elements belong.[25]

One of the experimental aims was that of creating new 'standards of relevance', and one way of doing this was to relate the elements of a work, not to each other, but to a controlling rationale. 'The thread going through the holes in the coin . . . is a necessary part of a thought system', said Pound.[26] The people wandering through the labyrinth of Dublin in Joyce's 'Wandering Rocks' chapter are cut off from each other, and their narratives are merely juxtaposed, but at the end the viceroy's cavalcade passes all of them, threading them together into a unit. In 'Marina', Eliot mentions four kinds of people:

> Those who sharpen the tooth of the dog . . .
> Those who glitter with the glory of the humming-bird . . .
> Those who sit in the stye of contentment . . .
> Those who suffer the ecstasy of the animals . . .

(p. 72)

These would seem to be related only by the animal imagery they share, if each of the lines did not end with the words 'meaning/ Death', which casts a loop about them and draws them into a design. But the unifying base of larger forms is often invisible, lying deeper than we expect or outside the work altogether. It is as if the figures in a painting faced away from each other, toward the frame, and were felt as a group only because they were included within the same border, so that the frame becomes the determining element of the design.

For, with some exceptions to be discussed later, discontinuity in experimental forms is part of a larger design. Generally speaking, the apparently unrelated fragments are at least influenced by some conception of unity. This unity is often arcane and inaccessible, and even when it comes into view the discontinuity of the parts remains an element of the final effect. What the reader experiences is not a triumph of form over unruly materials, but rather a meeting between chaos and a hypothetical order in which chaos loses none of its rights.

3 ANALOGICAL FORMS

Confronted with the fragments of a shattered culture, the experimental artists searched for new imaginative principles capable of gathering the incoherent experiences offered by modern life into unified and purposeful forms. One of the most influential of these was the type of analogy first proposed by Marinetti and the Futurists, a form of relationship more appropriate to a dynamic age than logic or syntax.

Futurist analogy differed from traditional analogy because it established relationships between widely different things, exploiting distance and discrepancy rather than proximity and resemblance. 'L' analogico,' wrote Marinetti, 'non è altro che l'amore profondo che college le cose distanti, apparentemente diversi ed ostili.'[27] To Marinetti, analogy was not merely a poetic device, but a master force capable of linking human consciousness with the physical world, and bringing all parts of the universe together, regardless of their diversity. In the statement of his views published in *Poetry and Drama* in September 1913, he wrote that the Futurist writer would not only express his intoxication with life in an outpouring of fragmentary, telegraphic language, but:

If, in addition to the power of lyrical expression, he has a mind full of general ideas, he will, involuntarily and at every moment, link up his sensations with those of the whole universe he knows and feels. To render the exact value and proportions of the life he has lived, he will create an immense net of analogies with which to envelop the world.[28]

Ultimately, the writer would achieve 'uno stilo orchestrale' having a range of expression that was no less than cosmic.

The great structural frameworks of the major modern works are animated by a very similar spirit. They employ far-reaching analogies, based on differences as much as similarities, to organize widely-scattered particulars into elaborate, detailed interconnecting patterns. Hulme devoted some thought to analogy and convinced himself that literature was not merely the transcription of experience, but a counter-logical activity of choosing and developing analogies. He observed that 'The progress of language is the absorption of new analogies', and went so far as to define thought itself as 'merely the discovery of new analogies' which simple statement was incapable of expressing. One of the values of analogy, he felt, was that of prolonging an effect until it developed the 'sense of novelty' which he was concerned with restoring to language. However, in a brief observation that suggests that the subject was leading him away from his usual insistence on precision, he said that analogies were not enough in themselves, but must suggest some mystic relationship.[29]

The integrating analogical designs used by the experimentalists can be divided into two types: abstract structures and organic frameworks. In the first, we find the material organized according to some more or less mechanical principle, as in the division of the chapters of *Ulysses* according to hours of the day, colours and organs of the body that is charted in the well-known *schema*; Joyce left no *schema* for *Finnegans Wake*, but similar principles operate in it, and Clive Hart has been able to construct a number of tables for it on the basis of internal evidence.[30] The framework or containing form that organizes the work according to some story, legend, document, or similar archetype has quite a different effect. It places the particulars in relation to one another, as the structures do, but it is also capable of generating transformational systems through the force of analogy. *Ulysses* as a whole is a suggested analogy, of the kind Marinetti favoured, the only key to its first term being its title. Once the Homeric correspondence is established, the naturalistic characters and events acquire a new dimension of significance, Bloom becomes Odysseus, Molly becomes Penelope, and so on. Similarly, the organization of *The Waste Land* according to the vision of spiritual life articulated in *The Golden Bough* and *From Ritual To Romance* gives such figures as Mme Sosostris, the women in the pub, and the wanderer in the desert affinities with each other and with specific historical characters. The time-cycles that are parts of both *Finnegans Wake* and the *Cantos* function both as structures and as frameworks; they lay the material out coherently in time, but they also set up analogical relationships among people and events.

These two types of form affect the language of a work in opposing ways. Insofar as words are used to make connections with other parts of the work, to establish rhythms, leitmotifs and thematic variations, they tend to lose their referential and narrative capacities and become abstractions. The element of 'meaning' subsides and a certain instrumentality obtrudes itself. This effect is noticeable even in the refrains of conventional songs, where the repeated lines clearly serve structural rather than expressive purposes, and it is emphasized in the fragmented structure of experimental works, where a context necessary for the understanding of what the words could communicate is often missing. The 'Wandering Rocks' chapter is an especially good example of this sort of structure. It consists of separate episodes, with stray details from one inserted more or less arbitrarily into others to establish simultaneity and other relationships. Thus, while Boylan is preparing for his assignation with Molly by buying fruit in a shop, a sentence looking forward to the account of Bloom searching through a bookstall appears: 'A darkbacked figure scanned books on the hawker's cart.' (p. 233) And while Ned Lambert is showing a visiting clergyman a historic underground chamber, there is an allusion to the lovers Father Conmee saw coming out of a field in the first episode. 'The young woman with slow care detached from her light skirt a clinging twig.' (p. 231). The sentence, 'The disk shot down the groove, wobbled a while, ceased and ogled them: six' (p. 229) is completely unintelligible until it appears again, in slightly different form, during Tom Rochford's demonstration of the machine he has invented for announcing the acts of a vaudeville show. These passages do not communicate; they have the function of linking episodes otherwise unrelated to each other.

The organic frameworks, on the other hand, tend to multiply and extend the expressive capacity of language, and the meanings of individual words. The description of the desert in *The Waste Land*, 'Here is no water but only rock' clearly acquires a general symbolic significance in addition to its descriptive effect because it is a part of the death and resurrection pattern, and in Canto XXX the lines.

> Seated there
>   dead eyes,
> Dead hair under the crown,
> The King still young there beside her.
>
> (p. 148)

are vivid enough in themselves, but their real meaning emerges only when they are seen within the framework of the story to which they refer. They describe the scene in which the young King Pedro of Portugal had the body of the girl he married when he was a prince, who was murdered by his father, exhumed and crowned as his queen. The murder was mentioned in a single line in Canto III; this account of the coronation of the dead is now introduced by the thematic statement, 'Time is the evil', and appears in a Canto that rejects 'Pity'. The King's action takes its place as a futile effort to resist time, with its pattern of renewal and rebirth, a major theme of the *Cantos*. Within this context, the concrete and objective words of Pound's description acquire complex overtones; 'dead eyes, /Dead hair' conveys an image of death rendered all the more ghastly by its attempt to counterfeit life, and 'still young' is felt as a premonition of the King's death, a meaning that miraculously reverses its literal sense.

The experimental forms differ from conventional unifying structures in a variety of ways. They are usually arbitrary, having no specific connection with the subject. Most of them are exceptionally rigid, and their mechanical regularity makes them seem inappropriate to the sprawling range of materials they are supposed to organize. Numerical organizations alone are unexpectedly prominent. Each of the *Four Quartets* has its five 'movements', *Finnegans Wake* and the *Cantos* are based on tripartite divisions of time, the eighteen sections of the 'Wandering Rocks' chapter reflect the eighteen chapters of *Ulysses*, and much of the structure of *Finnegans Wake* depends on numerical sets. There are twelve apostles, riddles and members of the jury, four judges, historians of Ireland, evangelists and bedposts, each of the ten thunder-words consists of exactly a hundred letters, (except the last, which has a hundred and one) and there are numerous doublets and triads that match each other. These abstract patterns and the material of the work exert reciprocal creative influences on each other. The patterns display organic irregularities as they sometimes take on the conformations of the subject, and also produce excesses of order that interfere with realism and plausibility.

The moderns favoured invisible forms. In spite of occasional hints, the structure is supposed to be intuited rather than consciously perceived, so that the different chapters of *Ulysses*, for example, can be felt to refer to the organs of the body, colours, and various arts, even if the reader is unaware of Joyce's plan. Traditional forms such as epic and drama offer themselves as 'nature methodiz'd', but Joyce's decision to have each chapter of *Ulysses* represent one of the arts, Hart Crane's adoption of the Brooklyn Bridge as the unifying symbol of *The Bridge*, and Eliot's use of musical forms in *Four Quartets* turn to patterns devised by man. Human achievements, we are being told, also contain sources of permanence.

The most ambitious of the experimental forms were designed as microcosms, miniature analogues of the universe. They are organized to exhaust the space of the mode in which they are conceived, so that everything can be placed and accounted for. Joyce took Ulysses as his hero because he was a complete man, and had performed the functions of husband, father, son and so on. He said, in a letter to Miss Weaver, that his novel was intended to be encyclopaedic, an index to all human life. Pound's universalizing tendencies are obvious from the very beginning of his work. In his series of articles, 'I Gather the Limbs of Osiris' written for the *New Age*, he said, 'The soul of each man is compounded of all the elements in the cosmos . . .' and art is the exposition of the artist's soul as a record of the human spirit.[31] The *Cantos* attempts to cover this record by examining the appearance of its themes in the three kinds of time, mythical, historical and the present. The pattern of death and resurrection adopted by Eliot from *The Golden Bough* for use in *The Waste Land* is also a unitary interpretation of human life, an image of the whole. Joyce dealt with space as well as time. The 'Ithaca' chapter begins by placing Stephen and Bloom with relation to their immediate surroundings, 'Starting united both at normal walking pace from Beresford place they followed in the order named Lower and Middle Gardiner streets and Mountjoy square, west . . .' (p. 666), and ends by relating them to the furthest perceptible points in the cosmos, the stars in the night sky which they see when they go out into the garden to urinate.

Traditionally, says Octavio Paz in *Children of the Mire*, analogy uses the similarities among things to reconcile us to their differences, but in the modern period it is confronted by the counter-force of irony, which drains it of its unifying power. This effect is central to Futurist and Dada imagery, and Paz finds that the agonizing contest between irony and analogy is especially prominent among the Anglo-American modernists where, for example, mundane modern equivalents to mythic themes transform analogies into ironic inversions. There is an interesting anticipation of this effect in the works of Lewis Carroll, which are thoroughly experimental in structure, as in so many other things. *Alice in Wonderland*, we recall, is a game of cards, and *Through the Looking-Glass* is a game of chess, and both are organized as dreams, so that there is an interplay between two sets of rules, one rational and the other irrational. The games illustrate systematic thought, but the folly displayed by the various cards and pieces in believing them-

selves to be real exposes the inadequacy of all such attempts to
impose a structure upon reality, including that of the most complex
game, language. In *Through the Looking-Glass*, the principle of
reversibility (possibly suggested to Carroll by various mathematical and scientific curiosities) exhibits an enormous potential
for ironic effects, as in the White Queen's insistence that the
punishment must come first and the trial afterwards.[32] When
they are seen as reversible, such analogies as those between Molly
Bloom and Calypso on the one hand and Penelope on the other,
and between Finnegan's fall from his ladder and the archetypal
Fall do not bring the terms of the parallel together, but have the
effect of elevating one while ironically diminishing the other.
Just as the disparity between the trivial and the heroic in mock-
epics affords access to a specific kind of satirical rhetoric, the
disproportions between the parallels employed by the modern
writers opens the way to new expressive resources by making
each member of the pair comment upon the other. The effects
achieved, however, are not always ironic, nor even specific.
The background presences of the *Inferno* in Cantos XIV and XV,
the legend of the golden bough in *The Waste Land*, the Viconian
time-cycle in *Finnegans Wake*, and the *Hamlet* theme in *Ulysses*
propose, in each case, a fertile and varied set of relationships.

    The Waste Land employs a handful of comparatively simple
patterns. The general movement of the poem from the desert of
spiritual sterility toward the salvation promised by the thunder
follows the sequence of death and resurrection described in
The Golden Bough. The related archetype of the Quest legend, as
it is described in *From Ritual to Romance* provides its main symbols,
but does not have a strong influence as a controlling form. *The
Waste Land* is not primarily a poem of change or movement,
however, but rather unfolds an unchanging pattern in human
affairs as Eliot's note suggests: 'Tiresias, although a mere spectator
and not indeed a "character", is yet the most important personage
in the poem, uniting all the rest. Just as the one-eyed merchant,
seller of currants, melts into the Phoenician Sailor, and the latter
is not wholly distinct from Ferdinand Prince of Naples, so all the
women are one woman, and the two sexes meet in Tiresias. What
Tiresias *sees*, in fact, is the substance of the poem.' (p. 52) Two
unifying elements are suggested here. The dissociated episodes
are the 'visions' or thoughts of the blind Tiresias, forming a kind
of interior monologue, and the persons, as in Joyce's comment
about the chapters of *Ulysses*, are counterparts or aspects of one
being. Cleanth Brooks has worked out the implications of
Eliot's note in a definitive article, grouping the characters into

archetypes, and parallel symbols that bring the ironies and correspondences of the poem to light. 'The complexity of the experience is not violated', says Brooks, 'by the apparent forcing upon it of a predetermined scheme.'[33]

The effect of the scheme upon the language of the poem is to deepen the semantic thrust of every word and image. The implications of the various frameworks, together with the many themes threaded into the poem from other works, produce a constant stir of augmented meanings. Madame Sosostris's comments about the Tarot cards ('Here, said she,/Is your card, the drowned Phoenician Sailor ...'), for example, are given an important dimension by the background presence of *From Ritual to Romance*, which describes the suit-marks of the Tarot as stylized fertility-symbols of ancient origin, and the cycles proposed by Frazer make her report, 'I see crowds of people walking around in a ring' a vision of universal history. The frameworks also enable Eliot to practice the art of juxtaposition. He can move without transitions from the gloomy greeting of spring that opens the poem to the speech of Marie, to the scene in the desert, the song from *Tristan und Isolde*, and the scene in the hyacinth garden, each written in a noticeably different style, exploiting the contrasts and parallels which arise. These fragments are not related to each other, but their meanings converge in their relation to the era of sterility symbolized by the death or sickness of the Frazerian god.

4 CONTROLLED FORMS

Pound had so little interest in the larger dimensions of the literary work that he was once tempted to assert that 'major form' was merely an Aristotelian conspiracy.[34] The *Cantos* nevertheless embody a number of concepts of form, the most fundamental ones belonging to Pound's Vorticist period, and to the time of his friendships with Gaudier-Brzeska and Wyndham Lewis, when he devised an image for the formalizing capacity itself. In an essay published in 1913, Pound observed that a magnet touched to the bottom of a plate on which iron filings are lying will move the filings into a circular pattern.[35] He took this to show that an invisible energy, like intellect, can bring order out of chaos, and that the order that emerges in turn manifests or 'expresses' the organizing force. Pound often reverted to this image; its key occurrence is in Canto LXXIV, where the water of Verlaine's fountain, because it is clear and rises steadily, is called 'a/property of the mind', and parallel images are offered:

Hast 'ou seen the rose in the steel dust

(or swansdown ever?)
so light is the urging, so ordered the dark petals of iron
we who have passed over Lethe.

(p. 449)

Closely related is the image of the vortex, a figure invented by
Gaudier-Brzeska, but modified by Pound to serve as the central
concept of Vorticism.

For Gaudier, the vortex was a centre of energy, ranging from
a person to a city or a culture. Sculptor-like, he assigned a significance to every part of its conformation, identifying its convexity
with maturity, its point with unity, and its spin with stability,
a quality lacking in the unsteady sphere. Most important, perhaps,
was the fact that it was an independent path of energy, capable of
swirling its way through any kind of matter.[36] In his 1914 essay,
'The Renaissance', Pound accepts Gaudier's idea of the vortex
as a cultural centre that gathers and generates creative energies.[37]
But in 'Vorticism', which appeared later in the same year, it
becomes the successor to the Image, a trope that causes 'form to
come into being', as the equations of analytic geometry do, independent of particular content. It is not an idea, rather 'It is a
radiant node or cluster; it is what I can, and must perforce, call a
VORTEX, from which, and through which, and into which,
ideas are constantly rushing.'[38]

The rose in the steel dust and the vortex have much to do with
the form and obscurity of the *Cantos*. In each Canto we see a
number of fragments that have been brought together in a way
that suggests a single point of convergence, yet this meeting point
is out of sight, like the magnet under the plate, or the forces that
determine the shape of the vortex. Hugh Kenner has observed
that it is difficult to discuss the organization of the *Cantos* without
using 'electromagnetic imagery', and one of the chapters of his
first book on Pound has the title, 'Fields of Force'. In describing the
various levels on which the elements of the *Cantos* interact with
each other, Kenner underlines the fact that the groupings are
'unformulable in conceptual terms'.[39] The patterns of the assembled fragments are shaped, not by the fragments themselves, but by
the energies of the ordering process which manifests itself through
them.

A third structure in the *Cantos* has to do with its quality as a
historical poem, and with its interpretation of time. Pound once
showed Yeats a photograph of the fresco by Cosimo Tura and
Francesco del Cossa in the Hall of the Months at the Palazzo
Schifanoia in Ferrara, explaining that the *Cantos* were organized

in a similar way. The fresco is divided vertically according to months, each vertical panel being divided into three horizontal parts. The top shows the triumphs of a deity appropriate to the month, the second the three zodiacal figures that belong to it, and the bottom, contemporary events, some of them taking place in and about the Palazzo itself. Pound said that the *Cantos*, too, would contain archetypal materials, like those in the top band of the frescoes, recurrent ones, corresponding to the zodiacal figures, and mundane or quotidian ones, like those in the lower panels. The mixture of legend, history and personal or current materials in the *Cantos* is thus an expression of this aspect of the poem's structure, the aligning of three kinds of time.

These abstract forms have a great deal to do with the way in which the language of the *Cantos* achieves meaning. Against the background of a representational structure or analogue, meanings undergo simple transformations. That is, in *Ulysses* Bloom is Odysseus and Stephen is Telemachus, and there are one or two points where they become each other. This method leads to incredible complications in *Finnegans Wake*, where each character is the prototype of numerous figures, but its principle is the same. Within the *Cantos*, however, the specific term must find its interpretation laterally rather than in depth, and its relation to the rest of the structure is less likely to be an identification with something else than the assumption of a position within a design. The idea can be demonstrated through the following vortex or circle of steel filings:

> Père Henri Jacques would speak with the Sennin, on Rokku,
> Mount Rokku between the rock and the cedars,
> Polhonac,
> As Gyges on Thracian platter set the feast,
> Cabestan, Tereus,
>   It is Cabestan's heart in the dish,
> Vidal, or Ecbatan, upon the gilded tower in Ecbatan
> Lay the god's bride, lay ever, waiting the golden rain.
>
> (p. 16)

The elements of this passage are: Père Jacques, the French Jesuit who hoped to converse with the Chinese spirits of nature on Mount Rokku; Polhonac, or Polignac, the French nobleman who wooed his own wife on behalf of a troubadour, singing the verses the minstrel had written for the occasion; Gyges, the Greek who was asked by a king to watch his queen disrobing, but who was caught by the queen and compelled to kill the deceitful husband and marry her; Cabestan, the twelfth-century troubadour,

lover of a nobleman's wife, who was killed and fed to her, and
Tereus, the seducer of Philomela, whose son was killed by his
jealous wife, Procne, and given to him in a cannibal feast.[40] Among
the energies that wrap these fragments into a single vortex—
apart from such obvious ones as pandering and cannibalism—
is the idea of sacrifice, which includes the Jesuit who was willing
to accept the gods of a rival religion and the mother who murdered
her son in order to revenge her husband's unfaithfulness. Another
is the element of human worth; most of the people mentioned are
talented or virtuous, and in Canto LXXXVIII Père Jacques is
described as actually talking with the Sennin, so that his sincerity
has been acknowledged.

On the other hand, a centrifugal energy is supplied by connections with other themes of the *Cantos*, such as that of deception or
self-deception. Just before the passage quoted we have been told
that 'No wind is the king's wind', that temporal power—whether of
kings or of gold—cannot command the forces of nature, whether
they are winds or gods. Just after it the priestess of Ecbatan is mentioned; she, like Danaë, awaited the golden visitation of a god, lying
atop the innermost, gilded tower of the ideal city; but because
mortals have no control over gods, she waited in vain. Yet
Cabestan's heart lies on the dish as she lay on the tower, and the
motif of deception is found in the stories of Gyges, the Viscount
of Polhonac, and possibly in that of Père Jacques, who also sought
a divine visitation in a high place. These are related, rather than
identified with each other, though the relationships seem to be
'unformulable in conceptual terms'. This structure emphasizes
the meaning each element has in relation to the others; each becomes intelligible—though not, perhaps, paraphrasable—within
the circle of the vortex or rose in the steel dust as a detail in a
pattern, and the vortex whirls faster as we note other possible
relationships, especially as connections with other themes of the
Cantos emerge.

The energies of the vortex are powerful enough to infiltrate
the materials and change them, it seems; it was not Gyges who
set a feast on a 'Thracian platter', but Procne, the vengeful wife
of Tereus. The displaced detail braids the two stories together.
The conformation presented by the passage cannot be reduced to
a single idea, but that does not mean that it is unintelligible. It
corresponds to the 'intensive manifold', Bergson's model of reality,
'whose parts interpenetrated in such a manner that they could not
be separated or analysed out'.[41] It forms a unit that is apprehended
intuitively as a cluster of shifting multiple relationships kept
together by a strongly-felt, but quite unspecifiable conviction.

In defending 'The Wreck of the Deutschland' to Bridges, who had complained that it was obscure, Hopkins suggested that he read it without insisting on complete understanding, saying that he often read poetry that way. 'Why, sometimes one enjoys and admires the very lines one cannot understand. . . . '[42] This possibility, he thought, was perfectly consistent with the nature of poetry, which was an object of contemplation with an interest beyond its meaning. 'Some matter and meaning is essential to it', he wrote, 'but only as an element necessary to support and employ the shape which is contemplated for its own sake.'[43]

Ulysses was conceived as a shape of this kind, an intricate pattern in search of the substance needed to flesh it out. Joyce's novel would have become a *Dubliners* short story if he had not decided to write it as an analogue of the *Odyssey*, and to connect each chapter with an hour of the day, a colour, an art, an organ of the body, and so forth. There has always been a certain amount of dissatisfaction with this set of organizational devices, though they serve both as a framework for stretching the novel to its full proportions, and as an armature for holding its parts in place. Generally speaking, the Homeric parallels have been treated more kindly. Eliot believed that Joyce, in patterning his novel on the *Odyssey*, had demonstrated how myth could survive in the modern world; and S.L. Goldberg has seen in the alternating correspondences and divergences between the mundane world of Bloom and the supposedly heroic world of Odysseus a universalizing device that is one of the sources of the calm, ironic clarity of vision the novel brings to bear on the human condition.[44]

But the more arbitrary and detailed influences of the *schema*, which shift the language out of normal channels in violent and distracting ways are somewhat harder to justify. The string of unintelligible phrases that opens the 'Sirens' chapter is there because the art of the chapter is music, and they correspond to an overture introducing the melodies of a piece. The names of the people present (Lidwell, Dedalus, Cowley, Kernan and Dollard) are shortened to Lid, De, Cow, Ker and Doll in a syncopated effect; the word order is often inverted or repeated as in musical patterns, and there is an imitation of what happens to words in operatic singing:

Miss Douce, Miss Lydia, did not believe: Miss Kennedy, Mina, did not believe: George Lidwell, no: Miss Dou did not: the first, the first: gent with the tank: believe, no, no: did not, Miss Kenn: Lidlydiawell: the tank.

(p. 278)

The 'Lestrygonians' chapter is filled with puns about food because it takes place at lunch-time, and Buck Mulligan is called 'Puck' in

'Scylla and Charybdis' because the chapter is about Shakespeare, and its art is rhetoric, including puns. 'Ithaca' tells its story through absurdly factual questions and answers, and 'Eumaeus' is a rambling tissue of intolerable triteness, in imitation of old narrative. These are Joyce's usual methods, in active use on every page, and most critics have felt that they are too deliberate, or insufficiently integrated into the narrative, and offer no more than an intellectual interest. But Joyce told Frank Budgen that he used them because ' . . . I want the reader to understand always through suggestion rather than direct statement'.[45] He seems to have been working according to a principle formulated by Hopkins (which he could not, of course, have known):

> The further in anything, as a work of art, the organisation is carried out, the deeper the form penetrates, the prepossession flushes the matter, the more effort will be required in apprehension, the more power of comparison, the more capacity for receiving that synthesis of . . . impressions which gives us the unity with the prepossession conveyed by it.[46]

Litz, we recall, showed that Joyce revised *Ulysses* by inserting thematic allusions and correspondences taken from notes into his early drafts in order to make the narrative participate more fully in the design set out by the *schema*.[47] He describes this as fairly mechanical, but 'the organisation is carried out' as Hopkins would put it, penetrating and flushing the matter with form. It is a procedure for integrating the controlling form into local texture by having it permeate every fibre, as if it were a dye, so that it is felt continually, if subliminally.

This process is carried much further in *Finnegans Wake*, where the union of 'content' and 'form' takes place within the words themselves. The dreaming mind that narrates *Finnegans Wake* assimilates the people and events of waking life to archetypal patterns. Innumerable characters and situations ranging from those involved in Joyce's own life to history and legend are superimposed upon each other, in accordance with the frameworks that control the novel. James S. Atherton has compared it to a photograph he once saw which combined pictures of thousands of women; W. I. Thompson has said that it is as if the eighteen chapters of the 'Wandering Rocks' chapter of *Ulysses* were narrated at once. Dreaming provides a model for a style which can refer simultaneously to numerous illustrations of a symbolic pattern. Atherton has cited a passage from Edgar Quinet's discussion of Vico which describes a motivation appropriate to this aspect of *Finnegans Wake* and underlines its psychological basis:

L'histoire, telle qu'elle est réfléchie et écrite dans le fond de nos âmes, en sorte que celui qui se rendrait véritablement attentif à ses mouvements intérieurs, re- trouverait la série entière des siècles comme ensevelie dans sa pensée. . . . J'aper- çus, pour la première fois, (on reading Vico) le nombre presque infini d'êtres semblables à moi, qui m'avaient précédé. . . [48]

Joyce's tendency to see individual experiences, even those of his private life, as instances of recurrent patterns is already fully apparent in the 'Scylla and Charybdis' chapter of *Ulysses*, where the father-son relationships of Stephen, Hamlet and Shakespeare himself are treated as counterparts of the apostolic succession. This method is carried much further in *Finnegans Wake*. There, the dream dissolves logical distinctions, and the people and events are related to each other through all sorts of fanciful and arbitrary patterns. These relations are notoriously flexible, so that parallels may become opposites, singles multiples, parents children and so on. The materials juggled in this game of constantly shifting rela- tionships are drawn from a seemingly limitless range of sources, including Joyce's life, his earlier books, the works of friends, acquaintances and rivals, popular songs, recent history, antiquity, and written material of every description.

At one extreme, such personal materials as those connected with Joyce's courtship of Nora enter. The name of the place where the two first met, Finn's Hotel, was too relevant to one of the book's main background figures, the legendary Irish giant, Finn MacCool, to be denied a place in it, but it is disguised in the form of 'Finn's Hot' (p. 420). On the other hand, material as remote from Joyce himself and the Earwicker family as the theories of Einstein and the Egyptian Book of the Dead are used. Distinctions of time, place and person disappear, so that the events of the story—when the original story can be distinguished—are buried in a swarm of counterparts from the legend of Tristram and Iseult, the *Arabian Nights*, *Alice in Wonderland*, the Koran, Le Fanu's novel, *The House by the Churchyard*, and the dozens of other sources Mr Atherton has brought to light. The individual characters are fragmented, generalized, multiplied, paired with historical charac- ters, blended with other members of their families, identified with features of the landscape, and subjected to every imaginable transformation. Differences and even oppositions are resolved, so that the brothers Shem and Shaun and their numerous analogues often merge and exchange places. These relationships have no status in logic, tradition or reality, but are the fabrications of mental processes akin to those that operate in dreams.

Joyce, we know, intended his integrating structures to be felt intuitively, but most readers report that they have an intrusive effect, and S.L. Goldberg has proposed that they might even be regarded as a substitute for the old convention of authorial commentary because they clarify the meaning of the narrative, and attract attention to the creative presence of the author. Something is seriously askew here. Joyce, after all, had Stephen, in *A Portrait*, describe the artist in a pose of supreme detachment, paring his fingernails, and the patterns controlling *Ulysses* and *Finnegans Wake* are clearly devices for escaping from, not expressing personality, in accordance with Eliot's observation in 'Tradition and the Individual Talent'. The refusal of many critics, even after half a century, to accept the 'merely' intellectual organizational methods of experimental works shows that the literary revolution has not entirely succeeded in accomplishing one of its major aims, linking intellectual and emotional responses. Hopkins had warned that the more complete penetration of the matter by form would require more effort from the reader. But there is an even greater difficulty inherent in the use of intricate structures.

Ortega y Gasset, in explaining why the majority of people never attend to the form of a work of art, but see only the subject, described it as an 'optical problem'. [49] Just as an observer cannot at the same time focus on a window-pane and on the scene outside the window, the art-viewer cannot encompass the subject and the form of a work simultaneously. If he becomes absorbed in the scene, those aspects of the work that counterfeit life, and responds to them as he would to life, he will not be aware of the window-pane through which he sees it, the technical qualities of the work. These call on feelings which are aesthetic or intellectual, and have no place in daily life. The modern artist is occupied with the work as the embodiment of an idea, or as an aesthetic form, to such an extent, as Ortega points out, that he is repelled by resemblances to living forms, and turns to abstract geometric patterns. *Ulysses* is obviously relevant to these observations, yet it has, in addition to the dehumanized form of its *schema*, the celebrated warmth and humanity of its characters. What could Joyce have meant by extending his art along two such incompatible lines?

A clue to his intentions, and to one of the broad ambitions of the early modern period, is found in a lecture given by Wilhelm Worringer, which was published in Eliot's *Criterion* in 1927. Worringer attributed what he took to be a decline in the visual arts to an effort which had, in spite of its essential failure, made a valuable contribution:

Our creative sensuous perception . . . has transferred itself to quite another channel and become sublimated; it has flowed into our intellectuality in order thence to become mind. The transition period of a sterile intellectuality . . . was perhaps necessary in order to produce intellect. Intellect not in the colourless sense, but nourished with blood of the whole creative sensuous perception of the time. In short mind as art, as the most vital and most sensuous organ of our existence.[50]

Reason and intuition have traditionally been separated from each other, and Ortega calls the intellectual emphasis on form 'dehumanization', but the experimentalists were trying to turn this corner, to bring both eyes of the mind to focus on a single point. It is a programme that corresponds with Blake's, and with the steady balance between reason and imagination that Coleridge described as an attribute of poetry. Why should this be so difficult to achieve? Once again, it is Hopkins who suggests an explanation, in a passage already quoted in chapter 3: 'The more intellectual, less physical, the spell of contemplation the more complex must be the object, the more close and elaborate must be the comparison the mind has to keep making between the whole and the parts, the parts and the whole.'[51] Subjects may lean for support upon reality, but form must assert itself through its own credentials. The spelling-out of analogues and patterns, even when it is carried so far that it involves the use of reference-books, translations and concordances may be a merely intellectual or mechanical process, but that should not darken the luminous pleasure of apprehending the proportions and relationships it discloses.

The dissociation of sensibility is not a habit that is easily overcome, and there were enough awkward passages as the experimentalists tried to navigate in what were still for them, as for everyone else, two worlds. The cases of Eliot and Pound, who were interested in social, political and economic questions as well as in 'mind as art' illustrate these hazards. But if we cannot agree with Pound about the virtues of Sigismundo di Malatesta or Mussolini, we are still open to what our sensibilities may discover about the structure and articulation of the *Cantos*. As we recall, the experimentalists took the view that form, not content, is the right road to immediacy. It is the elements of form in a poem, not its faint imitation of other things, that satisfy our need to touch reality, and the better they are understood, through such intellectual activities as study, analysis and even memorization, the deeper are the marks they make on our feelings.

5 OPEN FORMS

While the experimental writers appeared frivolous or whimsical to many of their contemporaries, it is now clear that they were giants of literary administration who were obsessed with patterns and order. Yet they also made use of a new premise about form that took them in the direction of indeterminacy. Frank Budgen reported that Joyce gathered material for *Ulysses* by watching for what he needed, and also made notes of stray curiosities, confident that he would have some use for them in his book.[52] The nature of the 'Circe' episode was determined by his meeting at Lago Maggiore with a woman who owned two islands in the lake and was called Circe, and who gave Joyce some material about sexual perversions. Joyce, says Budgen, believed in his luck, and there could hardly have been a better justification for his faith than this incident. If rigid intellectual patterning is one experimental attitude toward form, an openness to luck, an eye for the *objet trouvé*, for the gifts that chance sends, is another. Pound, as we have seen, had many structural intentions with regard to the *Cantos*; but he could not have planned the direction he took in the *Pisan Cantos*, where he allowed the events of his life to shape the course of his poem. Yet these events fitted in with the ongoing themes, and did not change the form in any essential way.

There are, in fact, two ways of accounting for the openness characteristic of the longer experimental works; one might say first that chance is allowed to take part in writing them. For example, William Carlos Williams wrote *Kora in Hell* and other early prose works as improvisations, fabricating them out of his thoughts of the day or even the moment, without any prearranged plan. *The Great American Novel* has some narrative aspects, but it is mainly about the thoughts of a man who is planning to write, seems to include events from Williams's own experiences at the time, and is nearly indefinite in form. These earlier works of Williams, mingling prose and verse, meditation and narrative, proceeded by exploiting whatever might arise in the writer's mind or daily life, and took their form, such as it was, from that. On the other hand, the forms of the great modern works, by virtue of their very abstractness, allowed almost any material to be fed into them, as if they were blanks to be filled in *ad libitum*. As Hugh Kenner has observed, Pound and Joyce used structures comprehensive enough to assimilate 'anything at all as it turned up' into the patterns of their books, and the same might be said of Williams's *Paterson*.

Elizabeth Sewell has observed a similar situation in Rimbaud's *Illuminations*, which contains particulars whose only connections with each other are those established in the poem itself. Unwilling to concede that the poem's process of combining the unrelated follows the dictates of chance, she concludes that Rimbaud's method induces a state of mind capable of assimilating any and all ideas into an imaginative unity.[53] Lévi-Strauss has shown that the sort of thinking that creates myths displays the same omnivorousness. Myths are intensively organized, as are the great modern literary works, according to unacknowledged principles, but there is room within them for the principle of construction Lévi-Strauss calls *bricolage*, the improvisational activity that allows a limited play of chance.

Lévi-Strauss finds in the activities of the hobbyist or home-handyman who makes use of whatever tools and materials he happens to have accumulated, many vital parallels to the processes involved in mythic thought and in art. The *bricoleur's* task is performed under a specific set of conditions. He begins with a finite collection of resources left over from other uses which are not adapted to his purpose, or to any particular purpose. They cannot determine the use he makes of them, but on the other hand, he must modify his intentions to make do with whatever is available. Hence, he carries on a sort of dialogue with his resources. The old spring, valve or bracket does not change its characteristics when it is fitted into the new project; but only a few of its characteristics come into play. Instead of being objects in their own right, these things now become means toward some new end, taking on new relationships. The once-handsome vase becomes a lampstand, the old newspapers which announced important events stuff the belly of a doll. In this way, the signified and the signifying exchange places, and percepts are transformed into concepts.

This is the opposite of what happens in a scientific experiment. The experiment begins with a 'structure'—that is, some hypothesis intellectually formulated—and transforms it into the 'events' of the actual testing procedure. *Bricolage*, on the other hand, takes 'events' from real life—the miscellaneous junk inherited from other activities—and builds them into a structure whose form they help to determine. The *bricoleur*, in endowing the objects he chooses from his collection with a specific function, transforms the random into the determinate, gives the meaningless a meaning.[54] This is another aspect of resemblance between the poetic state of mind, as it is described by Elizabeth Sewell, and *bricolage*— or its analogue, myth-making—for, by giving randomly-chosen materials specific places in the system of relationships seen in his vision, the poet, like the dreamer, transforms chance into necessity.

All writing is, of course, a form of *bricolage*. The writer, having formulated a purpose, reaches into the remnant bag of language, and does what he can with this extensive collection of second-hand, pre-used materials. 'Poetry', said Hulme, using an image that is unavoidable in thinking about much modern writing, 'is neither more nor less than a mosaic of words. . . .'[55] All writers must modify their intentions in accordance with what is available, as the *bricoleur* does; the conventional writer who does not depart much from previous practice will probably be less aware of the limitations imposed on his words by their traditional functions. But for the experimentalist, who proposes to put them to some new use, the qualities the words have acquired from their existence elsewhere obtrude conspicuously and the element of chance, uncontrollable life is introduced.

Finnegans Wake, which is itself an elaborate and engaging instance of *bricolage*, consistently exploits these apparently irrelevant associations. In describing the wall built by Finnegan as 'a waalworth of skyerscape of most eyeful hoyth entowerly', Joyce has modified the words to reflect the great height of the wall and to convey a sense of an Irish brogue. But these shifts release a torrent of random effects, so that the Woolworth building is associated with the wall, 'eyeful' is shown to have unexpected connections with 'awful' and 'Eiffel', and the brogue detects in 'entirely' the idea of a tower, and in 'height' an allusion to the Hill of Howth. Whenever elements of 'reality', such as quotations, contemporary events, details from the writer's life and facts connected with actual people and places are included in an imaginative work, similar chance relationships spring up, as they do in *bricolage*. Lévi-Strauss acknowledges that there is an element of chance in the *bricoleur's* transference of an object from its own function to a place within his design, for he looks to the object itself for some indication of the use made of it, but maintains that the artist does not surrender control of his materials, as Marcel Duchamp and Kurt Schwitters did.

Duchamp opened a crucial channel in modern art and literature through the invention of the 'Ready-Made', the acceptance as art of such humble objects as a bicycle wheel, a urinal and a bottle-rack whose raw and intrusive actuality captures the sort of attention hitherto reserved for deliberately created aesthetic objects. Duchamp was demonstrating, among other things, that beauty of form could appear as an unconscious by-product of utilitarian craftsmanship, and was driving a strategic wedge between form and use, or, as it would be called in literature, content. But the closest counterpart to *bricolage* in art is surely the form of *collage* practiced by Kurt Schwitters which he called *Merz*, the assemblage of works of art from discarded objects such as printed materials, driftwood, odd boards and mechanical parts. Schwitters worked from whatever came to hand, and one senses, in looking at his *Merzbilder*, both the previous use that his materials have served and the dialogue between the *bricoleur* and his resources to which Lévi-Strauss refers.

Lévi-Strauss himself distinguishes sharply between art and *bricolage*. Acknowledging that chance elements arising from the occasion or purpose of the work of art cannot be eliminated, and even have a legitimate place in it, he nevertheless maintains that an object capable of aesthetic effect can result only if 'events'— the uncontrolled accidents of experience—are balanced with 'structure'—a system of relationships which operates within the work to render them meaningful. The English and American experimentalists, who were strong traditionalists and had also been impressed by science, shared these views in principle; Joyce, as we know from the aesthetic theories of Stephen Dedalus, would certainly concur. Yet they often allowed chance a conspicuous, even a dominant place in their works, as if they agreed with the Surrealists that it had a metaphysical importance.

For the Surrealists did attribute positive metaphysical and aesthetic value to pure chance. Their feeling that it was innately creative was based on a doctrine they called 'objective hazard', the view that chance is an obscurely purposeful force, an abstract necessity that controls events, a kind of absolute. It operates in the mind as well as in the material world, and manifests itself when an observer recognizes some particularly pleasing or wish-fulfilling coincidence. André Breton interpreted chance phenomena in which material reality seems to conform to consciousness, such as coincidences and premonitions, as evidence of the existence in nature of forces which control both causal necessity and human desires. The language games the Surrealists played showed that language can participate in what Breton took to be the essential nature of reality—chance. Some of the forms of Dada and Surrealist art, such as automatic writing and the discordant image exploited the artistry of random effects, but also, the Surrealists felt, established contact with the ultimate reality of the universe.

These claims were generally met with contempt by their contemporaries, who felt that the Surrealists were exaggerating the importance of trivialities. But objective hazard has acquired general philosophic confirmation from a most unexpected source— nuclear physics. Werner Heisenberg's indeterminacy principle began with his discovery that the objective examination of small-scale physical phenomena is impossible because the measuring instruments cannot avoid influencing the behaviour of atomic particles. Their ordinary actions are therefore beyond direct observation and remain 'indeterminate'. Heisenberg speaks of a 'dividing line' between the observations that can be made and the real relationships the object is involved in, and thinks of this division as absolute. While it remains possible for physicists to predict the behaviour of atomic particles quite reliably through inference—in fact, the recognition of this limit of the knowable promotes the coherence of scientific findings—Heisenberg believes that 'the scientist will once and for all have to renounce all thought of an objective time scale common to all observers, and of objective events in time and space independent of observations of them'.[56] This plays into the Surrealists' hands in two ways. It shows that the basic actions of the universe are indeed, as far as human knowledge is concerned, 'random', and correspond with objective hazard. And it defines what is known about the physical world as the result of a mutual transaction between the observer and the observed in which both are parts of a single phenomenon. The human presence itself is a factor in the nature of reality; there is an inescapable bond between external forces and the inquiring mind, so that the profound harmony between mind and nature is confirmed.

The experimentalists became aware of the uncontrollable precisely because they aimed for complete control. Hopkins, in an observation that corresponds perfectly with the Surrealist view that the random is really an expression of nature, wrote: 'All the world is full of inscape and chance left free to act falls into an order as well as purpose. . . .'[57] His religious meditations led him to feel that chance is simply the name we give to causes we do not understand, for the word implies that events can come into being of themselves, an impossibility with all but first causes. Hulme noted that chance plays a significant part in the writing of a poem. Form and intention are controllable, but as they exert their influence upon the feelings to be expressed, ' . . . accidental phrases are hit upon. . . . The accidental discovery of an effect, not conscious intellectual endeavour for it'.[58] Eliot thought the passage of meaning from poet to reader was subject to all sorts of chance effects, and also willingly conceded that creation might prosper in a time when the poet gave up his habitual disciplines because of illness or weakness. Stephen Dedalus's aesthetic theories may be addressed to what is 'grave and constant' in human life, they may celebrate stasis and reject the notion that a cow hacked out of a piece of wood by accident may be a work of art, but Joyce himself after *A Portrait* depended more and more upon the random contributions of external events. *Ulysses* is built upon the events of a specific day chosen, apparently, by chance. The streets of Dublin, however they were laid out, were sufficient to provide a plan for the 'Wandering Rocks' chapter, and the Gerty MacDowell section was determined by what Joyce found in girls' magazines he asked his Aunt Josephine to send him. In showing how much of *Ulysses* is drawn from actual fact in *Surface and Symbol*, Robert M. Adams is also clearly showing that Joyce was willing to allow the tissue of random events we call reality to take part in the writing of his novel.

It should be noted that, except when they are onomatopoeic, words themselves are connected with their meanings only by chance. The series of accidents identifying a specific sound with a meaning is generally so remote that its result is best regarded as an established fact, but this is exactly what the Dadas and Surrealists say about the nature of reality itself. In basing the idiom of *Finnegans Wake* on puns and ambiguities, Joyce was acknowledging that language is fundamentally a product of chance. His diabolical ingenuity is undoubtedly the main source of energy, but sheer accident is an important condition of its operation. This will be shown more fully in the chapter on *Finnegans Wake*, but a few examples may be useful here. The legendary Irish giant who is one of the archetypes of Earwicker is *Finn* MacCool; another is King *Mark* of the Tristan and Isolde legend. These two, between them, suggest *Mark* Twain and his character, Huck *Finn*. The name Tristan lends itself to a pun on 'tree-stone'; Joyce takes advantage of this to transform his two washerwomen into a tree and a stone respectively. Further, the two sons of Earwicker, Shem and Shaun, are transmuted, in one passage, into 'stem and stone'. The scene of the novel is near Dublin. Its protagonist stammers, often reduplicating the syllables of words. He therefore has a 'doublin stutter'. In view of his creative use of the opportunities of chance, it is appropriate that Joyce should call Shem, his autobiographical character, a 'semi-semitic serendipitist'.

The appearance of obviously unplanned material in experimental works might also be explained by the fact that their forms are systems capable of filling all space or time or both, so that nothing can fall outside of them. Clive Hart speaks of Joyce's 'confidence trick' in adopting themes so universal and so numerous in *Finnegans Wake* that almost everything can find a place in it. But he points out that it is an unconcealed trick, that Joyce deliberately opened more associative possibilities than he could work out in order to promote the process of multiple relationships. Readers are always finding new relevancies in *Finnegans Wake*, often in connection with events occurring after it was written, and this process need never be brought to a close. 'The Work', says Hart, 'is eternally in Progress.'[59]

In spite of its intricate construction then, the form of *Finnegans Wake* does not preclude the action of chance. Structures of this kind transform language, as Elizabeth Sewell has pointed out, from a separating and distinguishing mechanism to an agglomerative one. Since random meanings circulate so freely, each word acquires wide potentialities of meaning, and the book as a whole reflects the contingent nature of reality itself. In this way it fulfills its aim of being, as J.S. Atherton has put it, 'an image, a model, a microcosm of the universe . . . in all its indeterminate complexity, although built not out of atoms but of letters'.[60]

Most of the major experimental works in English visibly combine determinate and indeterminate elements, following the general spirit of *bricolage* or objective hazard. The *Cantos* is especially interesting from this point of view. It was begun with definite notions of formal control, but these were seriously tested by the course of events in Pound's life, especially prominent in the *Pisan Cantos*, where the catastrophe of the war, Pound's imprisonment, and his loss of his working materials all represent a massive incursion of chance into the poem. These lead to significant departures, but the comparative universality of the formal designs established early in the poem assimilates the new elements fairly well, and associates many of them with themes carried forward from earlier passages. In the *Pisan Cantos*, there is a new centre of perception, 'ego scriptor', but Pound's personal consciousness is included in the patterns being elaborated, so that such language as 'Tempus tacendi, tempus loquendi' and 'a man on whom the sun has gone down' acquires a dimension it did not have before. Personal experiences appear in the earlier Cantos, but in the *Pisan Cantos* we have Pound's first acknowledgement that he is inside the course of history the poem has been examining. Connected with this is the effect of the immediate present penetrating the vortex, as if seen through apertures in the fabric of thought and memory of which the text consists:

> Berlin   dysentery   phosphorus
>   la vieille de Candide
> (Hullo Corporal Casey) double X or burocracy?
>   —Canto 74   (p. 438)

These are new effects, connected, however remotely, with the artistry of chance and *objet trouvé* invented by Dada artists a generation earlier.

V ABSTRACTION AND LANGUAGE

To THE modern artist, abstraction is the most extreme assertion of the rights of form over those of content. 'It must be abstract' is Wallace Stevens's first specification for the Supreme Fiction.

> It must be visible or invisible,
> Invisible or visible or both:
> A seeing and unseeing in the eye ...

> An abstraction blooded, as a man by thought.

Content, to follow Stevens's image, is the energizing fluid in the veins of form, a contingent necessity. The movement toward pure abstraction in art was an effort to escape this contingency, to grasp permanent significance. The claim that the normally representational arts could emulate mathematics or music, expressing ideas directly without the mediation of forms taken from life was one of those ideas as old as prehistory that the nineteenth century found revolutionary. The point of entry for it in modern painting is usually taken to be the work of Cézanne, and his observation that all objects can be broken down into such abstract shapes as cones, spheres and cylinders. The advent of abstraction in modern art is made visible in Picasso's *Demoiselles d'Avignon* (1907) where the figures on the left are more or less representational, but those on the right have faces resembling curving African masks carved out of wood, and bodies consisting of inorganic shapes defined with a few free-flowing lines. By 1914 the theorists of literary experimentation were fully aware of the importance of abstraction in the graphic arts, and were speculating on its significance for literature.

Abstraction is not a very specific concept in the field of art. In its more moderate forms it simply departs somewhat from the model, selecting and stylizing in ways that are hardly different, in principle, from normal painting conventions. Its non-representational aspects become more apparent when imagined shapes and patterns assert themselves, and the observer is frankly asked to take the work as a design rather than the rendering of a subject.

Abstraction may arise from two different kinds of motivation. The artist may feel that the primary responses can be evoked only by the primary elements of his art—shape, line, colour—and that the representational elements are, at best, a convenience for bringing the observer into contact with them. Or, on the contrary, he may feel that responses are as irrelevant as representation, and that abstract forms express permanent and universal truths which owe nothing to the observer's feelings or to the natural world. 'It took me a long time', said Piet Mondrian, 'to discover that particularity of form and natural colour evoke subjective states of feeling, which obscure *pure* reality. The appearance of natural forms changes but reality remains constant. To create pure reality plastically, it is necessary to reduce natural forms to the *constant elements* of form and natural colour to *primary colour*.'[1] Even on the theoretical level, these two views do not exclude each other, for the most objective attempt to record essential reality must be, in part, the work of a recording mind. Pound, as we have seen, thought that what he called 'the equations of eternity' inscribed themselves in the recurrent emotions experienced by mankind.

As Wyndham Lewis observed, the time before World War I witnessed a sudden enthusiasm for form, and with it a spirit of discipline and severity that counteracted both traditional natural-ism and the tendency toward artistic anarchy that Lewis associated with Bergson and the 'Time-spirit'. Lewis himself shared the new impatience with mere appearances, the urge to grasp essential, enduring elements that could be embodied only in abstract forms. In the 1915 number of *Blast*, he attacks the Cubists and the Futur-ists because they lean too heavily on their models, and calls imita-tion 'intellectual vacuity'. While admitting that a certain degree of representationalism cannot be avoided, he declares that exact rendering cannot get at the truth of an object. 'Nature itself is of no importance.' Recognizable shapes, he says, should be forbidden by act of Parliament.[2]

Hulme favoured abstraction in art because of what he took to be its religious implications. In a lecture delivered in 1914, he distinguished between the 'vital' and 'geometrical', finding in the latter an austere, objective concern with feelings for the absolute which transcend the weak, self-indulgent humanism of the former.[3] He made distinctions among the various types of abstraction, disapproving of Kandinsky's patches of colour, which seemed to call upon the observer only for a superficial admiration of form. Hulme, in opposition to Kant, denied that there was a specific aesthetic capacity to which pure form could address itself, and argued that the emotions form exploited were the ordinary human ones. The advantage of geometric forms was that they freed the artist from the imitation of mutable living things and enabled him to satisfy the need for stability, order and permanence. He might use nature as a source, but only to translate its limited and haphazard productions into forms that were universal and 'necessary'.

Many agreed that forms of this kind were likely to be found in machinery, whose shapes were adapted to accommodate and transmit primary physical forces. The possibility of biomorphic abstraction, such as is found in the sculpture of Jean Arp, seems to have escaped Hulme and his circle. For them abstraction meant the rigid and inorganic. Hulme saw this tendency toward geometrical form emerging as the dominant force in modern art through the work of such figures as the Cubists, Jacob Epstein and Wyndham Lewis. His essay is essentially a re-statement of the ideas of Wilhelm Worringer, whom he had met in Berlin in the winter of 1911-12 and whose thesis, *Abstraktion und Einfühlung (Abstraction and Empathy*, 1908) is a key document in the understanding of abstraction and modern art in general. It was Worringer's view that naturalistic art flourishes in times when people feel themselves to be in harmony with their environment, and seek satisfaction in empathy, in the pleasurable activity of identifying their feelings with organic forms that seem to reflect them. But this does not explain the abstractions and stylization which characterize many periods of art and which were often mistakenly regarded by historians as inept efforts at imitation. This sort of art, Worringer found, emerges at times when there is a general unrest in the face of nature, and people look beyond it to find sources of stability and faith. The abstractness of primitive art arises from the fact that nature seems threatening and chaotic, and the artist feels the need to exclude the transience and inconsistency associated with living things.

According to Worringer, the stylized representation of natural objects had two purposes. It was a way of redeeming something valuable from the chaos of nature and preserving it within the shelter of the laws of art. But the artist also demonstrated its connection with absolutes by imposing stable geometrical forms on it. This impulse can be seen even in sophisticated representational works, where conceptions of form and symmetry require that the figures in a painting or the parts of a sculptured body be arranged in conformity with some basic geometrical design. One of the most general characteristics of primitive stylization is the suppression of space. Since space is the element that links things to each other, making the cherished object prey to an infinite and unknowable continuity, it is felt as pain, and the primitive artist seeks to eliminate it. However, he does not simply take a flat cross-section of his subject, but seeks to preserve its details by bringing them into the two relatively controllable dimensions of a flat surface. The primitive artist's problem, observes Worringer in a key formulation with an obvious relevance to Cubism, was that 'depth relations had to be transformed, as far as possible, into plane relations'.[4]

The linguistic counterpart of Worringer's depth is *reference*. Linguistic representation organizes time in the way that pictorial representation organizes space. As Foucault has put it, 'Language gives the perpetual disruption of time the continuity of space, and it is to the degree that it analyses, articulates, and patterns representation that it has the power to link our knowledge of things together across the dimension of time.'[5] In conventional language, this power is implicated in the threatening, uncontrollable depth of referential meanings, and the experimental writers who lived in the period of World War I had adequate reasons for wanting to exclude it from consciousness, and for using words to create a separate realm of permanent and reliable values. They intuitively acted out Worringer's scenario, striving for the 'dehumanization' of formality and autonomy which Ortega y Gasset found to be characteristic of modern art. While they made abundant use of the 'nature' of tradition, history and past literature, they used these in ways that correspond to the primitive artist's selection and stylization of natural forms, salvaging their valuable parts by detaching them from the nightmare of history or the chaos of the present, and giving them new meanings within new formal organizations. The moments and places of *Four Quartets*, the Tristan legend in *Finnegans Wake*, the anecdote about Confucius in the *Cantos*, the snapshot descriptions of Williams's poems, and the numerous fragmentary quotations and allusions in experimental works all exhibit the urge, identified by Worringer, to redeem particular things of value from the chaotic background of actuality.

Further, the way in which these elements are given permanence within the design of the work is comparable to the projection of a multi-dimensional reality on a flat plane. They are not deprived of their original meanings; but these are assimilated into relationships determined by the themes and structure of the work, and so are shaped into something new. Sigismundo di Malatesta's directions for building his Tempio became a part of the pattern of true and false values that runs through the *Cantos*, and the ample, spreading legend of King Mark and the rival lover is bent into the shape of Earwicker's family situation in *Finnegans Wake*. Depth

relations, as Worringer puts it, are transformed into plane relations, as verbal reference is transformed into literary design.
Worringer enables us to see that the flattening out of time and
space, the elimination of those values captured by perspective
in the graphic arts and by consecutive narration in literature is
one of the most general impulses in experimental art and writing.

Pound's dictum, 'Go in fear of abstractions', is a warning against
feeble diction, and has nothing whatever to do with the artistic
process of transposing nature into stable forms which has the
misfortune to go by the same name. Pound was entirely sympathetic with the formalist, abstractionist tendencies of the period
1912–15, associated himself with some of their strongest advocates, such as Hulme, Lewis and Jacob Epstein, and incorporated
the principles of abstract art into his poetic. He was especially
responsive to the sculpture of Henri Gaudier-Brzeska, who was
killed in action in 1915, but left behind a spirited expression of
his attachment to the cause of abstraction in his letters and other
writings. Gaudier rejected the attractions of subject-matter in
favour of the capacity of forms and relations to grasp and project
concepts. Pound admired those works of his which established
authoritative plane surfaces, manipulated triangular or circular
forms in an interesting manner, or bore witness to the relationships between the vulnerable forms of actuality and their enduring
geometrical counterparts. Gaudier's work testifies to the innate
expressiveness of primary attributes. He wrote that while at the
front he stole an enemy rifle whose brutal shape interested him.
He broke off the wooden butt and carved it, but it is significant
that the shape he gave it was simple, corresponding to its original
one. Abstraction, for Gaudier, was not an allusion to permanence,
but the compact expression of instinct, 'the abstraction of . . .
intense feeling' comparable to the emotions of primitive men.
This feeling was conveyed through 'planes in relation' or 'an
arrangement of surfaces', phrases that recur in Gaudier's statements and letters and in Pound's writing about him.

Having spent two months at the front, and seen some of its
horrors, Gaudier reported that his feelings about abstraction in
sculpture had not changed. The war inspired, not pity, but a
determination to put his trust elsewhere than in human activities.
'I SHALL DERIVE MY EMOTIONS SOLELY FROM THE
ARRANGEMENT OF SURFACES', he wrote in a message
sent to *Blast*. 'I shall present my emotions by the ARRANGE-
MENT OF MY SURFACES, THE PLANES AND LINES
BY WHICH THEY ARE DEFINED.'[6] He had turned from a
threatening environment to abstraction, reliving the pattern
described by Worringer.

Through the influence of Wyndham Lewis, *Blast* went far toward identifying Vorticism and the artistic freedom it demanded with the abstraction informed by the spirit of an industrial age. Lewis felt that modern art ought to express primitive passions through forms generated by industrial civilization. He called for the extinction of the old human and natural forms, for a setting of 'steel trees' to replace the green ones that had been lost, for a hard, intelligent, scientifically crafted art, of the kind, one would think, that could be made with a lathe. Looking back at Vorticism in later years, he said that 'It was my ultimate aim to exclude from painting the everyday visual real altogether. The idea was to build up a visual language as abstract as music. The colour green would not be confined, or related, to what was green in nature ... a shape represented by a fish remained a form independent of the animal, and could be made use of in a universe in which there were no fish. ... I considered the world of machinery as real to us, or more so, as nature's forms ... and that machine-forms had an equal right to exist in our canvases.'[7] Even the self would disappear, merging with the congenial, controllable industrial environment. 'Dehumanization is the chief diagnosis of the Modern World',[8] said Lewis, anticipating both the message and the vocabulary of Ortega y Gasset.

A good part of Pound's 1914 exposition of Vorticism is a defense of the values of abstraction. The 'masses in relation' found in Wyndham Lewis's paintings and Gaudier-Brzeska's carved pieces gave him, he said, the satisfaction of an inner need; he felt that sheer form could be moving, and lamented the fact that most people cannot respond to 'an arrangement of planes'. Crediting the painters with discovering the advantages that form and colour, with their immediacy of effect, have over the symbols on which writers depend, he said that ideally, the emotions connected with the experience described in his poem, 'A Station of the Métro' should have been embodied in a non-representational arrangement of colours rather than in words. As we have seen, Pound felt that every mental event rises to consciousness in 'some primary form', and that this form dictates the appropriate medium for expressing it.[9] While this interest in abstraction may seem inconsistent with his emphasis on presentation it is actually an essential component of it. Art that strikes through particulars at universals in accordance with Pound's observation penetrates sense experience in order to grasp the necessary, unvarying relationships that exist independently of particular objects or events. If the poet is to feel the universal, recurring emotions of mankind as primary experiences, he must also apprehend them conceptually, as forms, removed from the contingencies of actuality, capable of being embodied in 'a sort of permanent metaphor', the Image, that, as Pound said, gives a sense of liberation from the limitations imposed by space and time.

In the analogue of the equation from analytic geometry which Pound used to clarify what he meant by intensity in poetry, the counterpart of the feelings generated by the poem is the abstract, disembodied curve generated by the equation. The parallel is still present in his review of a show of Brancusi's sculpture published in the *Little Review* in 1921, where Pound quotes the Vorticist doctrine, 'The beauty of form in the still stone can not be the same beauty of form as that in the living animal', and says of one of Brancusi's characteristic polished ovoids that it is 'form free from all terrestrial gravitation; form as free in its own life as the form of the analytic geometers. . . .'[10]

Pound employs this sort of freedom in such Imagist poems as 'The Return' and 'The Coming of War: Actaeon,' which, being mythical or quasi-mythical, begin by discarding specifically empirical intentions. But what is more important is their method of using a small number of essential and determinate particulars which act, much as the points in a geometrical field do in marking out a curve, to create an intuition that we recognize as capable of existing apart from the particulars. They do not describe, as, for example, '*Portrait d'une Femme*' does, through fullness of detail and emotional response. Instead, they approach the permanent, invulnerable stability of form which is one of the values of abstraction through particulars recognizable from common experience.

Ideally, an abstract literature would free itself of all referential tendencies. This was a project that suited the Dadas, who tried a number of ingenious experiments designed to empty language of all practical meaning. In 1917 Hugo Ball wrote and recited a 'sound-poem' consisting of nonsense-syllables which began:

> gadji beri bimba
> glandridri aluli lonni cadori
> gadjama bim beri glassala
> glandiridi blassala tuffm zimbrabrim. . . .[11]

Through this medium he expected to release energies that were suppressed by accepted linguistic rules. At a later stage of Dada, Kurt Schwitters invented the form he called 'Ursonate', which consisted of nonsense-syllables arranged in rather intricate patterns, and which he could recite with considerable effect. Perhaps less extreme than these, but certainly sufficiently abstract in the sense that they are nearly innocent of content, are the

Dada experiments with chance composition, the echoes and re-
duplications found in *Ubu-Roi* and imitated by the Dadas, and
the text of Tristan Tzara's *La première aventure céleste de Mr. Antipyrine*, which uses words (predominantly), but arranges them in
ways that make it impossible to take them referentially.

While the Anglo-American writers did not engage in a militant
campaign to drive meaning out of language as the Dadas did,
they made occasional investigations into the possibilities of
linguistic abstraction. Gertrude Stein was the most persistent
experimenter in this mode. There is a noticeable aversion, in
much of her work, to nouns; they are replaced, as far as possible,
by present participles expressing the continuous present. Her
vocabulary favours familiar colourless words. Such words as
'being', 'existing', 'repeating' and 'living' are treated as key words
at the beginning of *The Making of Americans*, and are repeated
incessantly; the effect of this is to set up oppressive rhythms in
the flow of the prose, and at the same time to empty it progressively
of meaning. The syntax has little subordination, but proceeds
by adding words on the same grammatical level, an effect comparable with the tendency among painters to move everything to
a single visual plane. *The Making of Americans* refers to clearly
identifiable characters, but in *Tender Buttons* the style becomes
nearly entirely detached from the subject matter.

But there is no disruption of the word itself, as there is in
Finnegans Wake. With surprising conservatism, Gertrude Stein
says that it is impossible to invent new words, because language is
a reality emerging from historical experience, 'an intellectual
recreation', and 'every one must stay with the language their
language. . . . ' In addition, maintaining the integrity of individual
words was essential to her aim of creating texts which would reflect
her childhood delight in diagramming sentences by establishing
interesting relationships among the words. Her idea was that
words should be set into groups that generated 'liveliness'. This
could apparently arise from either syntactic or phonic relationships, which could generate elaborate and original patterns not
entirely without meaning. Many such passages have become famous and are identified with Gertrude Stein's peculiar style. They
often succeed in bringing forward some unnoticed capacity of
their words and phrases, exactly in the spirit of self-reflexive
art. In the following sentence, for example, the juggling of the
same handful of words into different sequences sets up unexpected
syntactical relationships and dissociations, without having any
substantive meaning at all: 'And after that what changes what
changes after that, after that what changes and what changes

after that and after that and what changes and after that and
what changes after that.'[12]

Rather unexpectedly perhaps, in view of his attachment to
actual experience, William Carlos Williams shared Pound's
belief that the success of a poem depends on 'geometry', on its
capacity to embody abstract relationships. If we recall that his
interest in externals arose from the impulse to locate the resistant,
enduring quality of existence itself, it is not surprising that he
should feel that 'The forms/of the emotions are crystalline,/
geometric-faceted' (p. 64). Williams's passion for the purely
formal aspects of poetry is perhaps displayed nowhere so well
as in his essay on Marianne Moore. Observing that the apparent
fragmentation and confusion of modern poetry are only its most
visible aspects, he says: 'A course in mathematics would not
be wasted on a poet, or a reader of poetry, if he remember no
more from it than the geometric principle of the intersection of
loci: from all angles lines converging and crossing establish
points.' The pleasure of poetry lies in following this geometry,
in a movement over the body of the poem that is analogous, one
would think, considering Williams's interest in art, to the movement of the eye over the surface of a painting. Marianne Moore's
poems excel, not for their thought or content, but for their way
of managing these convergences with technical finish, for 'the
aesthetic pleasure engendered where pure craftsmanship joins
hard surfaces skilfully',[13] a standard of judgment that recalls
Gaudier-Brzeska's decision to put his trust only in abstractions.

But for Williams this decision was more problematic. He could
praise Gertrude Stein because she freed words of content, and
showed that movement and design had values independent of
any specific sense that might be attached to them, and he could
even say, 'That is the essence of all knowledge.' But he realized
that while Gertrude Stein had been forced to establish contact
with actuality in terms of an ascent 'to a plane of almost abstract
design', this manoeuvre conflicted with the need to represent and
interpret the reality encountered by the senses.[14] Williams recognizes that objects can be taken into the enclosure of the feelings
and assimilated into the design of a poem only if they undergo
stylization. He says, in 'The Rose': ' . . . to engage roses becomes
a geometry'. The trouble is, continues this poem, that each rose
petal ends in an edge, and at that edge the love it carries ends too.
But roses can be replicated in hard materials, such as metal and
porcelain; when this transformation is carried out,

From the petal's edge a line starts

that being of steel
infinitely fine, infinitely
rigid penetrates
the Milky Way
without contact—lifting
from it—neither hanging
nor pushing—

The fragility of the flower
unbruised
penetrates space

(p. 250)

so that the symbol of love can prevail and last when it changes its organic nature and is cast in an enduring form. The image Williams uses for Marianne Moore's poetry is a porcelain garden; it reflects nature only superficially, its real quality being totally different, hard, exact, compressed: 'It is the white of a clarity beyond the facts.'[15]

He admired Gertrude Stein's efforts to free language from the impediments of content because his own poetry undertakes a similar campaign. Referential as they are, the words of his poems turn away from their referential function once they have capitalized on it, to speak directly to the feelings, and to establish connections with other parts of the poem, thus acquiring the resistant, opaque quality that Williams valued. This effect is related to the way in which he internalizes space, making it a counterpart of bodily existence. J. Hillis Miller has shown that Williams thinks of space as being penetrated by the senses, so that objects are brought close, enfolded in the grasp of sight, touch or hearing, becoming known intuitively, as if they were bodily processes.[16] Within this continuum, all that is perceived becomes an aspect of the single experience of existence, and existence is identical with the sum of things perceived. The space between the eye and the object disappears, so that perception is transformed into a kind of touch, and the object is felt to share the reactions, strains and movements of the body. Within this arena consciousness multiplies itself, becoming distinct and various as it is articulated through externals. But objects also meet and merge, establishing invisible connections with each other just as different physical experiences meet in consciousness.

Miller enables us to see why Williams's treatment of objects should correspond with Worringer's analysis of abstraction. The space of his poems, where everything is contiguous to everything else, and equally accessible to perception, has no relation to our ordinary notions of space. It resembles the field of the Cubist paintings Williams found so meaningful early in his career. The Cubist's models were typically things that could be found at arm's length, the contents of a table-top, or the furniture and paraphernalia of the artist's room, and these objects, the guitar, the chessboard, or the wine bottle, participated in daily life by inserting their strong geometrical presences into it. The Cubist techniques extend and reinforce this familiarity by their elimination of depth. As they bend, warp, or even annihilate the space before the eye, blending the model with the wall in back of it, they claim it as a part of the two-dimensional reality of the canvas. Aspects of things irrelevant to their existence in this dynamic Flatland are eliminated; they are simplified and essentialized, perhaps hardly recognizable.

The objects in Williams's poems undergo similar transformations. They are not described, but detached from their ordinary backgrounds, brought into the radiant circle of the poet's awareness, immersed in his sentient and imaginative capacities. Once there, they are used, economically, as points of departure for words that form the design of the poem. Even an ostensibly narrative and representational poem of Williams's can be used to demonstrate this abstracting, anti-referential effect.

Good Night

In brilliant gas light
I turn the kitchen spigot
and watch the water plash
into the clean white sink.
On the grooved drain-board
to one side is
a glass filled with parsley—
crisped green.

Waiting
for the water to freshen—
I glance at the spotless floor—:
a pair of rubber sandals
lie side by side
under the wall-table
all is in order for the night.

Waiting, with a glass in my hand
—three girls in crimson satin
pass close before me on

the murmurous background of
the crowded opera—

      it is
memory playing the clown—
three vague meaningless girls
full of smells and
the rustling sounds of
cloth rubbing on cloth and
little slippers on carpet—
high-school French
spoken in a loud voice!

Parsley in a glass,
still and shining,
brings me back. I take a drink
and yawn deliciously.
I am ready for bed.

                          (p. 145–6)

This poem is not really about a visit to the kitchen, but about a drama of feelings, an interplay between the sense of order and security arising from the things at hand, and the alien, futile existence suggested in a chance memory. The referential qualities of the words are important mainly as support for their connotations. The things in the kitchen are serene, orderly, homely. On the other hand, the memory of 'crimson satin', 'little slippers' and high school French conveys artificiality and pretense. There are threatening elements of the disorderly and unaccountable in the remembered scene: vague smells and the untidy surface of a carpet contrast with the hard, smooth, precise details of the kitchen; the indefinite 'rustling sounds' contrast with the forthright, specific 'plash' of the water. As the two parts of the waiting moment fall into this antithetical design, the words take leave of their referents, and align themselves within this balance. One can almost see them being peeled from the surface of the objects to which they are normally attached and fitted into place in the poem. They are used, not primarily to mean anything in nature, but to generate abstract, intangible feelings that cannot be localized anywhere but within the self. Williams himself has explained this use of words very clearly:

When a man makes a poem, makes it, mind you, he takes the words as he finds them interrelated about him and composes them—without distortion which would mar their exact significances—into an intense expression of his perceptions and ardors that they may constitute a revelation in the speech that he uses. It isn't what he *says* that counts as a work of art, it's what he makes. . . . [17]

He found that Joyce used words in this way:

He forces me, before I can follow him, to separate the words from the printed page, to take them up into a world where the imagination is at play and where the words are no more than titles under the illustrations. It is a reaffirmation of the forever-sought freedom of truth from usage. It is the modern world emerging among the living ancients by paying attention to the immediacy of its own contact; a classical method.[18]

E.E. Cummings's poetry is usually considered vividly representational, but this aspect of his work is easily exaggerated; his linguistic innovations actually set aside the whole question of imitation, disengage words from their usual meanings, and free them to express private intuitions, or to take part in the design of the poem. It is true that many of his typographical devices are expressive or even representational; but they are used within the framework of stylized modernist conventions shared with William Carlos Williams, Marianne Moore and other poets of the time. The paradox involved in the new typographical conventions is very clear in Cummings's case. He said that he regarded the usual practices as affectations, and borrowed the custom of capitalizing only for emphasis and writing the first-person 'i' in lower case from the letters sent to him by Sam Ward, the caretaker of his New England farm, who is praised in poem No. 28 of *1 × 1* ('rain or hail').[19] He justified the uncapitalized 'i' on the ground of consistency, pointing out that no other language accords special treatment to the first-person pronoun. But, as has often been pointed out, these defiant departures are hardly natural and self-effacing, for they reject imperfect, but cherished traditional customs in favour of an obtrusive display of principle.

In spite of its apparent concreteness, Cummings's diction rather surprisingly exhibits a tendency toward abstract conceptualization. In an important analysis of Cummings's verse, R.P. Blackmur observed that certain favourite words in his vocabulary, such as 'flower' tend to become mere signals for private feelings, and to lose their referential and communal values. Blackmur's particular objection is that the ideas they are supposed to express remain inaccessible, and the reader becomes a bystander who observes the poem as a symptom of the poet's excitement, but cannot share it.[20] But one of Cummings's most conspicuous linguistic innovations, the transference of words from one grammatical role to another (in general, he makes nouns of them) exploits the abstraction Blackmur objected to with perfectly intelligible results.

In No. V of 'Sonnets-Realities' in *Tulips and Chimneys*, Cummings describes a girl as 'ducking always the touch of must and shall'. The same words are used with somewhat different values in the first line of No. 18 of *New Poems*, 'must being shall'. In using simple and familiar verbal auxiliaries as nouns, Cummings has found a disarmingly direct way of expressing ponderous notions. It would be no improvement to say that the girl in Sonnet V evaded both necessity and future consequences, or to paraphrase the line of No. 18 as saying 'the necessary is also the inevitable'. Cummings has not changed the meanings of the words, but he has given them unusual force, and made their meanings more visible. The success of this manoeuvre is no doubt partly due to the fact that it is not strictly original, but follows a pattern found in familiar speech: 'it's a must', 'he's a has-been'. At first glance what Cummings has done here seems to improve concreteness, for the words have been promoted from the status of mere grammatical aids to that of substantives, with solid meanings. But when they are compared with the nouns they have theoretically replaced, for example, 'ducking always her parents and the police', it becomes apparent that they are really abstractions, roughly equivalent to such words as 'compulsion' and 'obligation'. Poem XV of 1×1 tells the inhabitants of a warring world to scream

> ...till your if is up
> and vanish under prodigies of un)
>
> (p. 397)

so that 'if' occupies the position of a noun meaning something like hope. Accordingly, when Poem 2 of *No Thanks* speaks of the 'iflike moon', the coining means that the moon is full of promise. Transferences of this kind, which became much more common in the verse Cummings published after 1930, are vivid, direct and intelligible. But their effect is abstract. In lifting such words from their utilitarian roles and giving them more than their usual 'content', Cummings has also attached them to general concepts, using them to isolate and fix attitudes or ideas.

Transference augments the semantic force of such weak words as auxiliary verbs and conjunctions. With other words, however, it tends to limit the meaning to a concept appropriate to Cummings's immediate purpose. The first line of No. XXXIX of

I × *I* (p. 412), 'all ignorance toboggans into know' puns on the last word; intellectual knowing is a negative thing. But even without the pun, the blunt monosyllable is an effective exclusion of the favourable tone of 'knowing', a narrowing of its meaning. The poem ends by proposing that we move from a preoccupation with sterile history "into now;" the punning effect is still present, but this time the transference narrows the word's meaning in the direction of favourable connotations, escaping its neutrality to some degree. No. XL of *I* × *I* has a passage in which a verb becomes a noun and a proper noun a verb:

> let pitiless fear play host
> to every isn't that's under the spring
> —but if a look should april me,
> down isn't's own isn't go ghostly. . . .

> (p. 413)

Here 'isn't' seems to mean something like 'threat' or 'danger', and 'april', which is used in a similar way by Cummings elsewhere, means something like 'encourage'. The verb, therefore, has acquired the stronger meaning of a noun, but 'april' carries, not its meaning, but its secondary associations into the poem. Devices of this kind, whether they strengthen words that are comparatively blank, or specialize words with abundant meanings of their own, are conceptualizations that attempt to solve the problem of referring to sensation rather than to the external that generates sensation. If they were translated into conventional language of similar scope, they would be represented by words of little concrete meaning. A passage that depends heavily on grammatical transference will help to make the point. It is an account of paradise:

> . . . the green whereless truth
> of an eternal now welcomes each was
> of whom among not numerable ams . . .

> (p. 399)

Which might be paraphrased as meaning: the immanent truth of an eternal present welcomes each former identity of a person among an infinite host of existing beings. Cummings's neologisms have a double force; they strengthen the meanings of comparatively weak words; and each emphasizes a specific concept or quality which would be lost in a concrete reference. 'Was' and 'ams' mean approximately 'dead souls' and 'living selves', but the oddly-used verbs form a sharp, narrow contrast that less abstract language could not achieve.

Cummings's famous negatives are really instances of grammatical transference; part of the effectiveness of such coinings as 'unlife' and 'unrepute' is due to the fact that the prefix, since it is not generally used with nouns, acquires more substantial meaning than it ordinarily has. Cummings's ambition to make it more meaningful is made perfectly clear in such occasional independent uses as 'people/be/come/un', the statement that ends the first poem of *New Poems* (p. 333). Paradoxically, however, negative prefixes, while acquiring more significance themselves tend to turn substantives into abstractions. Examples appear in the pessimistic first poem of 1 × 1 :

> nonsun blob a
> cold to
> skylessness
> sticking fire . . .
>
> leaf of ghosts some
> few creep there
> here or on
> unearth

(p. 389)

The fact that 'nonsun' and 'unearth' refer to attributes rather than objects is exposed by 'skylessness', a negative with the appropriate form of an abstract noun, to which they are parallel. It should be added that Cummings shows an awareness of the abuses to which misplaced negatives can be subjected in a poem about a henpecked husband which describes him as 'one nonsufficiently inunderstood' (p. 287), an effective mockery of whimpering self-pity.

Many of these technical experiments, though ostensibly representational, really attract attention to themselves and to their way of handling the problems of imitation, thereby illustrating what appears to be a law connected with efforts to transcend the ordinary representational capacities of any art. When an art that operates in one mode or dimension departs from its usual limits in order to imitate a model that exists in another, the elementary nature of its own medium tends to emerge sharply, and to become the real subject of the work.

A passage from *Finnegans Wake* which uses a technique favoured by Cummings seems to be making this point. The letter from Boston, in one of its many incarnations, is pierced with holes by a professor using a fork. In what is apparently a satirical thrust at Worringer's theory of abstraction in primitive art, we are told that the professor did this in order to express a concept of time on a plane surface, and the language itself follows this up by offering an example of abstraction. The discovery about the professor, says the text, was made through the clue of

. . . the circumflexuous wall of a singleminded men's asylum, accentuated by bi
tso fb rok engl a ssan dspl itch ina. . . .

(p. 124)

Joyce has violated the convention that words are divided from
each other in order to imitate the broken glass and china directly
through language. Cummings uses exactly the same device:

. . . the paralyticwhose dod d e rin g partner whEEl shi min chb yi nch along. . . .

(p. 81)

and

. . . b etw ee nch air st ott er s thesillyold WomanSellingBalloonS

(p. 84)

These examples are perfectly intelligible when the words are
re-assembled, for the language turns out to be referential in two
ways—through the meanings of the words and through physical,
or visual imitation. Before this takes place, however, the nonsense-
syllables appear meaningful, as if they were the words of an
unknown language. When they have been assimilated into familiar
words, it becomes clear that this meaningfulness can exist independently, in the absence of actual reference, in abstract form, as an
inherent virtue of language. The nonsense-syllables temporarily
achieve the condition of abstract language, like the Dada 'Ursonate'
of Kurt Schwitters.

Violations of the mode of an art, even when they are imitative,
therefore, have a self-reflexive effect, calling attention to the
signifier rather than to the thing signified. Cummings does very
little to prevent this. He exacts close attention to his methods,
so that many of his poems are like puzzles, and their banal or
sentimental content often means that their values lies precisely
in the technical relationships which are the elements of the puzzle.
In some lines describing thunder, for example:

> at
> which (shal)lpounceupcrackw(ill)jumps
> of
>   THuNdeRB
>   loSSo!M iN
> -visiblya mongban(gedfrag-
> ment ssky?wha tm) eani ngl(essNess. . . .

(p. 250)

it is difficult to get any sense of thunder itself, though we can
easily lose ourselves in unravelling the typographical ingenuities
displayed. His practice of dividing constructions in order to

insert parenthetical interruptions also emphasizes mere structure; the device of intercalation, in which two elements interrupt each other, as in

strol(pre)ling(cise)dy(ly)na(
mite)

achieves an effect of simultaneity, but it also intervenes between the reader and the content of the poem. Some of the poems are completely fragmented and have to be read by being reassembled, like the famous one about the grasshopper. Many have to be read by referring closely from one section to another to gain a sense, not of their form, but of their meaning; significantly the two lie close together in such cases, and to decode the method of the poem is to have an experience of its form. In these instances, Cummings approaches, but does not achieve, the closure of the two elements that is possible in music or in graphic art that is completely abstract.

The coexistence in Cummings's work of imitative tendencies and formal abstraction is not exceptional in Anglo-American literary experimentation. Abstraction of language and form usually appears in conjunction with a certain degree of representation. Clive Hart has pointed out that Joyce employed leitmotifs with their flattening and self-reflexive effects as early as 'The Dead' and *A Portrait* yet both can certainly be read as if they had the 'depth' of stories whose main purpose is the representation of reality. In general, the experimentalists developed the abstract potentialities of language without absolutely opposing its normal referential function. They seem to have agreed, at least insofar as language is concerned, with Kandinsky's view that the abstract retains 'the timbre of the organic' rather than with Mondrian's idea that any allusion to natural forms interferes with a work's capacity to capture pure reality. They tended, therefore, to exploit meaning in the interests of abstraction instead of eliminating it, much as the sculpture of Gaudier-Brzeska and the Vorticist paintings of Wyndham Lewis used stylized representational forms to achieve the satisfactions of 'planes in relation'. Pound seems to have had this strategy in mind when, in an essay written more than ten years after the period of his strongest interest in abstraction, he distinguished the kind of poetry he called 'Logopoeia', which uses words in their ordinary meanings, but also exploits 'the aesthetic content which is peculiarly the domain of verbal manifestation' —that is, usage, connotation and association, calling this approach to poetry 'the dance of the intellect among words'.[21]

VI IMAGERY AND OTHER RESOURCES

THE SEEDS of experiment have always lain hidden inside the husk of traditional rhetorical theory. The recognized tropes and figures of speech are, after all, no more than names for the deviations from literal meaning and conventional practice that have always appeared in poetic language, and a full repertory of them would cover most of the irrational and inconsequent constructions found in the wildest experimental writing. But what were once regarded as ornaments of style were recognized, in the modern period, as examples of the autonomous power of language. Figurative language was regarded as an aperture in the carapace of literalism, a place where mind and matter met, a theatre in which the drama of perception and expression was performed. No single topic or term of art occupied modern theoreticians more.

Bergson considered image-formation indispensable to mental transactions with the physical world. *Image* is his usual term, in *Matter and Memory*, for the basic material the mind works with. It is both the primary impression that impinges upon the nervous system in naive perception, and the medium of mental activity. He says, ' . . . by positing the material world we assume an aggregate of images, and moreover . . . it is impossible to assume anything else. No theory of matter escapes this necessity,' and goes on to show that recent explanations of the behaviour of atoms are grounded in imagery.[1] The universe is one aggregate of images, the self another. In intuitive perception, the image is a rich composite of attributes, many of them drawn from memory. Most of these are suppressed when it passes into representation, for the artist makes a selection in accordance with his interests, but in spite of this loss, the representational image is more faithful to intuition than other forms of expression, and Bergson thought that a multiplicity of such images could approximate intuitive knowledge.

They cannot convey meaning independently, however, but must be put into relationship with each other by thought. In this crucial area, the spaces between and around images, the modern writers found opportunities for conveying new insights into the world and developing new linguistic possibilities. Suggestions of this kind came to them from many sources. The French Symbolists had demonstrated that objects can be more eloquent than ideas, and had explored the symbolic possibilities of things associated with industrialism and modern life. Rimbaud had suggested, in writing about the use of flowers in poetry, that one means of entering new spiritual realms was the irrational image—'Trouve des fleurs qui soient des chaises!'—and had compared lilies at evening to syringes. Freud's dream-images that could be read as clues to subconscious thought, Bergson's premise that primary intuitions manifest themselves in mental imagery, Ford Madox Ford's interest in the articles listed for auction, Eliot's analyses of metaphysical imagery, Fenollosa's poetic doctrine of the ideogram, the Futurist principle of the distant, suggestive analogy, and many other influences passed into the theory and practice of imagery, transforming accepted ideas about it.

In Anglo-American poetry, the period of modern imagery may be said to open with Eliot's

> . . . the evening is spread out against the sky
> Like a patient etherised upon a table.

Written no later than 1911, this simile abruptly violates conventional expectations. It relates two distant realities, uses a scientific term (in imitation of Laforgue), foregoes poetic resonance, and, as if in accordance with the Surrealist specification that an image should exit unimpressively, peters out with a deflationary close. The basis of the relationship between the two terms is either superficial or almost awesomely suggestive. Evening and patient are both twilight zones; but if their attributes are taken seriously, we are being told that the evening is unconscious, vacant, perhaps also diseased, like the patient. In 'East Coker', a poem written nearly thirty years later, the mind under ether is 'conscious but conscious of nothing', like Eliot's 'violet hour' that marks the close of a monotonous day in the wasteland of urban civilization. Most of the images that follow the simile of the patient in 'The Love Song of J. Alfred Prufrock' are equally venturesome, and show that in the modern period imagery could do more and mean more than at any time since the seventeenth century.

1 THE IMAGERY OF DISCORD

Traditionally, tropes depend upon a resemblance between two differing metaphoric terms. They employ Hopkins's general principle of rhyme, associating things that mingle similarity and dissimilarity, with emphasis upon the former. But Aristotle, in his discussion of metaphor, gives considerable prominence to the element of dissimilarity as well, defining metaphor as a grouping of two pairs of things having similar relations with each other. Any member of each pair can be substituted for the corresponding member of the other through the procedure carefully described in the *Rhetoric* as a substitution of one word for another that depends, not upon any specific resemblance between the two terms being exchanged, but upon the similarity of their relationship to the other members of their pairs. 'The Lord is my shepherd' equates its two terms only to the extent that the relation of the Lord to the speaker resembles that of the shepherd to his flock. A number of the qualities Aristotle attributes to metaphor have more to do with dissimilarity than with similarity:

(1)   It gives a 'foreign air'.
(2)   It gives names to things that have none by stemming from something akin to them.
(3)   It is a kind of enigma.[2]

These were the aspects of imagery that seemed most significant to the experimental generation. Differing motives lay behind this loose consensus. The imagery of discord was sometimes conceived as an attack upon conventional expectations and automatic habits of thought. Victor Shklovsky, denying that imagery is merely an economizing device, gave it a place in his theory of defamiliarization as a method of avoiding automatic perception, generating awareness and supplanting the mere knowledge of objects with fresh impressions of the world.[3] Sometimes such imagery is used to pry apart the rigid patterns of a rationally-ordered universe and reassemble the parts according to some new perception, 'through metaphor to reconcile/the people and the stones', as W.C. Williams wrote. It may serve to open poetry to unconventional materials from science, daily life and actual dreams (as opposed to romanticized ones). But the most vital function of such imagery was that of extending the possibilities of language, of creating new meanings through new affinities.

Motivations of this kind are especially explicit in the theory and practice of the Continental experimenters. Marinetti's proposal that Futurist poets write in chains of analogies that avoid obvious or immediate connections and also omit their first terms was certainly calculated to violate conventional ideas of coherence. He was also the first to make certain positive claims for this kind of imagery; it is, he said, an expression of love, a way of overcoming the antagonisms that exist in the universe. It enables the poet to align vast areas of thought with each other, and to bring forward unperceived multiple affinities. The imagery of Marinetti's own poetry, to be sure, seems belligerent rather than affectionate, and his use of the iconography of war and industry goes at least as far back as Tennyson and Baudelaire. But he manipulates his mundane imagery with the confident vigour of a mind to which nothing that is mechanical is alien; and his effortless assimilation of a maximum of disorder exhibits language in a condition of complete release.

By advocating the use of mathematical and other scientific symbols in poetry, for example, he seemed to imply that the scientific and poetic modes of thought could be merged, and that poetry was capable of a precision and assurance ordinarily considered foreign to its nature. But the idea raises interesting questions, some of which are illustrated by his use of the 'equals' sign to form a kind of metaphor. The 'equals' sign is narrower and more emphatic than the metaphoric 'is', for it denotes reversibility, and therefore complete equivalence; but it is less ambiguous and more open to critical examination. Sometimes Marinetti uses it to argue for the equal validity of psychological and material phenomena, as in this case, where an event is identified with the recollections it evokes:

> accensione di un veliero = lampada a petrolio +
> 12 paralumi bianchi + tappeto verde + cerchio di
> solitudine serenita famiglia
> (ignition (as in a motor) of a sailboat = oil-lamp +
> 12 white lampshades + green carpet + circle of loneliness
> family serenity)

A very different use occurs when the equivalence simply creates a tension between the incongruities:

> tenere in bocca tutto mare TONDO = nuotatore
> giocoliere + piatto porcellana (6 Km. diametro)
> fra denti[4]
> (to hold the whole ROUND sea in the mouth = swimming
> juggler + porcelain plate (6 Km. in diameter) in the teeth)

The first equation contradicts our belief that there is some difference between an event and the memories it illogically brings to mind; even if we are ready to admit that the paradoxical event aboard the sailboat led the poet to think of details of his home or childhood, we cannot accept the exact equivalence without first agreeing that both are psychological. In the second, the terms are alike because each is impossible or absurd; they would have been intelligible as the terms of a simile or metaphor, but, as in the first example, the 'equals' sign makes an assertion which forces us to grope for some extraordinary plane where this equivalence is possible.

The imaginative pranks of the Dadas in the field of imagery produced technical results of lasting value. Unhampered by the desire to communicate in the conventional sense, they reached for the most absurd and implausible effects, guided by two fairly contradictory motivations. On the one hand, such images demonstrated the absurdity of conventional associations; on the other, they expressed the feeling, which Marinetti also defined as the implication of Futurist analogy, that in an absurd world, nothing is too absurd to make a certain sense. Their lunatic imagery harmonized exactly with the variously-rationalized modern tendency to link dissimilars. They were not nearly so hysterical as they pretended to be, but loaded their apparently random shots with clear and deadly meaning.

Many of the best Dada images are graphic works, and some of these claim a certain literary quality because the metaphor is defined by the title. Francis Picabia, for example, gave a rather pleasing, crisply-rendered painting of some mechanical parts the title 'Paroxysme de la Douleur,' and a *collage* by George Grosz which was shown at a Dada exposition in Berlin in 1920, a portrait of a man whose face is encumbered by superimposed machine parts, a razor, and a large question mark is turned into a biographical document by its title, 'Remember Uncle August the Unhappy Inventor'. The suggestive power of Dada graphic art is well illustrated in Man Ray's classic construction of a handiron with a row of tacks fixed to its ironing surface; it is an incisive formulation of the essence of contradiction.

The Dada writers pretended that their madcap images were meaningless, no more than accidental or spontaneous parallels that mocked the emptiness of ordinary rhetoric. But they are often perfectly articulate. Richard Huelsenbeck's poem, 'End of the World' (1916) begins:

This is what things have come to in this world
The cows sit on the telegraph poles and play chess
The cockatoo under the skirts of the Spanish dancer
Sings as sadly as a headquarters bugler and the cannon lament
    all day . . .
Only the fire department can drive the nightmare from the
    drawing-

room but all the hoses are broken[5]

On the one hand, such imagery detaches the parts of the known world from each other and puts them into an entirely different sequence, as if to show that both arrangements are equally arbitrary. On the other, it is capable of suggesting very pointed meanings. The little parable about the fire department is clearly an allusion to the moral condition of Europe during the war years; but the disarming image of the chess-playing cows expresses a different feeling, suggesting an exuberant celebration of the diversity of life. As Huelsenbeck said in a later manifesto, poetry of this kind 'teaches a sense of the merrygoround of all things'. One of Tzara's innumerable images for Dada itself was 'virgin microbe'. The fact that this metaphoric term is purely imaginary does not interfere with the message that Dada is a new spirit of virtue that does its destructive work by invisibly infiltrating the cultural organism.

One article of the Surrealist heresy was the belief that there was positive meaning in the images of Dada. Imagery and doctrines connected with it were, in fact, fundamental to the Surrealist position. André Breton officially ascribed the origin of the movement to an image. In his *Manifeste de surréalisme*, he reported that one evening he became obsessed with a phrase which seemed to come from nowhere; Breton conscientiously admitted that he did not recall it exactly, but that it resembled 'Il y a un homme coupé en deux par la fenêtre', and that it was accompanied in his mind by an actual vision of a walking man cut through at his waist by a window perpendicular to his body. Trying to use that in his poetry, he found that it was followed by a stream of equally spontaneous images so rich that he felt he was losing control over his thoughts. This episode was followed by experiments in automatic writing conducted by Breton and Philippe Soupault, which resulted in texts containing, among other surprising elements, images of great originality and suggestiveness. Breton found an explanation for the effectiveness of these irrational productions in Pierre Reverdy's statement that the image results from a 'rapprochement de deux réalités plus ou moins éloignées', and that it increases in its emotive power according to the distance between the two terms. He followed this with his own specification that the Surrealist image consisted of simultaneously-envisioned realities which did not undergo a conscious *rapprochement* in the reader's mind, but on the contrary, produced a particular illumination through their differences. Association, insists Breton, is not involved in this phenomenon; the Surrealist image is not merely an elliptical rendering of a familiar relationship. The *Manifeste* takes such images to be the guides of Surrealist thinking, and identifies the most arbitrary, those most removed from ordinary channels of thought, as the most vital.

Louis Aragon defined Surrealism as the vice of 'the narcotic, *image*', whose use transforms the appearance of reality.[6] By asserting the continuity of the discontinuous, such images suggest a whole new order of things, free the mind from routine ideas, and open the imagination to new and limitless possibilities. The classic image of this kind, often cited by the Surrealists, is Lautréamont's '... beau comme la rencontre fortuite sur une table de dissection, d'une machine à coudre et d'un parapluie', which combines elements of mystery, chance, contradiction and indifference to reality, demonstrating that words can behave independently, creating a reality of their own. Sometimes this independence is asserted through a denial of the ordinary physical properties of things; Surrealist poetry mentions white leaves, twilights shaped like commas, and water with eyelids. Successful images of this kind, like dream images, resist conscious analysis, elusively suggest a latent content, and deny the reader access to their meanings unless he first becomes a convert to the visions they embody.

✶   ✶   ✶

It seems likely that Bergson's emphasis on the image passed into Hulme's critical idiom and thence into Pound's to become the name of the Imagist movement. However, not all of Bergson's ideas accompanied it on this journey. Hulme agreed with Bergson that the poetic image could not be more than an arrested version of the perceived one, but he did not, like Bergson, believe that it was possible or desirable for the artist to convey a sense of the fluctuating current of intuitive thought. By saying that 'Images in verse are not mere decoration, but the very essence of an intuitive language', he could not have meant that they reported intuition intact, but that they came as close as language could to preserving the individuality and immediacy of intuitive experience. There is an important qualifying phrase in his statement that the aesthetic effect of imagery depends upon 'the fact that it hands you over the sensation as directly as possible ... ' and he was satisfied to characterize it as 'a compromise for a language of intuition'.[7]

Hulme's comments on imagery give the impression that he is interested in it less for its value in presenting externals accurately than for its capacity to forestall the absorption of experience into abstraction. It causes the mind to linger on physical actualities, to fix itself upon individual sensations instead of slipping over the words into banal recollections of something similar. Although Bergson does not give representational imagery this emphasis, Hulme sees it as a means for preserving some of the intuitive qualities of perception. The images in his own poems are arresting and novel, but without much further ambition. The moon 'lean(s) over a hedge/Like a red-faced farmer' or 'Is but a child's balloon forgotten, after play', while God is asked to

> make small
> The old star-eaten blanket of the sky,
> That I may fold it round me and in comfort lie.[8]

Eliot's comments on the objective correlative and images in general suggest that they do their work best through processes that associate dissimilars. By saying, in his defense of Dante's allegory, that meaning is advantageous to an image, but it is not necessary for the reader to know what it is, he echoes Aristotle on the enigmatic quality of metaphor, and gives the unconventional imagery of modern experimentation a clear field. He praises an image from *Antony and Cleopatra* because, in contrast to one from Dante which has the element of visual precision, it is widely associative and difficult to paraphrase. The essay on the metaphysical poets (1921) defends the forced comparisons characteristic of the metaphysical conceit as a source of 'the vitality of language'. Eliot does not, however, surrender all notions of appropriateness, for in another place he cites some images from Marvell's 'Upon Appleton House', which would qualify very well as Surrealist images:

> Yet thus the leaden house does sweat
> And scarce endures the master great;
> But, where he comes, the swelling hall
> Stirs, and the square grows spherical

but dismisses them as absurd and unsuccessful. The discussion of the conceit in the essay on the metaphysical poets eventually leads him to the observation that, when a poet's mind is working properly, it is 'constantly amalgamating disparate experience'. Eliot notes that, in a particularly successful trope of the period, the first and second terms of the simile seem to unite effortlessly, so that a death becomes a journey; this is a feature sometimes found

in Surrealist imagery, where primary and secondary terms seem
to exchange places, so that it is impossible to distinguish material
from psychological reality. He observes that the conditions of
modern life, which compel the poet to make his language both
more inclusive and more indirect, give rise to something resembling the metaphysical conceit and metaphysical style.

These admissions that meaningful incongruity is the proper
mode of imagery for modern poetry are clear enough, but they
do not go as far as the images in Eliot's verse. He was, of course,
a master of the accurate, incisive image that recalls both neo-
classical precision and neo-classical savagery:

> A lustreless protrusive eye
>   Stares from the protozoic slime
> At a perspective of Canaletto.
>   The smoky candle end of time.
> Declines.
>
> (p. 24)

But he also employed images whose effects are powerful but
indefinite, owing something to Donne and the metaphysical
mode, to Baudelaire's iconography of the industrial city, to
Laforgue and his bold use of scientific diction, and to the
Symbolists generally. They link disparate things and make enigmatic impressions; their characteristic excellence is a combination
of visual (or auditory) precision and indefiniteness that somehow
prolongs itself into unlimited overtones of meaning, as in:

> Every street lamp that I pass
> Beats like a fatalistic drum. . . .
>
> (p. 14)

One of the methods of explicating metaphors and similes consists
of finding their 'base', the attribute which the two terms have in
common. There is no such connective here, and the passage from
visual to auditory sensation seems totally unjustified. But the
simile is marvellously successful in conveying both the *dementia*
of the speaker and his fear of the street-lamps. The problem of
its effectiveness can be solved if we turn to Aristotle's idea that
each metaphor involves a ratio, for the speaker is saying that the
street-lamp has the same threatening relation to himself that the
drum has toward some victim, as, for example, a man who is
about to be executed. This explanation does not exhaust its
mystery or its suggestiveness; on the contrary, it gives them a
firmer footing, and amplifies their effects. The next image (which
has its origin in Laforgue) presents no such problems, for it makes
the Aristotelian ratio perfectly clear:

Midnight shakes the memory
As a madman shakes a dead geranium.

(p. 14)

We have noted that, in defending religious intuition, Eliot advocated the sort of poetic creativity that approaches automatism.[9] Intuition, whether religious or secular, is the same phenomenon, and it is therefore not surprising that 'Ash Wednesday', his most overtly religious poem, should contain images that satisfy Surrealist requirements. I do not mean the three white leopards, the white-gowned lady and the figure in white and blue, which bring a certain heraldic clarity and elegance from their traditional origins. But the cluster of images connected with the stair is both disturbing and obscure, stirring up contradictory and unwanted implications, exactly as dream-images do:

the stair was dark,
Damp, jaggèd, like an old man's mouth drivelling, beyond repair,
Or the toothed gullet of an agèd shark.

(p. 63)

There are powerful sexual and sadistic overtones in this oppressive visual confrontation. The two kinds of imagery in the poem offer a mixture of the sinister and charming, and create an eerie sense that all this is familiar, an old conspiracy of subconscious associations.

Wyndham Lewis, in his play, *The Enemy of the Stars*, which appeared in the first number of *Blast* (1914), resorted to a new kind of imagery to express the brutalizing effects of modern industrialism.[10] The subject of his play is the pathetic weakness of self-conscious human egotism in a universe dominated by massive inhuman energies. The stage-directions contain numerous non-sentences that shoot out irrational, provocative and intensely discordant images conveying this vision. The scene, an industrial yard on a canal bank, is described in this manner: 'The Earth has burst, a granite flower, and disclosed the scene . . . A canal at one side, the night pouring into it like blood from a butcher's pail. Rouge mask in aluminum mirror, sunset's grimace. . . .' Machine civilization has perverted the animism which operates in most poetic imagery, so that reality is transformed into something inorganic and artificial instead of taking part in human feelings. The moonlight is described as an 'immense bleak electric advertisement of God', the stars are 'machines of prey'. On the other hand, everything that is living and organic has a repellent pathological quality. The characters' feelings are 'Fungi of sullen violet thoughts', and they are 'sickened by the immense vague infection of night'. Imagery of this kind forms a backdrop for a plot in which some minimal human beings try to emulate the brutality of their urban environment and fail.

2 IMAGERY: THE WORD BEYOND LANGUAGE

As his essay on Vorticism shows, Pound too expected much more from imagery than vivid representation. He had learned, in writing *Personae*, that mere self-expression was ineffective, for when one says '"I am" . . . with the words scarcely uttered one ceases to be that thing.'[11] The image as he now conceived it, however, offered an escape from this *impasse*. The statement on Imagism published in *Poetry* magazine in 1913 declares that the image is a fusion of elements, ' . . . which gives that sense of sudden liberation; that sense of freedom from time limits and space limits; that sense of sudden growth . . . ' which the 'masks' of *Personae* failed to achieve. Imagism, says Pound, is the practice of 'absolute metaphor'. In order to pass beyond the old limits of feeling, the image must also transcend the old limits of expression. 'The image is the word beyond formulated language.'[12]

There is more than a touch of obscurity in this, but Pound, who hated 'slither', and was always suspicious of the vague and amorphous, insisted that the image must achieve this transcendence without giving up its footing in the energizing visible world. As we know, however, Pound was interested, not in evoking 'new' feeling as the poets concerned with urban life were, but in renewing, as private experiences, the recurrent emotions of humanity. These are emphatically non-intellectual. They are not ideas. 'An idea is only an imperfect induction from fact.'[13] They belong to the elusive area of aesthetic, religious and imaginative experiences that the average lay mind finds hard to enter, but which is the ordinary context of shop-talk among artists. In his essay on Guido Cavalcanti, written about the same time as the Vorticist essay, Pound praised Cavalcanti's economy at the expense of Petrarch's ornamentation, and spoke of a time when strong traditions made it possible for images to launch clear feelings almost visibly into the air, of reproducing their sense of clarity and proportion in the minds of readers.

We appear to have lost the radiant world where one thought cuts through another with clean edge, a world of moving energies . . . the form that seems a form seen in a mirror . . . Not the pagan worship of strength, nor the Greek perception of visual non-animate plastic . . . but this 'harmony in the sentience' or harmony *of* the sentient, where the thought has its demarcation, the substance its *virtu* . . . [14]

Pound seems to have expected imagery to transfer the primary data of experience in this way, just as they were received in the poet's mind. 'The image is the poet's pigment. . . . An *image*, in our sense, is real because we know it directly.'[15] He did not make Bergson's distinction between perceived and expressed images, but sided with Hulme in believing that images could achieve an effective compromise in conveying intuitions.

Pound's Imagism comes to maturity in the *Cantos :*

> The empty armour shakes as the cygnet moves.
>
> (p. 15)

> The grey stone posts,
>   and the stair of gray stone,
> the passage clean-squared in granite;
>
> (p. 69)

> Flat water before me,
>   and the trees growing in water,
> Marble trunks out of stillness,
> On past the palazzi,
>   in the stillness,
> The light now, not of the sun.
>
> (p. 76)

These images can be explained as parts of the themes with which the *Cantos* is occupied, but they do their real work as abbreviated analogies, of the kind recommended by Marinetti. They are metaphors whose primary term is some feeling words cannot identify. To dissipate their mystery by fitting them into the narrative sequences of which they are a part would dull the sharp edges of their details. Therefore, Pound uses them as fragments, delaying intelligibility until they have had their effect as images.

Pound's discovery of Fenollosa's speculations about the Chinese ideogram in 1913, before he turned from Imagism to Vorticism, confirmed his view that the image grounded in external actuality could serve as a vehicle of augmented perception. Fenollosa, in his study of Chinese, had acquired the impression that it was basically metaphoric, using old signs for concrete things to convey meaning in a variety of ways. Through his study of translation he came to feel that the relations set up by English grammar conflicted with those projected by ideograms, which he took to be more authentic because they were based on nature and the real world. In this way, he encountered an issue that confronted the Imagists, William Carlos Williams, and other advocates of immediacy. The Imagists attempted to win a certain degree of freedom from mere 'associative' meanings by scrupulously attaching language to actuality, word by word and phrase by phrase. Instead of taking externals into the arena of feelings as the Romantics did through personification and similar methods, they tried to generate feelings through objective perception, finding 'No ideas but in things', as Williams put it.

L.S. Dembo has pointed out that they regarded the image, not merely as a transcription of experience, but as 'an idealized re-creation' of it, the vehicle of a 'transconceptual' insight into objects, and hence the agency of a special perception and a new aesthetic-ism.[16] There is some such emphasis in Fenollosa's praise for the ideogram because it keeps the object—or a version of it—before the eye while projecting its intellectual meaning, acting as vivid metaphor. 'Poetic language is always vibrant with fold on fold of overtones and with natural affinities, but in Chinese the visibility of the metaphor tends to raise this quality to its intensest power.'[17] According to Fenollosa, poetry, through metaphor, does consciously what the primitive mind does unconsciously. This is apparently a reference to the pre-rational use of language for connecting things as 'integral thoughts' which Shelley called 'vitally metaphorical', the mythic identifications accepted as fact by primitives which our literal use of language transforms into metaphors. Fenollosa felt that it was the responsibility of poets and scholars to discover the submerged metaphors that link words to nature, and to keep them alive in the language they used.

Fenollosa, said Pound, saved him time. His demonstration of what he took to be the metaphoric qualities of Chinese showed Pound what imagery should be—a concrete, objective rendering of subjective feelings and intangible relationships. When he moved from Imagism to Vorticism, he changed his idea of the functioning of particulars within a poem. Instead of merely identi-fying or embodying ideas, they are to be grouped in 'a radiant node or cluster' of more or less dissimilar constituents whose complex associations with each other activate a vortex or centre of energy.[18] The individual Cantos are much more like vortices than ideograms, for they emphasize the relationships among their particulars, not the meaning each may separately generate, and the relationships themselves are variable, not fixed. The image, as Pound originally conceived it, survives as an element of the vortex. For we do find in the *Cantos*, in greater abundance than ever, those sharp, visual renderings that project edges of feeling, like shadows or auras, beyond their physical borders, but they are grouped so that these auras overlap and intersect in complicated ways, providing channels through which, as Pound says, ideas may move without being fixed in the grouping of images as it stands.[19] As they circulate, they define the complex of relationships presented by the images, creating an abstract form. Canto IV, for example, offers no substantive message about Itys, Actaeon, Vidal and Cabestan; all underwent metamorphoses, but under different circumstances and for different reasons. Each figure takes his place, as an image, in a vortex of similarities and differences defined by the reader's mind as it moves among them, sorting them out. 'Relations', said Fenollosa, 'are more real and more important than the things which they relate'.[20]

William Carlos Williams paradoxically regarded accurate imagery as an indispensable point of departure for liberating words and poetry from the burden of reference. He considered the ordinary imagery of resemblance an obstruction to a true grasp of reality, particularly when it lent itself to conventional associations. For him, the aim of imagery was the sharp isolation of uniqueness in experience through ' . . . that power which discovers in things those inimitable particles of dissimilarity to all other things which are the peculiar perfections of the thing in question'.[21] This quality must be close to what Hopkins called 'inscape'; imagery that captures it would enable language to convey the private intuition emphasized by Hulme and the concrete particularity of Pound, and to establish the 'foreign air' of Aristotle. Williams went so far in his insistence on immediacy as to say that 'poetry should strive for nothing else, this vividness alone, *per se*, for itself'.[22] But since vividness can be had only as an attribute of the vivid, the poet gives the poem over to what is depicted, keeping his eye on the object, 'as to borrow no particle from right or left'. Williams would not have disagreed with those who point out that this principle does not avoid subjectivism, that the observing mind intervenes, so that the external becomes an aspect of internal reality after all.[23] But he felt that the imagination needs a field of clear, essentialized particulars for working out the designs which, as we have seen, he was willing to characterize as geometric and divorced from external experience.

Williams's image-making faculty is animated by the conviction that all things, in spite of their individuality, share the commonalty of sheer existence. 'There is no thing that with a twist of the imagination cannot be something else', he wrote in *Kora in Hell*, and much of the improvisation of this book is given over to associating experiences with each other through this universal metaphoric base. The resulting images draw their materials from everyday life; there is generally a wide disparity between their terms, which exhibits the power of the imagination to align them with each other; and they are often incomplete, leaving one of the terms to suggestion, so that the letter, if not the spirit of Marinetti's Futurist analogies is closely followed:

What can it mean to you that a child wears pretty clothes and speaks three languages or that its mother goes to the best shops? It means: July has good need of his blazing sun. But if you pick one berry from the ash tree I'd not know it again for the same no matter how the rain washed. Make my bed of witchhazel twigs, said the old man, since they bloom on the brink of winter.[24]

One has the sense that Williams is doing with images what he found Joyce to be doing with words, 'following some unapparent sequence quite apart from the usual syntactical one'.[25] The improvisational imagination skims quickly over particulars, following intuitive paths suggested by the method of automatic writing Williams was using. It is not impossible in this, and other cases, to reconstruct the movement of his thought. The mother and child are prosperous because they enjoy a fate as kindly as the July sun. The parable of the ash-berry warns us that good things are fragile. The old man, understanding this, prizes something that withstands destruction as long as possible. But even if they can be justified logically, the images of *Kora in Hell* depend for their effect on their incongruity. It is not surprising that Williams welcomed Surrealism, translated a book by Philippe Soupault, and recognized immediately that the Surrealists were liberating language from the dead accretions of practical and intellectual use and restoring it to the 'fantastic reality' of the imagination. 'Surrealism does not lie', he wrote in 1923. 'It is the single truth. It is an epidemic. It is. It is just words.'[26]

*   *   *

Though it is far removed from the early modern period in tone and philosophy, *Four Quartets* nevertheless resorts to enigmatic imagery to gain access to areas of meaning words cannot reach. In the world of *Four Quartets*, each atom of matter and moment of experience is felt to be a manifestation of divine permanence; yet when it is examined through the lens of the intellect, it exhibits unintelligible contradictions and discontinuities. Eliot's task is to remove these divisions, to convey the unity of a cosmos in which particulars are indistinguishable from universals, so that 'history is now and England'. Language, it is clear, cannot do this, for it shares the modalities into which sense and intellect have carved the world. It exists in time, and is impermanent:

> Words move, music moves
> Only in time; but that which is only living
> Can only die.
>
> (p. 121)

It reflects human fallibilities.

> Words strain,
> Crack and sometimes break, under the burden,
> Under the tension, slip, slide, perish,
> Decay with imprecision, will not stay in place ...
>
> (p. 121)

Poetry is not exempted from these failings, as Mallarmé thought it was. The poet himself regards his efforts to use words as a failure, because they seem to serve only

> For the thing one no longer has to say, or the way in which
> One is no longer disposed to say it.
>
> (p. 128)

(Pound, we recall, testified that one only had to say 'I am', to cease to be that thing.) It is impossible to make progress in the poetic venture, for each effort is 'a raid on the inarticulate/With shabby equipment always deteriorating', and whatever areas of expression one may win have already been discovered by others. The composite poet who speaks in 'Little Gidding' says that language is vulnerable to time and must be constantly renewed. But what he has to say in a privileged diction motivated by Mallarmé's idea that the poet's mission is 'To purify the dialect of the tribe', is only a warning about the folly of looking to old age for satisfaction.

Eliot acknowledges that language bears no special responsibility for its own inadequacy, for ' ... to apprehend/The point of intersection of the timeless/With time is an occupation for the saint—' or rather, a divine mercy beyond human effort. Nevertheless, there are moments 'in and out of time' which replicate the experience of the absolute in human experience. Since they overcome the divisions imposed upon the world by the intellect, we are bound to say that they are moments in which what we call contraries are reconciled, and what we call dissimilars are seen as the elements of a single universal permanence. The speaker who visits the deserted garden of 'Burnt Norton' has painful thoughts of the unfulfilled wish that he might have entertained certain guests

there, and of the disappointment of his actual loneliness. The
drained pool, which paradoxically looks filled with water bearing
a lotus when the sunlight shines on it, is an image both for 'What
might have been and what has been.' It is fitting that the one
object should reflect both possibility and actuality, for together
they 'Point to one end, which is always present'.

Other images embody similar reconciliations. The paradox
of 'In my beginning is my end' which opens 'East Coker' is resolved
in three metaphors: the sequences of construction, in which new
houses replace the old, the vision of the ancient ceremony in an
open field, and the identification of the poet with a vision of the
sea at dawn: 'I am here/Or there, or elsewhere.' Salvation may
arrive at moments of helplessness and passivity; when the darkness
descends between scene-changes in a theatre, when the underground train stops and the conversation of the passengers fades
away embarrassingly, when an anaesthetic empties the mind of
thought. At times like these, when conscious effort is set aside,
and the mind has surrendered to the pointlessness of ordinary
life, it may regain a sense of purpose: 'So the darkness shall be the
light, and the stillness the dancing.' All of these are counterparts
of Eliot's cosmic image, the wheel of the world turning upon an
unmoving mystic centre, which is the still source of all movement:

> And do not call it fixity,
> Where past and future are gathered. Neither movement
>   from nor towards,
> Neither ascent nor decline.

(p. 119)

Eliot's images of divine communion, like Surrealist images,
unite the disparate and irreconcilable. Their purpose, as also in
Surrealist imagery, is to generate a fall of dominoes in which the
upsetting of one opposition leads to an upsetting of all, so that
conventional notions of order are destroyed. If the darkness in
the theatre can be identified with the light of God, the image must
secrete a potion capable of curing the intellectual disease of contradiction. Hence,

> In order to arrive there,
> To arrive where you are, to get from where you are not,
>   You must go by a way wherein there is no ecstasy.
> In order to arrive at what you do not know
>   You must go by a way which is the way of ignorance.
> In order to possess what you do not possess
>   You must go by the way of dispossession.

(p. 127)

Speaking technically, therefore, and without regard to substantive ideas, Eliot's use of mystic imagery in *Four Quartets* corresponds to Surrealist principles. Eliot is Breton reversed. The Surrealist brings together disparate things in order to suggest another plane of being on which the two can co-exist. Sewing machine and umbrella have nothing to do with each other as we know them, but their meeting tells us that there is some realm beyond our capacities where they are related. With Eliot the sense of the absolute is a prior intuition and situations manifesting what we take to be contradiction have the function of making us aware of it by associating 'two distant realities' with each other. 'Time the destroyer' is also 'time the preserver'. 'The bitter apple and the bite in the apple' presents pain first as an abstraction contemplated from a distance, then as a lived experience. The rock in the water may act as a seamark in good weather, but in a storm it 'is what it always was'. These polarities that fold into each other mark the edge of permanence, where contradiction ceases to exist. Images embodying them cannot articulate what lies beyond, but they can suggest that it is there.

> The wild thyme unseen, or the winter lightning
> Or the waterfall, or music heard so deeply
> That it is not heard at all, but you are the music
> While the music lasts. These are only hints and guesses . . .
>
> (p. 136)

3 PARODY

The use of borrowed materials in ways that conflict with conventional notions of originality and self-expression is a striking general tendency of modern experimental literature. Both the material borrowed, which often comes from factual or utilitarian prose, and the methods used to bring it into the work, which include quotation, allusion, parody, translation, summary and annotation may be difficult to identify with imaginative literature. Of the 434 lines of *The Waste Land*, at least seventy-five are quotation, translation, parody and the like, forty are dramatic monologues spoken in a voice other than the poet's, and the rest of the poem is sown with significant allusions. Pound's *Mauberley* has about 450 lines; at least sixty of these are quotations or translations or (more usually) involve allusions to works in Latin, Greek and French as well as English. The *Cantos* opens with a translation of a translation, faithfully documented, and, like *Paterson*, makes important use of quoted documents from American history. Many of Marianne Moore's poems are built around quotations from humble contemporary sources which are carefully integrated into the text. None of these practices is new, of course, but the experimentalists found entirely new uses for them; their parodies are not simply mockeries of originals, their quotations are not ways of adducing evidence, and their allusions are more than enrichments drawn from traditional sources. There is some feeling of *collage* in all this, as well as an element of depersonalization. But its main significance is that it makes all the functions of language, even the most utilitarian ones, available to literature.

Some of the parody in modern works follows the traditional mode of satire, but much of it is used to exhibit the reality of style, so that it replaces content as the focus of attention, and becomes a vehicle of ideas. Parodic language exhibits thought instead of transmitting it. It is not an aid to meaning, but the embodiment of meaning itself. It exploits what Bergson called 'the motor diagram', the features of a discourse that tell the audience what attitude to adopt toward it. Bergson denies that the impressions we receive in reading or listening depend simply on memory, and suggests that we interpret what we learn in accordance with signals given in the discourse itself.

> Do we not . . . feel that we are adopting a certain disposition which varies with our interlocutor, with the language he speaks, with the nature of the ideas which he expresses—and varies, above all, with the general movement of his phrase, as though we were choosing the key in which our own intellect is called upon to play? The motor diagram . . . shows our thought the road. It is the empty vessel, which determines, by its form, the form which the fluid mass, rushing into it, already tends to take.[27]

Modern parody employs this capacity of linguistic form to shape expressive energies by matching a familiar mode with a novel content, and exploiting the varied and subtle tensions that arise over the distance between them. The strong jocular contrast of traditional parody is replaced by a wide repertory of effects, many of them not at all amusing. In the parody of Enobarbus's speech from *Antony and Cleopatra* which occurs in the second section of *The Waste Land*, Eliot uses the traditional parodistic effect of contrast to depict a shrunken modern Cleopatra. There is no humour; all the changes are quietly reductive. The barge which 'burned on the water' becomes a modern chair which 'glowed on the marble'; the Cupids in the original are real boys; in Eliot's passage they are carved gilt figures. The colours, movements and perfumes of Eliot's passage and the speaker herself are languid echoes of vigorous originals in Shakespeare's description, where the people and the objects share a common vitality.

On the other hand, Pound's use of the Omar Khayyám quatrain toward the end of Canto LXXX to condemn the violence of English history does not, like the passage from *The Waste Land*, depend on contrast alone. A line of traditional parody attacking both Browning and Winston Churchill occurs somewhat earlier in the Canto: 'Oh to be in England now that Winston's out.' But the Omar Khayyám imitation does not mock FitzGerald's poem. Instead, the epigrammatic quality of the distinctive quatrain serves Pound for expressing a different, but hardly a contrasting feeling:

> Tudor indeed is gone and every rose,
> Blood-red, blanch-white that in the sunset glows
> Cries: 'Blood, Blood, Blood!' against the gothic stone
> Of England, as the Howard or Boleyn knows.
>
> (p. 516)

The genial fatalism of FitzGerald's poem is not denied, but assimilated into Pound's contentious irony. The prosodic parody is parallelled by a shift in the symbolic function of the rose. FitzGerald's rose, in addition to being a traditional symbol of life and beauty, draws its vitality from woe, from the bleeding of 'some buried Caesar'. Pound, assisted by the symbolism of the rose in the Wars of the Roses and in Tudor iconography, takes up and develops these associations, so that his roses embody the violence of English history.

As Vivian Mercier has shown, Joyce, the master parodist of the modern period, is best seen against the backdrop of ancient traditions, especially that of the blasphemous medieval parodies favoured by the Goliards, which includes some Gaelic examples, and provided models for such important parodic works as *Don Quixote*. Parodies of this kind generally emerged from conflicts between such groups as lay poets and clerics; Joyce employed parody in its traditional way, to mock the clergy, but also, in his treatment of Bloom, to attack the influence of pseudo-science on the average mind.[28] Parody was more than a tradition for Joyce; the popular literature of his time and place abounded with it— Oliver St. John Gogarty, the original of Buck Mulligan, was himself a formidable parodist—and it was natural for Joyce to try his hand at it.

The first parodies in his published work expose the dullness and vulgarity of his Dubliners. The verses recited by Hynes in 'Ivy Day in the Committee Room', and the newspaper account of the death of Mrs Sinico in 'A Painful Case' skilfully exhibit the attitudes of their writers through their styles. In *A Portrait* the parodic method becomes central. The quatrain written by Stephen's schoolmate Fleming, the villanelle Stephen composes, the retreat sermon and Stephen's diary entries all function to give evidence of states of consciousness having a bearing on Stephen's intellectual destiny. Parody also appears surreptitiously in the direct discourse of the novel, when certain of Stephen's emotional reactions are described in a swooning, ninetyish prose.

There are numerous instances of parody in *Ulysses*, including the letters of Milly and Martha Clifford, the newspaper headlines in 'Aeolus', and the interior monologue of Gerty MacDowell, but the most important are, of course, the virtuoso performances of the 'Oxen of the Sun' chapter. Joyce's intention of recapitulating the history of English prose, with the analogue of the developing foetus in mind, may be partly jocular: in any case, the pattern does not emerge strongly because the succession of styles does not make an impression of progress. The one place where there is a sense of specific change is toward the end, where the marvellous miscellany of slang, foreignisms, conversational tags and other perversions signals the collapse of stylistic control. Many of the styles do perform the traditional function of parody, mocking an excessive or pretentious original, but they also exhibit the variety, flexibility and expressive power of language. They remind us that language, in spite of the deadening uses to which it is so often put, is still capable of reflecting the peculiarities of the mind with astonishing fidelity. They demonstrate that style goes far toward controlling meaning, that reported events acquire a definitive colouration from the way they are reported.

Perhaps even more remarkable than the parodies of *Ulysses* are its newly-fabricated styles. These do not imitate the technical peculiarities used by other writers, but instead reflect some state of consciousness directly through a newly-invented idiom. The two chief examples of this odd genre are the inset passages of 'Cyclops' and the 'Eumaeus' chapter. The 'Cyclops' insets imitate gigantism, as Stuart has pointed out, through the device of inflation. They do not follow any specific principle, but comically exaggerate whatever feelings may be connected with the subject. 'Eumaeus' on the other hand, practices a kind of deflation in a remarkably flat, matter-of-fact, unoriginal style completely lacking anything startling or noteworthy. In both of these, clichés and standard phrases play an important part, and sentences are extended to enormous lengths so that such syntactic affectations as parallelism and subordination can take part in the comedy.

These stylistic demonstrations are particularly characteristic of modern experimentation because they define states of consciousness through the technical aspects of language rather than actual thoughts or actions. It is all a question of diction, sentence structure, tone and connotation; whatever these passages accomplish is done with the resources offered by language itself.

4 BORROWING AND QUOTATION

Herman Meyer's study, *The Poetics of Quotation in the European Novel*, by showing that quotations perform vital structural functions in the works of such novelists as Rabelais, Cervantes, Sterne, Wieland and Fontane, offers considerable support to their use as a serious artistic resource.[29] Meyer argues that recognizable quotations can be fully assimilated into the fabric of novels, and make essential contributions to their meaning. In *Tristram Shandy*, for example, Sterne, by citing some of Locke's descriptions of the operation of the mind, shows how inapposite they are to the chaotic thought-processes of his characters; by having Mr Shandy quote Burton, he demonstrates both his obsession with words and his failure to appreciate the reality around him. In *Don Quixote*, the numerous quotations from the literature of chivalry represent the area of illusion which collaborates with the novel's realistic scenes in forming the dialectic structure of the book.

Modern experimental texts use quotations in similar ways; the borrowed elements are often indispensable to the whole structure of the work, forming crucial relationships with other parts of it. Meyer observes that while every work borrows cultural elements, these are ordinarily thoroughly assimilated, and their sources forgotten; but the recognizable quotation brings with it a sense of its origin, so that a link is established between its source and the new work. The author seeks an effect composed of two sensibilities, the one represented by the quotation (or summary, paraphrase, etc.), and his own. The subtlety and variety of these linkages constitute a genuine augmentation of linguistic resources, a foray into a new area of poetic expression.

The echoic devices which appear in strength in *The Waste Land* also play important parts in other early poems by Eliot, such as 'Gerontion'. The old man thinks of contemporaries, enigmatic figures named Silvero, Hakagawa, Madame de Tornquist about whom we know little except that they are apparently aesthetes and cosmopolites. But his train of thought has begun with the quotation 'We would see a sign!' the demand made by the Pharisee in Matthew 38 for some evidence of Jesus' divine affiliation. It is this scepticism, this rejection of faith in favour of verifiable knowledge which infects Gerontion and the people he thinks about, and which leads him to ask, 'After such knowledge, what forgiveness?' In *The Waste Land*, the line of German toward the beginning, 'Bin gar keine Russin, stamm' aus Litauen, echt deutsch', has the earmarks of an actual bit of conversation lifted from real life and inserted into the poem, carrying with it all the implications of *collage*. The quotations from *Tristan und Isolde* which follow soon after are both more problematic and more suggestive. They are obscurely connected with the Wagnerian figures of the Rhine-maidens from *Götterdammerung* in 'The Fire Sermon', who are counterparts of the modern girls, victims of seduction, who speak toward the end of the section. These borrowings defy any simple interpretation. Bracketed by the sailor's cheerful song from the beginning of *Tristan* and the observation about the emptiness of the sea, they say something about the deceptiveness of earthly love. This is in turn connected with the idea of decline in the wailing of the Rhine-maidens, the sorrows of the English girls and the scene of modern civilization as a whole. The words taken from Wagner's text, particularly since they are accompanied by memories of the music, function as sensuously-apprehended *things* within the framework of the poem, partly enigmatic, like all real objects, yet capable of throwing off meaning in many directions.

The quotations at the end of *The Waste Land* are all expressions of the sense of loss, a feeling that Eliot finds especially appropriate to the spiritual poverty of modern life. The words themselves are meaningful, but the real strength of the feelings involved can be known only through the contexts from which they have been borrowed—the children's rhyme, the *Purgatorio*, the *Pervigilium Veneris* and so on. The reader is called upon to assemble these, as if in a mental anthology, as a way of setting the lands of his cultural heritage in order through appropriate parallels, contrasts and historical connections.

In beginning Canto VIII with 'These fragments you have shelved (shored)', Pound is apparently reproaching Eliot for using quotations in an antiquarian spirit, then acknowledging in the parenthesis that they do serve the purpose for which he intended them. Certainly no one has amplified and exploited the methods of *The Waste Land* more fully than Pound. The *Cantos* is, to a very considerable degree, a poem made of borrowed materials.[30] Its literary and historical sources are not those of ordinary, or even extraordinary culture. Pound himself had only a casual know-

ledge of many of them, and the reader of the *Cantos* should know
not only his sources, but even more urgently the distortions he
subjected them to, either deliberately or through error. Pound is
more or less reliable when he deals with Western literary materials,
although his prejudices exaggerate the importance of the *trouvéres*,
and minimize that of classical Greece. But he is self-taught in
economics, history, Chinese, Egyptian, anthropology and the
numerous other specialized subjects which the *Cantos*, perhaps
the most presumptuous of all poems, presumes to illuminate.[31]

The translation from the *Odyssey* that occupies most of the
first Canto broaches one of the major themes of the poem (and
one of Pound's life-long interests) both through the symbolism
of its content, and through its status as a translation. It is Pound's
English version of the passage describing Odysseus's descent to
the underworld found in a Latin translation by Andreas Divus,
a sixteenth-century author known only by his name. In 1935,
while corresponding with W.H.D. Rouse about the latter's prose
translation of the *Odyssey*, Pound said that he felt a special antiquity in the 'Nekuia' or descent. On the other hand, the *Odyssey*
is '3000 years old and still *fresh*', and a translation must capture
this freshness through its own originality of language.[32] This is,
of course, the principle of Pound's own translations and much of
his scholarship, the transmission of an older author's individual
quality through a modern style devised for the purpose. The
culture of the past cannot be opened to modern readers through
imitation or mechanical transcription, but only through a process
of metamorphosis, the re-infusion of the original spirit into new
forms of language equivalent to those used in the original. Daniel
D. Pearlman has suggested that the blood sacrifice described in
the passage is taken by Pound as a symbol of this cultural renewal.[33]
The translation dramatizes the process of transmission that Pound
envisioned by passing Homer on from an intermediate renewer.

The end of the Canto subtly calls attention to this process.
The Latin words 'Venerandam . . . Cypri munimenta sortita est'
are a quotation, pieced out with some English, from a Latin version
of one of the Homeric hymns. This can be associated with the
Nekuia on thematic grounds, since in it Aphrodite is described
as carrying the golden bough of renewal which Tiresias bears in
the passage from the *Odyssey*. But there is another, more illuminating connection as well. After publishing something much like
Canto I as the third of 'Three Cantos' in *Poetry* magazine in 1917,
Pound used his translation from Divus, the Latin original, and the
Latin version of the passage from the Homeric hymn in an article
on the problems of translating Homer which appeared in the

Egoist in September, 1918.[34] Dealing with the question of whether two nineteenth-century scholars who translated the *Odyssey* into Latin might not have made use of Divus's translation, Pound gives, as evidence of possible plagiarism, the passage from the Homeric hymn, together with the very close imitation of it published by one of the suspect translators as his own. Thus, the translations and quotations in Canto I, particularly since they are accompanied, in entirely unconventional fashion, by documentation in the text itself, are connected with questions concerning the process of cultural transmission. The Canto might almost be understood as an abbreviated version of the article. The opening of the *Cantos* fully justifies itself as poetry; but Pound also had a scholarly purpose in putting this translation twice removed in its conspicuous place. He was concerned to see that the golden bough of renewal did not lose its magical powers.

The multiple sources of Canto I produce a layered impression in which various historical periods are brought into relation with each other. This is one of the most common effects of Pound's borrowings, but it is not one which the poem can achieve on its own powers. For example,

> The pines at Takasago
> grow with the pines of Isé!
>
> (p. 15)

from Canto IV is one instance of a repeated leitmotif whose significance Walter Baumann has explained:

At Takasago in Japan stand two famous pine trees inhabited by the spirits of a married couple whose love endures for ever. . . . At Isé, another Japanese sanctuary, there are two shrines sacred to the worship of the Japanese emperors and the sun-goddess, their progenetrix. These shrines are apparently in a pine grove . . . probably according to a Japanese tradition, these two groups of sacred pines are believed to be mysteriously connected with each other . . . in Pound's eyes the connection between the pines is of the kind which the classical world assumed to exist between the Nile and the river Inopos in Delos.[35]

This is not the end of this chain of allusions, yet without going further it is obvious that even the best-equipped mind would not have these elements of Eastern and Western traditions at hand for easy recall. Pound is asking his reader to familiarize himself with the specific ages and phases of the world's culture, so that he can grasp the design his poem creates out of the relationships among them. It is an activity which begins with intellectual effort, but ends with aesthetic experience, joining the two in a unity which was one of the aspirations of the experimental period.

The *Cantos* often counts on leading the reader to an important context through the slightest of allusions, sometimes consisting of only a single word. The handful of references to Browning's *Sordello* are the vestigial remains of Pound's original intention of writing a poem modelled after Browning's, but the scanty allusions must be carefully investigated if this fact is to emerge. Pound's lingering on the steps of the Dogana in Venice at the opening of Canto III parallels the passage in Book Three of *Sordello* where Browning breaks off his narrative to describe himself sitting 'on a ruined palace-step' in Venice, looking at some peasant-girls. Browning wonders which of them will be his queen, and Pound, taking up his thoughts about 'those girls', says that he has one, not many, in mind. While he says nothing about Browning or *Sordello* in this passage, it is plain, once his allusion is clarified, that Pound is adding a stroke to the connection he has mentioned before between his poem and Browning's. There are passages in the *Cantos* where brief and enigmatic allusions of this kind form discontinuous mosaics of fragments drawn from different cultures and periods of history, a device that becomes increasingly common in the Pisan and later Cantos. They give the impression that all of world culture is a single city with avenues radiating from widely scattered centres.

5 TYPOGRAPHICAL EXPERIMENT

Departures from conventional typography, as we have already seen, may be used for widely differing effects, but it is possible to make one generalization about them: they are, like *collage*, incursions of physical reality into the imaginary realm of the work. Regardless of their expressive functions, they offer an experience of immediacy by calling attention to the physical aspects of print. Mallarmé considered the shapes of words and letters, the form of the poem on the page, and the spaces left between the words as important elements of 'Un Coup de Dés'. In his essay, 'Quant au Livre', he dwells on the physical qualities of the book, which he regards as nothing more nor less than 'expansion totale de la lettre'. The shape of the volume, the black-on-white appearance of the page, even the need for cutting the pages open with a knife, so reminiscent of a sacrificial act, are significant aspects of the experience of reading.[36] These considerations are, of course, generally regarded as irrelevancies. In fact, print is supposed to have the advantage of standardizing them and thus preventing them from intervening between the word and the reader. But the experimental writers sensed that if the features of the book which printers normally tried to neutralize could instead be rendered meaningful, they would have the direct force of objects.

Typographical experimentation was motivated by numerous intentions; by using it, writers hoped to evoke responses outside the range of normal printed material, overcome various dissociations of sensibility, and establish a dimension where feeling and intellectual activity can meet. In addition to penetrating the curtain of convention set up by print, many of the typographical innovations obviously attempt to achieve some of the effects of graphic art. Lessing had separated art and poetry on the ground that the former exists in space and the latter in time; but in a period when the concept of space-time was formulated, it was perhaps natural to think of joining the two as a way of showing that the two dimensions are not cut off from each other. Experiments with typography were also a way of overcoming the deeply rooted habits which lead people to look at writing in one way and at pictures in another. Writing is expected to be transparent and utilitarian, to exist for the sake of the meaning that can be seen through it; pictures are supposed to be opaque and non-intellectual, to provide terminal experiences. Hence, it can be seen that the typographical experimenters were trying to do from one end of the art-literature spectrum what the Cubists were trying to do from the other—to create works that encouraged the merging of sensuous and intellectual elements into a single undivided response.

The typographical innovation of the early modern period falls into two categories: the founding of new conventions, and the use of typography as an independent expressive resource. The first category includes the elimination of capitals at the beginning of the verse line, the omission of punctuation, very short lines of poetry, new rules for indentation, and the use of devices seldom found in the poetry of the past, such as mathematical signs, the slash, abbreviations and so on. These gave the printed text a 'modern' look when they came in about 1915, and exhibited the poet's intention of detaching his work from traditional supports. They were not always purely conventional, for some of the new arrangements were backed by good reasons. Williams's short verse lines gave his words a necessary isolation, and the two-part line often found in the *Cantos* seems to put the material in the indented line on a lower level of emphasis.

Most typographical innovations, however, were expressive, developing a tradition that goes at least as far back as George Herbert, whose 'Altar' and 'Easter Wings' have shapes that correspond with their subjects, an innovation that would be radical at any time. The case of Mallarmé, the founder of the practice in modern times, is peculiar, for the printing modifications he used in 'Un Coup de Dés' were intended to provide an escape from the verbal level of the poem, and to appeal directly to the eye; but in doing this they acquired another kind of symbolism. The white spaces of the page are the emptiness of the sea and sky, and the descending lines of verse represent the fall of the dice. Marinetti, who was critical of Mallarmé, nevertheless took up his ideas about typography, and developed them imaginatively writing Futurist poems that appeal to the eye with every conceivable variation of type, spacing, and arrangement. One of Marinetti's prose poems describes a steep street in this way:

<pre>
                strada scendere
        scendere
                scendere
                        scendere
                                scendere
                salire
        scendere   scendere
                pianerottolo d'un torrente
        scendere ancora[37]
</pre>

While a scene of warfare is rendered

<pre>
            SOLE + PALLONE
            FRENATI

      fiamme giganti   colonne di fumo   spirali di scintille

            villaggi   turchi   incendiati[38]
</pre>

During his brief alliance with the Futurists, Guillaume Apollinaire became convinced of the usefulness of the new typography. His 'Manifeste-synthèse', 'L'Anti-tradition futuriste', published in the Italian Futurist journal, *Lacerba*, and dated 29 June 1913, was printed in display type of various sizes arranged in ornamental or expressive groupings, and was imitated in the following year by Wyndham Lewis's journal, *Blast*. But his main contribution to the exploitation of typography was his volume *Calli-grammes* (1918), which contains poems printed in shapes suggestive of their subjects, carrying the practices of George Herbert, Mallarmé and the Futurists much further. These picture-poems blend the graphic and literary arts in a spirited aesthetic game, transforming typography into a fluid, lyrical medium. They were of enormous historical significance because they broke through a number of barriers, and brought forward new expressive possibilities, anticipating Pound's use of ideograms, and the typographical ventures of such poets as E.E. Cummings and William Carlos Williams.

Unlike Apollinaire's printing experiments, which use a wide variety of printing devices, Cummings's are creations of the typewriter. Instead of seeming mechanical, however, they are convincing demonstrations that an artist can employ a machine to assert his individuality against the regularity of mass production. To the familiar practices of modernist typography, Cummings added some of his own; while dropping punctuation in places where it is ordinarily called for, he uses it in his own way, to slow down or emphasize, even inserting it between the letters of a word. Capitals are used for emphasis; the verse line is not metrical, but isolates and groups word and phrases. Usages of this kind expand the expressive capacity of print, but since they are more or less regular, they merely substitute new conventions for old ones.

Many of Cummings's innovations are simply intended to guide pronunciation, and often make the poem look more peculiar than it really is, following the traditional idea that poetry is an oral art, and that the page of verse has the same relation to a poem that a score has to a piece of music. But Cummings also wrote for the eye alone, a practice that R.P. Blackmur in his review of *50 Poems* characterized as 'the sin against the Holy Ghost'. In committing this heresy, Cummings followed the examples set by Mallarmé and the Futurists. It was a part of the modernist revolution to acknowledge that in the twentieth century literature normally appears in print, and there is something to be said for a poetic style which accepts this and makes use of it, instead of modelling itself on archaic oral conventions.

Cummings's typographical ventures often succeed in altering or expanding conventional meanings. One of his favorite devices is that of isolating an unnoticed word in the middle of another. *No Thanks* opens with 'the (/Wistfully/ dead . . . ' who become 'wistFully dead' and later, 'wistfulLy dead'. This effect can also be achieved by spacing and line division, as in 'its elf' (p. 230) and 'the kno/wing spirit' (p. 231). What might loosely be called

parenthetical effects sometimes divide grammatical constructions
and even words. No. 1 of *ViVa* is a poem over a page long bracketed
between its first and last lines which are, respectively, 'mean-'
and 'while;' Sometimes this sort of interposition is mutual,
producing an effect of simultaneity through a self-interrupting
alternation of constructions:

> . . . than dream more sing
> (buoyant & who
> silently shall to rea-disa)
> ular
>   (ppear ah!Star
>   whycol
>
> our
>   ed
> shy lurch small

> (p. 251–2)

Parenthesis marks sometimes separate but they are often used
simply to put some words on a different level of attention, and
must be read through. An extreme example, where the marks
come into the middle of the words, illustrates this:

> . . . tug?g(ing intently it
> refuses.
>   to refuse;
> just, look)ing dead . . .

> (p. 280)

In one of his uses of parenthesis, Cummings begins a parenthetical
construction which then joins the main one, so that the first parenthetical mark counts, but the second one does not.

> when
>   from a sidewalk
>   out of (blown never quite to
> -gether by large sorry) creatures out
> of (clumsily shining out of) instru-
> ments, waltzing . . .

> (p. 317)

In this passage 'large sorry creatures' and 'shining out of instruments' are clearly part of the message; the effect has been to achieve
a double statement, one in which a separate beginning joins with
the main statement being made. Another kind of expressiveness
is developed when the behavior of the letters, if that is the term,
reflects some concept. No. 40 of *No Thanks* is a cryptic assertion

that vapours like fog and smoke have a life of their own and seem capable of generating their own landscapes in space. The smoke, says Cummings, flickers, and itself 'makes world'. But the last line is arranged, typographically, to reflect the gradual coming into being of this world out of the rising and circling smoke:

mmamakmakemakesWwOwoRworLworlD

(p. 303)

Cummings's premise that visual effects can participate in the verbal life of the poem is even more crucial when the device is pictorial, impressing the eye, not with an abstract effect, but with a representational one. He seldom follows the example of Herbert and Mallarmé in arranging type in recognizable shapes (although the dedication to *No Thanks* gives a list of publishing firms in the shape of a goblet), but attempts to use letters or marks of punctuation to suggest objects. We have already mentioned the line that repeats the word 'of' to suggest circles of sunlight coming through the leaves of trees, and the acrobatic activities of the words and letters in the poem about the grasshopper, (p. 286). Other illustrations of this method are the capitalized I's in 'theraIncomIng' (p. 250) which are no doubt meant to suggest the falling rain; the description of a harem queen dancing, 'stealing body ex-/pending gathering pouring upon itself stiffenS' in which the final S reflects the sinuous bendings of the dancer's body; and, in one of the best of Cummings's many poems about sex, the simile of sand coming through a chute visually emphasized by two capitalized letters:

> her
> flesh
> Came
> at
> meassandca V
>   ingint
>   oA
> chute

(p. 96)

Cummings's typographical effects are genuine expansions of the possibilities of language, not puzzles to be solved and set aside. They prevent the sort of reading which vapourizes words into concepts, and give his poems the status of objects whose specific features must be attended to. They are also a part of the modern effort to undo Lessing's division of the arts between time and space, and to achieve the spatial structure which Joseph

Frank has seen as one of the aims of modern literature. He went further in his typographical experiments than Mallarmé or the Futurists, and was the predecessor, in turn, of the vigorous resurgence of what is now called 'concrete poetry' after 1950, which emerged in many countries, developed various styles, and often merged with graphic art to become a striking legacy of the early modern period.[39]

Nearly all of the experimental writers responded in some measure to the atmosphere of freedom in printing conventions that had been created by the example of the Futurists. The *Cantos* touches upon typography as one of the crucial skills of civilization; Canto XXX includes an excerpt from a statement by the Renaissance printer, Gerolamo Soncino, which tells how he hired skilled workmen to cut dies for new type-faces, including Greek and Hebrew; and John Adams, in Canto LXXI, laments that this sort of enterprise is lacking in America in his time. Most of the innovative uses of typography in the *Cantos* are intended to emphasize the sense of immediacy through imitative rather than pictorial means. In his frequent quotations, translations, or paraphrases from documents, Pound goes to some lengths to suggest the appearance of the original by spacing, abbreviations, and similar devices. For example, in paraphrasing the agreement that set up the bank of the Monte dei Paschi in seventeenth-century Siena (Canto XLII), he reproduces the cross in the margin, the name of the scribe and the date. Apparently, the method of emphasizing A.V., the abbreviation for 'Altesse Votre' was to double the letters, making them AA. VV. Pound jocularly imitates this in his translation, writing 'YYour HHighness', and devotes an enigmatic parenthesis to the non-explanation: (AA. VV. = YY HH)'. The birds seen on the wires of the fence around the DTC in Canto LXXXII, which struck Pound as resembling musical notes, are represented by letters of the scale placed as they would be on the musical staff, and some medieval musical notation is handsomely reproduced at the beginning of Canto XCI. It might be argued that these scraps of music, together with the 'Canzone degli Uccelli', reproduced in manuscript form in Canto LXXV, extend the poem into the musical, as well as the visual mode. Canto LXXXVIII ends with a visual comment on the poem's great theme of time, the marks of the four suits of cards (which are reproduced in colour in the Faber and Faber edition), accompanied by the observation that the year too is divided into fifty-two units organized into four groups.

The Chinese ideograms in the *Cantos* (and, in later Cantos, the Egyptian hieroglyphics) conveniently illustrate the effects of unconventional typography at their most extreme. A reader ignorant of Chinese or the history of China is bound to miss the major significance of the ideograms, but there is a sense in which he is the proper reader for them. The Chinese reader sees little that is remarkable in them, except their size, which is more appropriate for display than for reading. But the Westerner who knows no more about them than what he can gather from the hints in the text approaches them as visual experiences. To him they are both obtrusive and impenetrable, opaque objects rather than words. The fact that Pound often uses Chinese words in transliterated form suggests that with the ideograms he is aiming at an effect that is to some extent pictorial. In some cases the Western reader can make out the visual metaphor on which the ideogram is based. But most of the words, especially the names of the emperors, do not involve any such metaphor, so that the ideograms speak directly to the eye as vivid concrete forms in contrast to the English words beside them, which are primarily symbolic. As forms, they carry cultural and historical associations. This effect is also created by much of the Latin and Greek that appears in the *Cantos*, for since these are often translated (or transliterated), the presence of the original word (and, in the case of Greek, the original letters) seems to offer a physical connection with their original contexts.[40]

It is clear that throughout the *Cantos*, and most obviously in the later ones, the regularity of print is no more than a notion providing a sort of contrapuntal basis for Pound's constant variations. A random page from *Thrones*, for example, presents a radically different appearance from the conventional page of verse of 1915 or so. Varied levels of indentation, different type-faces, careful spacing, the presence of ideograms and other alphabets, marginal additions, abbreviations, numbers and other variations of the comparatively limited resources of type differentiate the texture of the poem from line to line. These have expressive functions, sometimes related to other parts of the poem, which show that they are no longer merely mechanical or matters of editorial discretion.

Apart from following the Continental convention for printing dialogue by using dashes rather than quotation marks, Joyce made few ventures into innovative typography until *Ulysses*. The device of affixing journalistic headlines to sections of the narrative in 'Aeolus' enables the reader to compare the event with its caption, and tellingly suggests the inescapable disparity between actuality and its representation in print. There is a consciousness of typography again, though not as a part of the book's own medium, when Bloom sees Patrick Dignam's name spelled backwards as it appears in the type set up for his obituary. The typographical departures found in *Finnegans Wake*, though conservative and scanty in comparison with those of other experimental works, are not without significance. Some are merely imitative; for example, when the textbook prose says that something must be 'greater than or less than' something else, the letters of the two 'than's' diminish and increase in size (p. 298). The discussion of the hen's letter (pp. 111–23) emphasizes the physical aspect of writing through its hilarious references to the lines ruled across the page, the stains made by the refuse from the dump, and its wildly illegible calligraphy. In this passage (p. 119) it is explained that the trilithon, a capital E printed horizontally with its legs pointing downward stands for Earwicker, and the delta or triangle for Anna Livia. These suggest that the explanations of the letter are also explanations of the *Wake* itself, for they were among the signs Joyce used in his notes for the book, and appear in a footnote in the textbook chapter as 'the Doodles family', (p. 299). This chapter contains most of the typographical curiosities in the *Wake*. By arranging it as if it were a textbook (a device introduced after the original publication in *transition* in February, 1928), Joyce is able to bring in the comments of the three children through marginal notes and footnotes. Perhaps the most significant typographical departure in the *Wake* is the omission of opening and closing punctuation conventions, which establishes, with great simplicity, the continuity between the text and the reality outside it.

The diversity of typographical arrangements in *Paterson* reflects the diversity of its materials. There is considerable prose consisting of letters, excerpts from newspapers, and the like. One of its elements of originality, the student soon finds, is that the pages of the first edition's five volumes are not numbered, though the sections into which the poem is divided are. Williams employs a complex, though apparently inconsistent convention of line-indentation, sometimes used to analyse the verse into units, sometimes to establish subordination. Part I of Book Two, for example, which describes the sights seen by Paterson while he is strolling in the park, has the word 'Walking' flush with the left margin of the page from time to time, and the descriptive material is indented (for the most part), as if included under it. At a point in Part III, the typography imitates the meaning, much as it does in *Un Coup de dés* or a Futurist poem:

She was married with empty words:

                            better to
                          stumble at
                            the edge
                             to fall
                                fall
                and be
                —divorced

The most unusual typographical venture is the page with its lines askew, reflecting the tilting of objects on the waves of a flood. It is clear from *Paterson* that the poet considers the printed page an active participant in his work, and has constant specifications for short lines, spacing, divided words and the like, some of them making exceptional demands upon printing technology. We can see from it that Williams thought, not only in words, but also in terms of the visual impression made by his page.

These typographic ventures reflect the general nature of verbal experimentation. Traditionally, print, like the rules of language, is immune to the writer's control; it seems to serve its purpose best when it is least noticed, and few thought of calling attention to it by breaking out of the stringent limitations imposed on it. Yet the experimental writers observed that it could serve as a source of expressive energy if it were freed from the usual conventions, and could be transformed from an unregarded vehicle into a valuable literary resource.

VII THE LANGUAGE OF FINNEGANS WAKE

The Lady of the Lake went to Rock herself to sleep on Arthur's seat and the Lord of the Isles coming to Press a Piece and seeing her Assleap remembered their last meeting at Cony stone Water so touching her with one hand on the Vallis Lucis while [t]he other un-Derwent her Whitehaven, Ireby stifled her clack man on, that he might her Anglesea and give her a Buchanan and said. . . .

This is not a passage from *Finnegans Wake*, but a sample given by Keats of the chatter of his friend, Charles Brown, during a walking-tour in Scotland in 1818.[1] It suggests that the inventive energies which erupted in *Finnegans Wake* and the linguistic revolution, and which found their way into print in the works of Lewis Carroll and Edward Lear had been accumulating for a long time in the oral forms of language. It also suggests that while *Finnegans Wake* was the last, the most sustained, and in many ways the most extreme example of the verbal experimentation of the period ended by World War II, it cannot be accounted for as if it were simply a product of the contemporary forces we have been examining.

In fact, literary historians usually distinguish sharply between *Finnegans Wake* and the other experimental works of its time. Clive Hart has even said that Joyce's innovations are less radical than the linguistic disruptions found in the works of his contemporaries.[2] It is true that *transition* featured excerpts from 'Work in Progress' as the chief exhibits of its campaign to free language in nearly every one of the twenty-seven issues published between 1927 and 1938, but there was a considerable disparity between the aims of the periodical and those of Joyce's text. As A. Walton Litz has observed, *transition* was interested in the expression of unconscious ideas, while for Joyce dream-thoughts were only material which he subjected to eminently rational control.[3]

Nevertheless, *transition* defended Joyce vigorously in numerous polemic statements, many of them later collected in the volume called *Our Exagmination*, which put some of his aims before the public for the first time. Eugene Jolas, Samuel Beckett, John Rodker and others described *Work in Progress*, as it was then called, as an instance of the transformation and amalgamation that languages inevitably undergo, a renewal of linguistic vitality, and a successful attempt to record dreaming; they also tried to place the work historically, developing parallels between it and the writing of such forerunners as Vico and Carroll on the one hand and such contemporaries as the Surrealists on the other.[4]

After the forty years of intensive study that have followed the publication of the completed *Wake*, there is little difficulty in perceiving at least the main principles underlying its use of language. The book as a whole is the discourse of a dreaming mind stocked with a seemingly inexhaustible knowledge of history, languages, literature, geography and odd, unclassifiable facts. The atmosphere of the dream dissolves logical discriminations, so that anything can be identified with almost anything else through linguistic deformations. As the dreamer tells of the small world of the pub in Chapelizod, the Earwicker family, the patrons in the bar, and the events of the recent past and the day itself, he uses an idiom that identifies them with the people and events of all other times and places. Individual words are distorted to acquire double or multiple meanings, to establish links with the numerous leitmotifs and themes of the book, and to embody the metamorphic character of language.

The multiplicity of identities which is one of the main structural premises of *Finnegans Wake* is stated by Stephen in *Ulysses*: 'We walk through ourselves, meeting robbers, ghosts, giants, old men, young men, wives, widows, brothers-in-love. But always meeting ourselves.' (p. 213) The self and its experiences appear in constantly shifting disguises of memories and associations borrowed from all of Western culture. To the dreamer of the *Wake*, Earwicker ('giants, old men'), Anna Livia ('wives, widows'), Shem and Shaun ('brothers-in-love') and the other characters are the prototypes of a vast range of historical, legendary, psychological and fictional counterparts.

The fact that its language has multiple meanings is conveyed through the numerous explanations of the Mamafesta, or letter from Boston, which is first described as a 'proteiform graph . . . a polyhedron of scripture' (p. 107). After a first rendering of its contents, the commentator, acknowledging that it is far from clear, explains;

Well, almost any photoist worth his chemicots will tip anyone asking him the teaser that if a negative of a horse happens to melt enough while drying, well, what you do get is, well, a positively grotesquely distorted macromass of all sorts of horsehappy values and masses of meltwhile horse. Tip.

(p. 111)

It is a language of plural references that has its own literal way of fulfilling Pound's requirement that poetry should consist of 'language charged with meaning to the utmost possible degree'. The celebrated puns and portmanteau words may be used for the sake of isolated effects, to form local patterns, or to participate in major themes, thereby multiplying and extending their referential capacity, sometimes to an astonishing degree. As the reader of the *Wake* quickly perceives, the jocularity of the puns and the seriousness of the work they are called upon to perform do not interfere with one another. The most convincing examples are perhaps the multiple puns which enfold numerous meanings within a single ingeniously compounded word or term. The name of the giant who appears early in the book, 'Comestipple Sacksoun', (p. 15) is a variant of a presumptive name, 'Constable Saxon', which involves 'comestible' and the idea of drinking suggested in 'tipple' and 'sack', an association supported by the time of year, which is identified as 'junipery or febrewery'. A river is parenthetically described as 'olympiading even till the eleventh dynasty to reach the thuddysickend Hamlaugh', (p. 84). The word before the last includes not only 'thud', 'sick', and 'end', but 'thirty-second', and in conjunction with the 'eleventh dynasty' gives the date 1132, when the twins Shem and Shaun were born, a date that plays a vital part in the numerical structure of the book. In *Ulysses*, Bloom thought of 'thirty-two feet per second per second' as the speed of falling bodies, a relation which gives a special point to 'thud', 'sick', and 'end', especially since the archetypal Fall is one of the major motifs of the *Wake*. Multiple meanings also appear in puns that spread over numerous words, instead of being folded into one. The time of the encounter between HCE and the cad is the racing season, a time when 'the wetter is pest, the renns are overt and come and the voax of the turfur is hurled on our lande', (p. 39) in which the language of the *Song of Songs* forms the basis for a number of insinuations about bad weather, poetry ('renns' are verses), dishonest racing practices and the Irish sport of hurling. Foreign languages come into play in these elaborate puns, as in 'Who ails tongue coddeau, aspace of dumbillsilly?' (p. 15), a rendering of the French 'où est ton cadeau, espèce d'imbécile?'

Joyce's puns may be immediately amusing and ingenious, but

they often have the sober purpose of establishing links with the general theme of a sentence, a passage, a chapter, or the book as a whole. The cad's wife's maiden name, 'Maxwelton' connects with the 'annie lawrie promises' she makes later in the paragraph (p. 38). In the sequence of the Mookse and the Gripes, the Mookse is identified with Popes and with Rome generally, and this connection is strengthened when one of his actions is described through a series of papal names, 'by turning clement, urban, eugenious and celestian in the formose of good grogory humours', (p. 154), while 'formose' joins the many insect-allusions of the passage through the French *fourmi*, 'ant'. The cad is described as 'Gaping Gill, swift to mate errthors, stern to checkself', (p. 36) a charming design of puns playing on chess ('mate', 'check',) Augustan writers ('swift', 'stern',) and alluding to Thor, the god of thunder, which is one of the central structural themes of the *Wake*, because Vico attributed to the clap of thunder the origin of all human culture. Similarly, 'the umpple does not fall very far from the dumpertree', (p. 184) links a number of leading themes. It is about the Fall, which is the archetypal event of the *Wake*, the counterpart of HCE's disaster; it alludes to Humpty Dumpty, who had his own fall and who, as an egg, has a connection with the hen who found the letter from Boston; and 'dumpertree' refers to the dump or midden in which the letter was found, identifying it with the Tree in the story of the Fall. Many of the puns seem to be isolated, and simply speak for themselves, like 'notional gullery'; but it is dangerous to accept this conclusion in any particular case, for the persistent reader of the *Wake* is always finding patterns of meaning which take in apparently isolated words.

The vocabulary consists largely of hybrid words which seem to be participating in a vast metamorphic process. Joyce, as Clive Hart explains, was less interested in completions than in the shifts and transformations of ongoing processes, as is shown by his effort to recapitulate foetal development in the 'Oxen of the Sun' chapter in *Ulysses*. 'There is', said Samuel Beckett in his article on 'Work in Progress' in *Our Exagmination*, 'an endless verbal germination, maturation, putrefaction, the cyclic dynamism of the intermediate.'[5] This dynamism is, of course, an element of language itself. A first awareness of it occurs in *A Portrait* when Stephen, after feeling revulsion at the empty words he sees on shop signs and hears in the silly rhyme he has invented about ivy whining on the wall, finds that the word 'ivory' springs to life in his mind as part of the sequence, 'Ivory, ivoire, avorio, ebur'. It has been transformed from a mere referential counter to a cell in the growing organism of language. The shifting forms

of the word, suggesting differing countries and cultures, paradoxically keep an unchanging meaning before the mind. Joyce
must have examined many such sequences in *Skeat's Etymological
Dictionary*, one of the favourite books of his youth, and *Finnegans
Wake* exploits the flexibility of language he saw recorded there.
Its eccentric distortions are no more than exaggerations and ex-
tensions of the normal processes of language-change. But Joyce's
virtuosity intensified this flexibility, giving the impression that
any word or expression is inherent in almost any other. His distortions recall Lewis Carroll's game of 'Doublets', where the contes-
tants are called upon to transform a word into a different one of the
same length by changing one letter at a time. Carroll's first example
(which Joyce could hardly have seen) demonstrates how 'head' can
be changed into 'tail', an exercise that would have suited the
antithetical pattern of the *Wake* perfectly.

The metamorphic process going on in the language of the
Wake does not lie simply between the book and conventional
English, but continues within the book itself. An explanation of
the letter from Boston warns that 'every person, place and thing
in the chaosmos ... was moving and changing every part of the
time ... the as time went on as it will variously inflected, differently pronounced, otherwise spelled, changeably meaning vocable
scriptsigns' (p. 118). Accordingly, the words, phrases and sentences of the *Wake* undergo constant transformations, continuing
and sometimes recapitulating the process they have already
undergone before arriving at the modern English lexicon. The
changes Joyce introduces are not merely phonetic, as in the case
of 'ivory ... ebur', but involve changes in meaning as well. Like
actual language-shifts, they generally reflect some cause, the
accent of the speaker, the context of the word, the assimilation of
some idea.[6]

In certain passages however, the principle of transformation
takes on an independent life as it moulds words to new uses in
accordance with some pattern of permutation. For example, when
a painful thought strikes the restless ALP in her dozing, she has
a glimpse of the future: 'the windr of a wondr in a wildr is a weltr
as a wirbl of a warbl is a world' (p. 597). She thinks of a stable political order as 'a socially organic entity of a millenary military mari-
tory monetary morphological circumformation in a more or less
settled state of equonomic ecolube equalobe equilab equilibbrium'
(p. 599). These word-chains make it hard to believe that Joyce
was unaware of the diary entries in which Hopkins argued that
similar words were variants of a single idea, a principle that is
applied in his poetry, and can be felt behind many of his allitera-

tive effects. The *Wake* contains one sequence that comes astonishingly close to one of Hopkins's examples The poet's diary entry reads:

Flick means to touch or strike lightly as with the end of a whip, a finger, etc. To *fleck* is the next tone above flick, still meaning to touch or strike lightly (and leave a mark of the touch or stroke) but in a broader less slight manner . . . *Flake* is a broad and decided fleck, a thin plate of something, the tone above it. . . . Key to meaning of *flick, fleck* and *flake* is that of striking or cutting off the surface of a thing. . . .[7]

A description of ALP in the *Wake* has:

Here . . . she comes, . . . with peewee and powwows in beggybaggy on her bickybacky and a flick flask fleckflinging its pixylighting pacts' huemeramybows . . .   (p. 11)

The parallel suggests that Hopkins's principle that controlled differentiations of sound generate similar differentiations of meaning is also one of the principles of the *Wake's* language.

If the verbal distortions of the *Wake* could be reduced to a single principle, it would be the one formulated in a word that occurs in the marginal notes of the children's textbook: 'mutuomorphomutation' (p. 281), which would mean a process in which things interact, changing their shapes through influences that are both given and received. These influences can operate either over a limited area of the text, or throughout the *Wake* as a whole. Instances of the first occur where some principle is temporarily present as a controlling element. These can appear in dialect passages (pidgin: 'no fella he go make bakenbeggfuss longa white man', (p. 41), parody ('for ditcher for plower, till deltas twoport', p. 318), and the quasimagnetic effect that Stuart Gilbert called 'foliation', in which a series of words is pulled out of shape by the presence of a dominating idea;[8] there is a Moslem or Near Eastern aura in 'abhout that time stambuling haround Dumbaling', (p. 33–34), and one of insects in the section about the Ondt and the Gracehoper which reads, ' . . . he was always making ungraceful overtures . . . to play pupa-pupa and pulicy-pulicy and langtennas and pushpygyddyum and to commence insects with him . . . behold a waspering pot' (p. 414). Almost the opposite effect is developed when a word appears in different parts of the text, varied to reflect entirely different meanings. Among the variants for Shem's name, for example, are Shun, Shames, Jem, Jim, and many more. Proverbs, lines of songs and familiar sayings are repeated in disguised form. For example, 'Polly put the kettle on' appears in 'And the duppy shot the shutter clup . . . And they all drank free.' (p. 23) 'While the dumb he shoots the shopper rope. And they all pour forth' (p. 372), and 'Anny, blow your wickle out! Tuck away the tablesheet! You never wet the tea!' (p. 585)

The word 'Dublin' undergoes numerous variations appropriate to differing contexts. On the first page of the *Wake* it appears in the phrase 'doublin their mumper', which refers to the town of Dublin, Georgia, whose motto is 'Doubling all the time', a pun exactly reflecting the spirit of Joyce's linguistic experiment.[9] The *Wake* refers to itself as 'the book of Doublends Jined' (p. 20), a book about cycles, but also about Dublin. A part of the address of the letter on page 66 is 'Edenberry, Dubblenn'. The Gripes is called the Mookse's 'Dubville brooder-on-low' (p. 153). The Gaelic pronunciation of the word appears in 'Dyfflinarsky', (p. 13), and in 'Dyfflinsborg' (p. 582). It acquires the aspect of a Russian city in 'Novo Nilbud' (p. 24), and is the answer, in the anagrammatic form, 'Nublid', to the question of which city has 'the most expensive brewing industry in the world' (p. 140). In a letter to Miss Weaver in 1925, Joyce offered as an example of verbal coincidence the fact that Sir Benjamin Lee Guinness, the brewer, had once been Lord Mayor of Dublin, and that the Gaelic name for the porter he manufactured was *lin dub* or *dub lin*. This coincidence is exploited on page 553 in 'my granvilled brand-old Dublin lindub, the free, the froh, the frothy freshener. . . .' Like nearly everything else in *Finnegans Wake*, Dublin appears in one of the suggested titles for ALP's Mamafesta as 'Hear Hubty Hublin' (p. 105), and also in the title given to Brian Boru by Mutt: 'Brian d' of Linn' (p. 17). The list is by no means exhaustive; I have located about thirty variations of the word 'Dublin' with the aid of Clive Hart's *Concordance*, and would guess that this number could easily be quadrupled in a thorough search.

Somewhat less ubiquitous, but nearly as crucial, for it signals one of the book's central events, the fall of HCE, is the phrase *felix culpa*. The original Latin never appears in *Finnegans Wake*, but is represented in a series of ingenious variants (twenty-eight, according to Bernard Benstock) which have been adapted to merge with other themes. HCE is called 'O foenix culprit' (p. 23) because his 'fall' took place in Phoenix Park. The phrase appears in the list of Mamafesta titles as *Ophelia's Culpreints* (p. 105); one of the names rejected for the signboard of the tavern in answer to the third question of chapter IV is 'O'Faynix Coalprince' (p. 139). On p. 246 appears the perverse motto, 'felixed is who culpas does'; Earwicker begins his explanation of the crime of which he is accused with 'Guilty but fellows culpows!' (p. 363), and a fashion

in women's dress draws the exclamation 'O', felicious coolpose!'
(p. 618)

It is thoroughly characteristic of *Finnegans Wake* that these two
verbal sequences, which I thought I had chosen arbitrarily, should
turn out to be related to each other. In his *Reader's Guide to
Finnegans Wake*, W.Y. Tindall discloses that 'the hearsomeness
of the burger felicitates the whole of the polis' is one of many
Joycean renderings of the motto of Dublin, 'Obedientia civium
urbis felicitas'. The last word is, of course, a derivative of *felix*,
and Joyce strengthens this etymological bridge by introducing
'O foenix culprit' immediately after his first translation of the
motto. In this way, the happiness of the original fall into sin and
that of Dublin's obedient citizenry are joined as examples of the
incorrigible good humour of mankind. This connection is an
instance of the principle of *anastomosis*, the establishment of links
between systems that accounts for much of the structure of
Finnegans Wake. As Clive Hart observes, Joyce used the word to
describe the act of intercourse, and employed other figures, including cross-pollination and mental telepathy as instances of the same
concept.[10] It must have been the labour of establishing connections
of this kind that he was describing when he reported in one of his
letters to Miss Weaver that writing the *Wake* was like tunnelling
toward a centre from various directions.[11]

Joyce did not have to rely on verbal resemblances to create the
links that he needed. (The description of Shem as a 'Europasianiz-
ed Afferyank' for example, owes nothing to verbal similarities.)
Nevertheless, the correspondences that bind the *Wake's* fabric
together are, it should be noted, often dependent on the words
themselves. The possibility of relating referential or conceptual
meanings must often have been suggested to Joyce, in the first
instance, by some verbal resemblance, so that it is perfectly accurate to say that the words, as words, exert a controlling influence
upon the structure of the *Wake*. The discovery of these links is
one of the experiences of reading the *Wake*; it enables the reader
to re-live the encounters with coincidence that Joyce experienced
while he spun his intricate web, or, rather, dug his tunnels through
to their meeting-place. For example, the similarity between the
names Humphrey and Humpty-Dumpty leads to the motifs of
walls, falling, and eggs; the latter, in turn, is connected with the
hen who presides over the midden where the letter is found. Again,
the associations of Chapelizod led Joyce to the Tristram and Iseult
legend, or he may have chosen the locality for his setting because
of this connection. In any event, the fact that the name 'Tristan'
can be broken up into the elements 'tree' and 'stone' leads to the

impressive imagery of the 'Anna Livia Plurabelle' chapter, in which the two washerwomen are gradually transformed into these natural objects, and to such marvellous minor developments as the mutation of 'tree' and 'stone' into 'stem and stone' and thence into 'Shem and Shaun'. Although Joyce did not follow the Dada principle of abandoning the responsibilities of composition to chance, he certainly welcomed the interventions of chance in fulfilling his design.

Joyce had incredibly embarked on *Finnegans Wake* without knowing the work of Lewis Carroll. When the parallels between his own ideas about words and dreams and those of Carroll were pointed out, he read *Sylvie and Bruno*; he might well have been puzzled about the resemblances that had been perceived, because *Sylvie and Bruno* contains very little of the word-play and dream-magic of the Alice books. But it offered some useful connectives nevertheless. The little boy who appears in it has the same name as Giordano Bruno, one of the presiding presences of the *Wake*; and the little girl to whom the book is dedicated (and who was eventually to play the part of Alice on the stage), Isa Bowman, had a first name resembling that of Joyce's character Issy, or Iseult, a name drawn from the scene of the story, Chapelizod or Chapelle d'Iseult. Joyce soon read the Alice books, and their characters, as well as Carroll himself, became important strands in the network of *Finnegans Wake*. Joyce, like Shem, was a 'serendipitist'; it is perfectly clear that happy discovery was an integral part of his method.

The *Wake*-language is, of course, an original creation, and its originality is enhanced, rather than diminished by the influences Joyce accepted in developing it, such as those of Vico, Bruno, Lewis Carroll, the Swift of the *Letters to Stella*, and the Book of Kells. If we consider the love of word-play Joyce encountered in traditional Irish humour, his two predilections for words and heresy, and the moments of verbal experimentation in *Ulysses*, it is almost possible to be persuaded that the appearance of just such an idiom as that of the *Wake* was inevitable in his development. It embodies three of his passions: subtlety, intricacy and ductility.

Joyce's favourite element, like Bloom's, was water. The best passages of *Finnegans Wake* are those connected with ALP and the Liffey, and the 'Ithaca' chapter of *Ulysses* contains a great prose ode about water. We find Joyce saying in an early critical piece, a review of Ibsen's *Catalina* written in 1903, ' . . . the imagination has the quality of a fluid, and it must be held firmly, lest it become vague, and delicately, that it may lose none of its magical powers'.[12] Water may well have come to occupy a central position in Joyce's imagination because its ductility and flexibility were the physical counterparts of the qualities he valued most in language and the imagination. In the idiom of *Finnegans Wake*, single syllables and even letters can be detached from their words and re-assigned to others; they drift about, like freely-circulating liquid molecules, in the vast sea of its language. Among the reasons for Bloom's love of water are its 'universality . . . vastness . . . profundity . . . preserving penetrativeness'; he also admires it because of its 'capacity to dissolve and hold in solution all soluble substances', 'infallibility as paradigm and paragon', and 'metamorphoses as vapour, mist, cloud, rain, sleet, snow, hail'. These are all attributes of language, the attributes emphasized and magnified in *Finnegans Wake*. Joyce said, in explaining that he needed factual *données* for his work on *Ulysses*, that he lacked imagination; *Finnegans Wake* might be seen as an effort to make language do the work of imagination, to exploit the Coleridgean fusing and transforming powers it has in common with its metaphoric equivalent, water.

Although Joyce's *transition* allies may have exaggerated the parallels between *Work in Progress* and some of the other texts they published, there are some general affinities between the mission Joyce assigned to language in the *Wake* and the aims of certain contemporaries. There is something like Dada humour in it; it is a hoax in the sense that it is far more serious than it appears to be. It uses language to reflect the dream-work, in a way that resembles, yet is different from, the methods of the Surrealists. In it language becomes Cassirer's 'independent activity of the imagination', freeing the mind from conventional channels of thought, associating disparate things with each other, forming structures having no models in actuality. It achieves the effect of spatialization and simultaneity found in other major experimental works, rendering things divided by historical time mutually accessible to each other.

It is true, however, that some of Joyce's most sympathetic contemporaries failed to catch the drift of *Work in Progress*. After reading some of it, Pound wrote to Joyce: 'I will have another go at it, but up to present I make nothing of it whatever. Nothing so far as I make out, nothing short of divine vision or a new cure for the clapp can possibly be worth all the circumambient peripherization.'[13] William Carlos Williams, on the other hand, responded to it enthusiastically. 'Reading Joyce last night when my mind was fluid from fatigue. . . . I saw! . . . The words are freed to be understood again in an original, a fresh, delightful sense. Lucid they do become. Plain, as they have not been for a lifetime, we see them.'[14] Marcel Brion reported that the *transition* instalments gave him a sense of emancipation, the impression that 'we seem to be present at the birth of a world. In this apparent chaos we are conscious of a creative purpose . . . which has razed every conventional dimension, concept and vocabulary, and selected from their scattered material the elements of a new structure'.[15] Robert Sage explained that Joyce was telescoping together all humanity and the times and places in which it has appeared; 'the uninitiated reader', he wrote 'will understand at the outset that he is faced with a revolutionary four-dimensional conception of the universe, that the "characters" . . . are composite, that time plays no part, that Joyce reaches out into all space to take what he for the moment requires.'[16]

When the implausible notion of translating *Finnegans Wake* into French occurred to some members of Joyce's circle in 1930, one of the most enthusiastic participants was Philippe Soupault, who had collaborated with André Breton about ten years before in writing the first Surrealist automatic texts. While his presence constitutes a genuine link between the *Wake* and the European experimentalists, Soupault admired Joyce for exercising a control and discrimination that were entirely opposed to the spontaneity of the Surrealists. 'Before my eyes', he reported, 'Joyce, his index finger raised, saying nothing, repeating a word, a phrase, criticizing, rejecting, taking back an entire fragment, destroying pages already on the point of being printed. . . . '[17]

The *Wake* makes numerous overt allusions to Joyce's contemporaries in the literary revolution, including Hulme, Bergson and Gertrude Stein, as well as older figures such as Rimbaud and Mallarmé. Pound appears as a 'parsonifier propounde' (p. 378) and as 'Esra, the cat' (p. 116), and there are uncomplimentary allusions to his emphatic manner, his American accent and his Chinese interests in 'A maundarin tongue in a pounderin jowl? Father ourder about the mathers of prenanciation. Distributary endings? And we recommends.' (p. 89) There are numerous references, direct and oblique, to Eliot and his works, including what is apparently a description of a woman in a nightgown: 'Thou in shanty! Thou in scanty shanty!! Thou in slanty scanty shanty!!!' (p. 305), after the closing 'Shantih shantih shantih' of *The Waste Land*. There seem to be no references to André Breton, Tristan Tzara, Philippe Soupault, Marinetti, Kurt Schwitters or other Continental writers; on the other hand, certain painters such as Paul Klee and Hans Arp—who was also a poet— do appear. The most sustained allusion to a contemporary is also the only episode where Joyce deals in his own way with a philosophical issue of the experimental period.

The long lecture on the 'dime-cash' problem with which Professor Jones answers the eleventh riddle on pp. 149–68 of the *Wake* is part of an exchange between Joyce and Wyndham Lewis.[18] Although this section did not appear in *transition* until September, 1927, the month in which Lewis's *Time and Western Man* was published, Joyce must already have heard something of Lewis's attack on philosophers and artists (including Joyce) who were overly concerned with time, and his advocacy of the more stable and intellectual sort of art which articulates itself in spatial terms. Jones is undoubtedly the same Professor who, in an earlier passage, punctured a version of the letter from Boston with his fork in an effort to follow ideas about art of the kind propagated by Worringer and Hulme.

In his lecture, the Professor inveighs against such representatives of time as Bergson ('the sophology of Bitchson', p. 149), Einstein ('the whoo-whoo and where's hairs theory of Winestain', p. 149), says that he is working on a 'quantum' theory of his own, and criticizes 'all that school of neoitalian or paleoparisien schola of tinkers and spanglers' (p. 151). To clarify his meaning, he resorts to the fable in which the Mookse represents the Popes of Rome and the Gripes various enemies of theirs within and without the church; but the former also represents the interest of the permanent and timeless, as Lewis advocated them, and the latter the temporal, as it was represented by Bergson, Einstein and their supposed followers.

The Mookse's story begins 'Eins within a space' (p. 152); he walks in 'parsecs' (p. 152)—a unit of space-time consisting of about two light-years—and is outraged when the Gripes, repeating the question put by the cad to Earwicker, asks, 'By the watch, what is the time, pace?' (p. 154) The indignant Mookse answers, 'Is this space of our couple of hours too dimensional for you, temporiser?' (p. 154), which is exactly the sort of question the spatially-oriented Lewis might have put to his time-obsessed enemies. The Professor goes on to say that his opponent's aim is ' mere cashdime' or space-time, for to him 'dime *is* cash'. His spatial preferences continue to show when he proceeds to the tale of Burrus and Cassius, in such locutions as 'until I can find space to look into it' (p. 163) and 'I shall have a word to say in a few yards' (p. 165). He identifies himself again as Lewis by mentioning 'gentlemen's spring modes' (p. 165), an allusion to Lewis's 1917 short story, 'Cantleman's Spring Mate'. There is another reference to this title in a later context, 'cattlemen's spring meat' (p. 172) followed by 'His liver too is great value, a spatiality!' perhaps an allusion to Lewis's bile, certainly to his advocacy of space. The professor ends with a disguised allusion to another contemporary. He promises to entertain a friend in a ship with the name *Noisdanger* (p. 168), which can hardly be anything but a reference to Pound's Canto XX, with its anecdote about the interpretation of the word '*noigandres*' from a poem by Arnaut Daniel.

In spite of Lewis's attack on him as a representative of the Bergsonian time school, it is clear that Joyce's work participates in the spatialization characteristic of modern art, and that much of the originality of the *Finnegans Wake* idiom is due to this tendency. Its major devices, parody, compounds, blends, and portmanteau words, are means for eliminating sequential effects and achieving simultaneity. The cyclic Viconian pattern renders the movement of time nearly trivial, since each age is a return to some previous stage of culture. Hence, a single event has universal implications, and the things that take place during the few hours the reader of the *Wake* spends in and around Earwicker's house, bar and bedroom are enough to represent huge stretches of historical time. The intricate cross-connections that make up the fabric of the book suggest that ideally, it is all to be held in the mind at once, and also as Robert Sage observes in *Our Exagmination*, and as the manuscripts of the *Wake* show, that all parts of it were written concurrently, new material being added in various places as Joyce thought of it. ' . . . the *Wake*', says W.I. Thompson, 'is the eighteen sections of "Wandering Rocks" written at once; it is the point outside the space-time system, the point at which God observes the absurd carnival of history.'[19] Clive Hart has shown that the *Wake* is organized according to a number of intricate time-schemes, but that all of these are ultimately resolved into the eternal now of traditional mysticism.[20]

As we have seen, the French Surrealists Roger Vitrac and Robert Desnos had already exploited the punning transposition of sounds. Desnos' 'jeux des fous qui mettent le feu aux joues' follows exactly the same principle as Joyce's 'lice nittle clinkers' (p. 29). In analyzing a passage of *Les Champs magnétiques*, Rosmarie Waldrop has shown that automatic writing is controlled by associative methods resembling those that operate in the prose of the *Wake*. The sequence 'avance . . . avale . . . avarice' depends upon similarity of sounds, a feature basic to Joyce's style. Some of the language can be attributed to the influence of words that do not appear in the text, but exert an influence upon it through implied puns, so that, for example, when the narrator sees 'bouts aeriens' in 'endroits marécageux', the connection turns upon 'boue', which sounds like 'bouts', ends, and has a meaning, 'mud', related to 'marécageux', swampy.[21] A similar magnetism of the unexpressed is often manifested in Joyce's distortions. For example, in 'And bids him tend her, lute and airly. Sing, sweetharp, thing to me anone!' (p. 224) three of the words are pulled out of shape by the underlying idea of music.

These resemblances are due to the principle which the *Wake* shares with the Dadas and Surrealists, that words themselves should be given priority over their rational or referential functions, and should be treated as primary realities. But the operation of this principle in the *Wake* does not reduce the expressive power of language, as it does in some other contexts. Alfred Jarry and the Dadas distorted words as a means of ridiculing their pretensions, Kurt Schwitters wrote *Ursonate* in meaningless vocables, and Gertrude Stein, Marinetti and Michel Leiris thought words could appeal directly to the feelings or evoke associations simply through their sounds. The *Wake* does share with these the aim of freeing language by demoting reference; however, it does not discard reference, but assigns it an important place as a vital secondary function. When the camp-followers or 'jinnies' of Napoleon's army are said to go 'boycottoncrezy' (p. 9) about Wellington, for example, the new word does not lack meaning. Besides 'boy-crazy', it means the Irish land agent whose name has come stand for economic isolation, 'cotton', because much of the passage is about clothing, and the Battle of Crécy, in accordance with the idea of warfare, which dominates it. Still, the word does not 'refer' to anything that has independent existence, but participates in the themes, some of them quite abstract, that interweave in the passage where it is found.

Similarly, the names Tristopher and Hilary (p. 21) are the products of a purely verbal union between familiar Christian names and a motto from Giordano Bruno, *In tristitia hilaris, hilaritate tristis*.[22] In the *Wake* they refer to the two sons of the Jarl van Hoother, who correspond to Shem and Shaun, instances of the archetype of pairs based on Bruno's principle of the identity of opposites. Far from seeking to eliminate reference, Joyce uses the unconventional tools of the pun and the portmanteau-word and the conventional ones of archetypes and symbols to accumulate extensive areas of meaning and relate them to each other in original ways. But these meanings are not in themselves communicative. They form parts of the design of the book as a whole. The language of the *Wake* has in common with the Surrealist use of language a capacity to assimilate objective reality to the purposes of thought. The nature of the thought is entirely different, for Joyce is conscious and calculating, while automatic writing attempts to tap subconscious processes. But for both, objective reality is an appendage to language, not its model, and language changes it by rendering it capable of acquiring the fluid, ambiguous qualities of thought.

There has always been some difference of opinion about Joyce's attitude toward the operation of chance in *Finnegans Wake*. Clive Hart has said that Joyce did not insist upon absolute control, but welcomed the coincidental meanings unlocked by his manipulation of words, and even chance effects. It was, he says, part of Joyce's intention to accept readings he did not himself intend.[23] Bernard Benstock, on the other hand, maintains that while Joyce made full use of pre-existing linguistic accidents (such as the identity of names in Finn MacCumhal and Huckleberry Finn), he controlled them strictly, and admitted few coincidences into the *Wake* itself.[24] Benstock's view is supported by the deliberate workmanship found in Joyce's intricate cross-connections, but there is also considerable evidence to suggest that Joyce had some regard for what the Surrealists called 'objective hazard', the artistry of nature manifested through chance. He certainly took verbal coincidences that occurred in actuality seriously, and it is hard to see why he should rule them out of his book. He sometimes actively invited chance effects. In 1926, for example, he invited Miss Weaver to give him some specifications for a portion of his book; she sent him photographs of the giant's grave at St. Andrews in Penrith, together with a pamphlet about it, and Joyce composed a passage using these materials.

Some of the people around Joyce believed that his text included such chance additions as the errors made by typists and remarks overheard while he was writing. One anecdote has him saying 'Come in' in reply to a knock on the door while he was dictating to Samuel Beckett; Beckett included these words in what he was writing, and Joyce let the chance interpolation stand. If this anecdote is true, its possible result may be 'What does Coemghen?' (p. 602) Similarly, Padraic Colum reported that while he was typing parts of the *Wake*, Joyce invited him to propose more complex substitutes for some of the words, and apparently used some of the suggestions while rejecting others.[25] Everyone who reads the *Wake* finds that it seems to allude to his friends, his personal affairs, or other matters outside Joyce's field of knowledge. Joyce seems to have liked this odd form of universal significance, and welcomed the possibility that his work might acquire unforeseen meanings from future events. In a letter of 1940 written in French, he claimed that his title had predicted the outbreak of the Russo-Finnish war in which 'le Finn again wakes'.[26]

The Surrealists, as we have seen, regarded coincidences as the spontaneous fulfilments of wishes or other psychological images, as demonstrations that the mind and the material world are governed by the same determinism. Though there is no such principle in Joyce's use of chance, the feeling of general unity is certainly present in the *Wake*. Instead of responding with wonder, however, Joyce responds with comic inventiveness, with the motive of demonstrating the relationship of all things to each other through the inexhaustible meaningfulness of language. He is not interested in such effects of pure chance as those produced by the Dada practice of writing a poem with 'words from a hat', or by such later exploitations of accident as the 'cut up' method used by William Burroughs and Brion Gysin, but rather in the opportunities presented by accidents for creating a controlled design.

The element of chance in *Finnegans Wake* is related less to Surrealism than to the component of randomness found in such relatively purposeful techniques as *bricolage, collage, Merz* and *objet-trouvé*. As we have seen (chapter 4), Joyce used the words in the dictionary as the *bricoleur* uses the remnants in his attic, releasing latent qualities in them by adapting them to new uses. His achievement is not a conquest but a compromise; their old meanings are not eliminated, but survive as witty contrapuntal effects within the imaginative design. Earwicker's story corresponds to the invented 'project' of the *bricoleur*, but Joyce tells it through such pre-existing remains from other stories as the figures of Adam, Wellington, Humpty-Dumpty and so on, and these in turn provide him with new chances for extending and elaborating his original intention. All of the transformations typical of *bricolage* occur in the *Wake's* use of language: chance resemblances become the determinate elements of an organized pattern; words that were originally terminal products are used as means to another end; and the merely actual and utilitarian acquires the aura and suggestiveness of the imagined. Like *collage* and its various developments, the *Wake* is an intersection of imagination and reality. It is, says Clive Hart, 'the most outstanding example of what can be done with *objet-trouvé* collage in literature',[27] Hart finds that Joyce did not subordinate his fragments of reality to his design, but deliberately left them incompletely assimilated, so that they would still have a connection with the actual world outside his book. The *Wake*, in fact, exploits the complex paradoxes involved in joining the actual and the imagined, deriving its validity from both. Each modified or distorted word is both a part of the ordinary vocabulary and something else, an object that has been 'found', and then adapted to the purposes of art, acting both as a bridge between actuality and artifice and as a demonstration of their ultimate incongruity.

Complaining, in the course of his effort to gain a greater liberty for language, that writers used only tame comparisons, Marinetti said, 'They have compared for example a fox terrier to a very small pure-bred Altri . . . I would have compared it instead to a turbulent river.'[28] This is, of course, exactly the sort of analogy used in *Finnegans Wake*, where Anna Livia is identified with the Liffey, Earwicker with the Hill of Howth, and Shem and Shaun with tree and stone, and Ondt and Gracehoper. Marinetti had proposed that the poet create 'an immense net of analogies with which to envelope the world'.[29] It would be hard to find a more apt description of the general structure of the *Wake*, whose major characters and situations are identified with counterparts of all times and places. *Finnegans Wake* may not have been what Marinetti had in mind, but it cannot be denied that it fulfills his aim of organizing reality according to new relationships perceived intuitively. Through their metamorphic qualities, the words establish relations with each other across great distances. Anna Livia's farewell as she goes out to sea on the last page includes the word 'Avelaval'. Early in the book, speaking of the household cat, Kate says, 'It's an allavalonche that blows nopussy food' (p. 28), in which 'lunch' and the French meaning of 'avalanche', 'swallowing' are both involved. The word is moved close to a river-meaning as one of the washerwomen at the ford exclaims 'Allalivial, allalluvial!' (p. 213) It reverts to the first use in 'saving grace after avalunch' (p. 240), and 'his avalunch oclock snack' (p. 406). 'Ave' appears in the list of addresses to which Shaun tries to deliver Shem's letter (p. 420). Whether it is an abbreviation for 'avenue', or the Latin for 'farewell', indicating that the person to whom it has been sent is no longer there, is wittily left completely unclear. On p. 600 is an account of a pool, 'Innalavia', of which it is said, 'whereinn once we lave 'tis alve and vale', which seems to mean that washing in it brings death. The whole complex of related words is a minor thread contributing a number of associated meanings to Anna Livia's word of farewell. Through methods like this, developed on a much more elaborate scale, the *Wake* maintains its great structural analogies such as those between the fall of Earwicker and the fall of Adam, between the letter from Boston and literature in general, and between Shem and Shaun and the innumerable polarities they represent.

Marinetti found that the revelations of modern physics about the nature of material reality suggested new linguistic resources, and Joyce seems to have been influenced by similar ideas. Marinetti had said:

One must express . . . the infinitely small that encircles one, the imperceptible, invisible, the agitation of atoms, the Brownian movement, all the inspiring hypotheses and explored controls of the ultra-microscopic. . . . I want to introduce into poetry infinite molecular life, which must be mingled, in a work of art, with the spectacles and dramas of the infinitely great, so that this fusion will constitute the integral synthesis of life.[30]

Here again is a poetic ambition of the Futurists that *Finnegans Wake* seems to fulfill, though less pompously. Its portmanteau-words and puns oscillate between meanings, giving a very good imitation of the Brownian movement. When we read, for example, that among the bric-a-brac in Shem's house are to be found 'quashed quotatoes, messes of mottage' (p. 183), it is impossible to exclude from the meaning either food or words. The *Wake* has even been described as an attempt to imitate the atomic reactions of matter in words capable of generating 'a chain reaction of meaning',[31] an aim which corresponds with Marinetti's recommendation. In describing something seen on the television set in Earwicker's bar as 'the abnihilisation of the etym', Joyce identifies the splitting of the atom—or some such event—with parallel developments in language. He can be thought of as working in terms of this analogy, reaching into the interiors of the atoms called words, splitting them into various meanings by letter-substitutions, added syllables and similar distortions, and linking these minute intra-verbal elements to his large themes in order to weave 'a net of analogies' that would, in Marinetti's grandiose terms, 'constitute the integral synthesis of life'. Joyce's feeling for the correspondence between ultra-microscopic and psychological phenomena goes back at least to *Ulysses*, where Stephen thinks: 'Molecules all change. I am other I now' (*Ulysses* p. 189), thus providing a physical basis for Rimbaud's '*Je* est un autre.'

The structural elements of the *Wake* do not resolve its verbal ambiguities, but confirm them, opening multiple levels of meaning. This radical indeterminacy, one of the book's most revolutionary aspects, seems appropriate to the age of Heisenberg, but it may well have had its source in the world-view of an older philosopher, Giordano Bruno, a figure Joyce had admired since his student days as a daring and original thinker, as well as a heretic.

Bruno mentions Daedalus, Joyce's 'fabulous artificer', as his own ideal of intelligence in the first lines of the dedicatory epistle to one of his chief works, *De l'infinito universo et mondi*. Joyce referred to Bruno, a citizen of Nola, as 'the Nolan' in the opening words of his 1901 essay, 'The Day of the Rabblement', wrote a review of J. Lewis McIntyre's *Giordano Bruno* for the *Daily Express* of Dublin in 1903, and seems to have read odd passages of Bruno's extensive works for practice in Italian while he was writing the *Wake*.

He found Bruno's doctrine of the reconciliation of opposites especially congenial. According to Bruno, as Joyce learned from McIntyre's book, the minimal conditions of opposing primary experiences will be found, on examination, to be identical. Minimal cold and minimal heat meet at one point of temperature, and each moves away from this point as it increases. Similarly, Bruno taught that such opposites as love and hate, generation and decay, poison and its antidotes have basic principles in common which connect them with each other. 'Profound magic it is to know', wrote Bruno, 'how to extract the contrary after having found the point of union.' Joyce saw reflections of this doctrine in Tristan's device of disguising his name by reversing its syllables, and in the fact that the genders of Norwegian-Danish are neither masculine nor feminine. The idea of the coincidence of contraries is the model for the many sets of opposites that appear in the *Wake*; Bruno himself is often introduced, and is identified, in a typical verbal association, with the firm of Dublin stationers, Browne and Nolan.

However, the reconciliation of opposites was only one aspect of the majestic general cosmology which Joyce found outlined in McIntyre's study. Bruno was, after Nicholas of Cusa, who is also mentioned in the *Wake*, an advocate of the theory that the universe is infinite and contains an infinite number of worlds. Since no boundary to creation is conceivable, argued Bruno, expounding a view that contradicted the teachings of the Church, it can have no centre; every point in the universe is equally central, and the various positions in it cannot be distinguished from each other. 'If point does not differ from body, centre from circumference, finite from infinite, the greatest from the least, then the universe, as we have said, is all centre, or the centre of the universe is everywhere. . . .'[32]

Since the universe is radically unified, not contraries alone, but all objects share each other's nature.

Our philosophy . . . reduceth to a single origin and relateth to a single end, and maketh contraries to coincide so that there is one primal foundation both of origin and of end. From this coincidence of contraries, we deduce that ultimately it is divinely true that contraries are within contraries; wherefore it is not difficult to compass the knowledge that each thing is within every other. . . . All power and act which in origin is complicated, united and one is in other things explicate, dispersed and multiple.[33]

Bruno was an atomist in the tradition of Democritus and Lucretius, and believed that there is a uniform element which circulates among the far-flung worlds of the cosmos, so that each object eventually becomes every other through the interchange of matter. Each specific thing, as McIntyre explains, is in potentiality all of reality, a temporary form in the process of passing into some other kind of existence. 'Matter, weary of old forms, eagerly snatches after new, for it desires to become all things, and to resemble, as far as may be, all being.'[34] In another passage from the same work, Bruno says: 'Whoever considers well, will recognize that we have not in youth the same flesh as in childhood, nor in old age the same as in youth: for we suffer perpetual transmutation, whereby we receive a perpetual flow of fresh atoms. . . .'[35] This idea seems to have suggested Stephen's observation in *Ulysses*: ' . . . the mole on my right breast is where it was when I was born, though all my body has been woven of new stuff time after time. . . . '

As James S. Atherton has shown in *The Books at the Wake*, the language of *Finnegans Wake* may be usefully regarded as a linguistic counterpart of Bruno's vision of the cosmos. 'The universe being infinite', wrote Bruno,

and the bodies thereof transmutable, all are therefore constantly dispersed and constantly reassembled. . . . Whence we deduce that if this earth be eternal, it is not so by virtue of the stability of any one part or individual, but through vicissitudes of many parts, some being expelled therefrom and their place taken by others. Thus soul and intelligence persist while the body is ever changing and renewed, part by part.[36]

Stephen, we recall, thought of 'Ivory, ivoire, eborio, ebur', a word manifesting the persistence of soul with the change and renewal of its body. The puns and compounds of the *Wake* bring together the elements of two or more words, just as the things of Bruno's world participate in each other's existence. The letters and syllables that represent variations from English correspond to atoms that have migrated from one object to another. The words are temporary forms on their way to acquiring new identities under the influence of a metamorphic energy like the one that dominates Bruno's cosmos. Joyce's language is multivalent because it is a dream-language, and he connects both Bruno and Nicholas of Cusa with dreams in a speech by a character named Sordid Sam: 'Me drames, O'Loughlins, has come through! Now let the centuple celves of my egourge as Micholas de Cusack calls them . . . by the coincidance of their contraries reamalgamerge in that indentity of undiscernibles where the Baxters and the

Fleshmans may they cease to bidivil uns and ... this outandin brown candlestock melt Nolan's into peese!' (p. 49–50). Nicholas of Cusa, merged with Michael Cusack, the 'citizen' of the 'Cyclops' chapter of *Ulysses*, is offered here as an authority for the multiplicity of selves characteristic of dreams, and Browne and Nolan, Joyce's verbal link from Dublin to Bruno, appear in the suggestive passage about the 'candlestock'. Bruno is reverted to persistently later on this page as 'Father San Browne', 'Padre Don Bruno' and 'hornerable Fratomistor Nawlanmore and Brawne'.

Bruno's theories helped to free the Renaissance mind from the Aristotelian notion of a finite universe and the geocentric cosmology of the middle ages. They introduced the conception of infinite worlds as an inspiriting recognition of the unlimited abundance of God and freed the intellect to wander speculatively over his vast and varied creation. Joyce's idiom in *Finnegans Wake* impinges upon conventional language very much as Bruno's theories impinged upon the medieval cosmos. It emancipates the word from its traditional service to a focused, localized meaning, and develops the potentialities that have always been inherent in words for conveying multiple ideas and forming elaborate, many-tiered structures. It shows that the possibilities of verbal expression are far greater than they seem, that they are, if not unlimited, at least inexhaustible. Strother B. Purdy has calculated that, following Joyce's methods, seventeen letters forming a single word can be rearranged into combinations numbering no fewer than 370 billion. Nevertheless, he disagrees with those who say that no reading of a passage in the *Wake* can be wrong; he insists that the multiplicity of meanings it is possible to derive from its text must be limited by its themes and structure.[37]

The *Wake* is not infinite; but it discloses a universe of language which is. It is an example of the sort of structure that Jacques Derrida has described as characteristic of recent times, 'a field of infinite substitutions in the closure of a finite ensemble', and displays some remarkable affinities with the sensibility that informs the structuralist analysis of the period after World War II. It is Derrida's view that previous ideas of order have had centres or points of origin, forms of certitude that generated governing principles, but that the consciousness of structure and investigations of signification have revealed structures without such centres, systems without external determinants, goals or separable significations. Myths, for example, can be seen as non-referential fabrics of interwoven themes, developing meaning through the relationships of their elements as they engage in 'an interplay of absence and presence'.[38] In *The Decentered Universe of Finnegans*

Wake, an illuminating application of structuralist critical principles to Joyce's work, Margot Norris shows that the *Wake* generates meaning in this way, through the 'intricate and devious connections' among its words and ideas rather than through a substantial content, and that its idiom is the language of such a decentred system as Derrida describes.[39]

When the *Wake* is examined from Derrida's point of view, its characters, settings and events are seen, not as particular identities, but as the interchangeable elements of mythic, fictional and historical patterns. This aspect of it is made especially clear in Adaline Glasheen's *Second Census of Finnegans Wake* through the chart entitled 'Who is Who When Everybody is Somebody Else', which shows that Joyce used the Earwicker family as a template for transpositions, so that when HCE is Shakespeare, Shaun is the W.H. of the sonnets, Shem is his son Hamnet, Issy is his daughter Susanna, and ALP is, of course, Ann Hathaway: when he is Caesar, the sons are Burrus and Caseous, the daughter is Cleopatra, and ALP is Fulvia. The punning, metamorphic language sustains these patterns without committing itself to any specific content. Its parallels are not disguises for any particular significations; in fact, the multiple identifications cancel each other out, as they take part in a game of endless substitutions. According to Derrida, the decentred system increases the possibility of what he calls *freeplay* among its elements; there is probably no literary work with a greater degree of this than *Finnegans Wake*.

Ultimately, the *Wake* will probably be recognized as an unbroken series of parodies. Every passage seems to have an identifiable manner of speech or style of expression as its basis, and there are none in the neutral style of an objective author. The opening adopts an epic tone: 'What clashes here of wills gen wonts. . . . Assiegates and boomeringstroms. . . . Sanglorians, save! Arms apeal with larms, appalling.' (p. 4). This is followed by a different voice, that of one of the mourners at the wake: 'Shize? I should shee! Macool, orra whyi deed ye diie?' (p. 6) A new style, that of a pedantic lecturer, soon appears: 'Yet may we not see still the brontoichthyan form outlined aslumbered. . . . ' (p. 7) There have been at least three different speakers, then, by the time we hear Kate, the guide at the Wellington Museum, begin her speech with: 'This is the way to the museyroom. . . . ' (p. 8) These imitations are generally based on subliterary forms, many of them oral: the museum-guide's speech, the letter from Boston, the lecture on the dime-cash problem, the textbook of the nursery chapter, stage directions describing a couple in bed, the bar room anecdote of the Russian general, and so on. The *Wake* carries

forward a technique whose possibilities were only broached in
The Waste Land; it assembles a large repertory of different speaking styles, so that the Dublin accent, pidgin English, children's
talk, the lisping of a girl detective, the muttering of the drunk,
and many more can be heard through the interference of its
linguistic distortions.

The originals on which the parodies of the *Wake* are based
range from general styles like these to specific works and even
passages. The fable is parodied in the two tales of the Mookse
and the Gripes, and the Ondt and the Gracehoper, and the play-
summary in the story of Honuphrius. (p. 50) There are some verses
in the metre of Browning's 'How They Brought the Good News
from Ghent to Aix', and innumerable parodies of songs, proverbs,
traditional sayings and passages from literature:

. . . meed of anthems here we pant!   (p. 41)
Maid of Athens, ere we part . . . (Byron)

Brawn is my name and broad is my nature   (p. 187)
Gamp is my name and gamp is my nater. *(Martin Chuzzlewit)*

. . . was Parish worth thette mess   (p. 199)
Paris vaut bien une messe. (Henri IV)

The groom is in the greenhouse, gattling out his. Gun! (p. 377)
The king was in the counting-house
Counting out his money.

Add lightest knot unto tiptition   (p. 561)
And lead us not into temptation.

half a league wrongwards   (p. 567)
Half a league onwards (Tennyson)

Guld modning, have yous viewsed Piers' aube?   (p. 593)
Good morning, have you used Pears' soap?

Among the parodies of specific originals is the case of a French
sentence from a work on history by Edgar Quinet, a thoroughly
exceptional instance which has been analysed in detail by Clive
Hart; it dwells on the fact that the flowers that bloomed in antiquity continue to flourish, in spite of the changes civilization has
undergone. Joyce rewrote this sentence five times and inserted
it at different places in the *Wake*, altering its content each time to
suit his context, and connecting it with new themes. As Hart says,

this is not really parody, but 'an altogether different art for which no adequate term seems to exist'.[40]

It can be seen, in fact, as a further development of modern parody, which differs from the traditional kind in adapting the expressive resources of its original to a new use instead of mocking it. In the *Cantos* and *The Waste Land* as we have seen, the echoes of recognizable styles often aim at rehabilitation rather than repudiation. The original is not discredited, but is heard as a part of the new text, so that an effect of multiplicity, which need not be ironic, is achieved. By imitating a specific expressive manner, the modern parodies isolate style from content. Like other modern techniques, they direct attention toward the medium and its capacities, and away from the subject. The reader's main experience with the parodic passages of *Finnegans Wake* consists of an identification, not with the characters and events of the story, but with the activity of the language, as it moulds, connects, amplifies or reverses its original. This experience is another instance of the 'dehumanization' Ortega y Gasset perceived in modern art which focuses upon matters of style; and its most conspicuous principles are those of *bricolage*, the rules that must be followed if old things are put to new uses. The parodies of *Finnegans Wake* thus represent a significant expansion of the resources of literary expression which moves in the same direction as many of the other modern techniques.

As Clive Hart has observed, much of the parody in the *Wake* is self-parody. Joyce's manuscripts show that he intended to include parodies of his earlier works in it, but limited himself to the sort of parodies of the text of the *Wake* itself that are inherent in the metamorphic development of the book. Joyce uses parody, says Hart, to deny that any way of expressing an idea can be the final one.[41] Vivian Mercier in *The Irish Comic Tradition*, connects the parodic elements of the *Wake* with Joyce's sense that Vico's cyclic view of history, and the general notion of repetition in history have their comic aspects. These observations, together with the nature of the *Wake's* affinities with other experimental works, tend to confirm what should be obvious: that what Joyce has accomplished with relation to language is the creation of a great verbal comedy. In the *Wake* no one meaning is ever fixed, no word ever achieves a stable form, no locution is ever final. Its idiom is fluid, uncommitted, ambiguous, like the dream images exploited by the Surrealists. It is independent of time, achieving a massive simultaneity through the dense interrelationship of its parts. Because the language participates in a kind of *bricolage*, it has the playfulness and tolerance of the chance effects found in

Dada and Surrealist creations. Through something resembling Futurist analogy, it regards all things in the cosmos as potentially identifiable with each other, so that even incongruities can be joined.

The analysts of the *Wake* usually conclude that there is no message to be found in it, no general statement about the spectacle of human life. That is because it has the purpose of freeing language rather than binding it to specific commitments. By terming the *Wake* 'a single gigantic anti-epiphany',[42] Northrop Frye elliptically makes the point that, while it focuses the diversity of history into a short length of time, it paradoxically opposes the epiphany's pretension that the meaning of life can be concentrated into the experience of a single moment. Instead, it takes the comic view that life is marvellously diverse and changeable, full of an uncontrollable vitality that assumes unpredictable forms which escape any single formulation. Its innovations express toward language that sense of freedom, openness and proportion which the great comic writers like Rabelais, Cervantes and Fielding express toward life. Joyce laughs aside the narrow fanatical notion that language is a medium of communication that matches material reality. For him, as for Cassirer, it is an expression of mind and spirit. It has no more specific animating idea than the comic vision: a mingling of intelligent perception and humane laughter capable of establishing vital new relationships, patterns and rhythms among the elements of a cosmos where the old ones have gone dead. In the *Wake*, Joyce says that he sees no inevitable doom for the word, the English language, or the universe of words as a whole, but finds them as open to renewal as the imagination itself.

NOTES

Where more than one date of publication is given, the edition used is usually the most recent reprint.

Introduction
1 F.M. Ford, 'Chroniques', *Transatlantic Review*, 2 (Dec. 1924) p. 683.
2 O. Paz, *Children of the Mire*, Harvard U.P. Cambridge, Mass. (1974) p. 134.
3 See R. Poggioli, *The Theory of the Avant-Garde*, Harvard U.P. Cambridge, Mass; Oxford U.P. (1969). Poggioli's terms for the four attitudes characteristic of the avant-garde are: *activism, nihilism, antagonism* and *agonism*.
4 T. S. Eliot, 'Contemporanea', *The Egoist*, 5 (June-July 1918) p. 84.
5 M. Foucault, *The Order of Things*, Tavistock, London; Pantheon, New York (1970) p. xx.
6 Poggioli *op. cit.* pp. 131–7 for discussion of experimentalism.
7 E. Pound, *Polite Essays*, Faber, London (1937) New Directions, New York (1940) p. 149.
8 T. S. Eliot, 'The Social Function of Poetry', *On Poetry and Poets*, Faber, London (1957); Noonday Press, New York (1961) p. 7.
9 N. Frye, *Anatomy of Criticism*, Atheneum, New York (1966) pp. 97–8.

Chapter I : Experimental Motives
1 E. Cassirer, *The Philosophy of Symbolic Forms*, trans. R. Manheim (1953) Yale U.P. New Haven and London, 3rd printing (1961) vol. I, p. 78.
2 *Ibid.* p. 93, 111.
3 E. Pound, 'The Serious Artist', in *Literary Essays*, (ed.) T.S. Eliot, Faber, London; New Directions, New York (1954) reprint (1968) p. 44, and 'Vorticism', *Fortnightly Review*, 96. n.s. (1 September 1914) p. 465–6.
4 S.L. Goldberg, *The Classical Temper*, Chatto & Windus, London; Barnes & Noble, New York (1961) p. 262.
5 R. Barthes, 'Écrivains et Écrivants', *Essais Critiques*, Paris (1964) pp. 150–1.
6 R. Barthes, 'Writing and Silence', *Writing Degree Zero and Elements of Semiology*, Editions du Seuil, Paris (1953) trans. A. Lavers and C. Smith, Jonathan Cape, London (1967) Beacon Press, Boston (1968) p. 78.
7 M. Foucault, *The Order of Things*, Tavistock, London; Pantheon, New York (1970) p. 298.
8 E. Pound, *Literary Essays*, p. 21.
9 W.C. Williams, 'A 1 Pound Stein', in *Selected Essays of William Carlos Williams*, Random House, New York (1954) p. 164.
10 E. Pound, 'Vorticism', pp. 461–71. What I am loosely calling the autonomous mode in the arts is an essential concept in experimental poetics, yet it is too large and varied a manifestation to be discussed effectively here. Accounts of

it which I have borne in mind in examining linguistic experiment include the following general discussions: R. Shattuck, 'The Art of Stillness', chapter 11 of *The Banquet Years* (1958) reprint Doubleday Garden City, N.Y. (1961); J. Ortega y Gasset 'The Dehumanization of Art', *The Dehumanization of Art and Other Writings*, Doubleday Anchor Books, Garden City, N.Y. (n.d.); W. Sypher, 'The New World of Relationships: Camera and Cinema', in *Rococo to Cubism in Art and Literature* (1960) reprinted Vintage Books, New York (1965); R. Poggioli, *The Theory of the Avant-Garde*; and the following discussions of autonomy in literature: S.K. Langer, 'Poesis', chap. 13, *Feeling and Form*, Scribner's, New York; Routledge & Kegan Paul, London (1953); E. Vivas, 'What is a Poem?' in *Creation and Discovery*, Noonday Press, New York (1955); Y. Winters, *In Defence of Reason*, Alan Swallow, New York (1937) reprinted, Denver (1947); F. Jameson, *The Prison-House of Language*, Princeton U.P. (1972); G.L. Bruns, *Modern Poetry and the Idea of Language*, Yale U.P. New Haven (1973); S. Burkhardt, 'The Poet as Fool and Priest', *ELH*, vol. 23 (1956) pp. 279–98; O. Paz, *Children of the Mire*, trans. R. Phillips, Harvard U.P. Cambridge, Mass. (1974). The possibility or desirability of autonomy in literature remains a subject of active debate. See, for example, G. Graff, *Poetic Statement and Critical Dogma*, Northwestern U.P. Evanston (1970); E. Wasiolek's introduction to S. Doubrovsky, *The New Criticism in France*, trans. D. Coltman, Chicago U.P. (1973).

11 E.M. Forster, 'Anonymity', *Calendar of Modern Letters*, 2 (Nov. 1925) p. 150.

12 D.D. Paige (ed.) *The Letters of Ezra Pound 1907–41*, Harcourt, Brace, and World, New York (1950), Faber, London (1951) p. 90.

13 G.M. Hopkins, 'Parmenides' and 'Notes, February 9, 1868', *Journals and Papers*, (eds) H. House and G. Storey, Oxford U.P. London (1959) pp. 129, 125.

14 W.C. Williams, *Spring and All: Imaginations*, (ed.) Webster Schott, New Directions, New York; MacGibbon & Kee, London (1970) p. 117.

15 See R. Barthes, 'L' Activité Structuraliste' in *Essais Critiques*, pp. 213–20.

16 E. Muir, 'James Joyce: The Meaning of *Ulysses*', *Calendar of Modern Letters*, 1 (July 1925) p. 347.

17 M. Abrams, *The Mirror and the Lamp*, Oxford U.P. London and New York (1953) reprinted The Norton Library, New York (1958) pp. 272–5.

18 R. Poggioli, *op. cit.* p. 38.

19 J. Ortega y Gasset, *op. cit.* pp. 35, 34.

20 W. Stevens, 'The Noble Rider and the Sound of Words', *The Necessary Angel*, Knopf, New York (1951) p. 32.

21 C. Lévi-Strauss, *The Savage Mind*, Weidenfeld & Nicolson, London (1966) reprint Chicago (1968) pp. 29–30.

22 See M. Krieger, *A Window to Criticism*, Princeton U.P. (1964) pp. 3–70 for a critical survey which describes some of this debate.

23 M. Foucault, *The Order of Things*, p. 103.

24 W. Kandinsky, 'The Inner Necessity', *Blast* no. 1 (June 1914) p. 123.

25 L. Wittgenstein, *Tractatus Logico-Philosophicus*, German text, trans. by D.F. Pears and B.F. McGuinness, Routledge & Kegan Paul, London (1961) p. 15.

26 M. Black, *A Companion to Wittgenstein's Tractatus*, Cornell U.P. Ithaca, N.Y. (1964) pp. 331 ff.

27 W.C. Williams, *Spring and All: Imaginations*, p. 129.

28   W.C. Williams, Prologue to *Kora in Hell : Imaginations*, pp. 16–17.
29   W.C. Williams, *Spring and All : Imaginations*, p. 111.
30   *Ibid.* p. 149.
31   E. Pound, 'Prefatio aut Cimicium Tumulus', *Polite Essays*, Faber, London (1937); New Directions, New York (1940) p. 151.
32   W.C. Williams, *Spring and All : Imaginations*, p. 149.
33   C. Bernard, *An Introduction to the Study of Experimental Medicine*, trans. H.C. Greene, Henry Schuman, New York (1949) p. 32.
34   V. Shklovsky, 'Art as Technique' in *Russian Formalist Criticism: Four Essays*, trans. with intro. by L.T. Lemon and M.J. Reis, Nebraska U.P. Lincoln, Nebraska (1965).
35   O. Barfield, *Poetic Diction* (1928) reprint Faber, London (1952) p. 107.
36   E. Kris, 'Aesthetic Ambiguity', *Psychoanalytic Explorations in Art*, Schocken Books, New York; Baily, London (1952) reprinted Schocken Books (1964) pp. 251–5.
37   W.C. Williams, 'Caviar and Bread Again', in *Selected Essays*, p. 103.
38   O. Paz, *Children of the Mire*, p. 148.
39   M. Foucault, *The Order of Things*, pp. 251–2.
40   S. Gilbert (ed.), *Letters of James Joyce*, Viking Press, Faber, London (1966) vol. I, p. 140.

Chapter II : Toward Reality
1   W. Lewis, *Time and Western Man*, Chatto & Windus, London (1927) reprinted Beacon Press, Boston (1957) p. 113.
2   L. Aragon, *Le Paysan de Paris*, Paris (1926) p. 69. In a review of this book in *transition*, April, 1927, Robert Sage interpreted the poem as meaning that Aragon finds only the syllables of reality 'artistically usable', and believes that reality itself is a hallucination. The poem is quoted—not quite accurately—in William Carlos Williams's *Paterson*.
3   W. Worringer, *Abstraction and Empathy*, trans. M. Bullock, Routledge and Kegan Paul, London; International Universities Press, New York (1953) p. 11.
4   W.C. Williams, Prologue to *Kora in Hell; Imaginations*, p. 14.
5   W. Lewis, *Time and Western Man*, op. cit. pp. 165–6.
6   *Ibid.* pp. 304–5.
7   T.S. Eliot, *Knowledge and Experience in the Philosophy of F.H. Bradley*, Faber, London (1964) p. 18. For the influence of Bradley's views on Eliot's poems, see H. Kenner, *The Invisible Poet*, Obolensky (1959) reprinted Citadel Press, New York (1964) pp. 43–69; reprinted W.H. Allen, London (1960).
8   T.S. Eliot, 'Leibniz', Monads and Bradley's Finite Centres', *Monist*, 26 (Oct. 1916) pp. 566–76.
9   H. Bergson, *Creative Evolution*, trans. A. Mitchell, Modern Library, New York (1944) p. 14.
10   H. Bergson, *Matter and Memory* trans. N.M. Paul and W.S. Palmer (1911) Doubleday Anchor Books Garden City, N.Y. (1959) p. 192. Original French publication, 1896.
11   A.N. Whitehead, *Science and the Modern World*, Cambridge U.P. (1925) reprinted New American Library, New York (1964) pp. 84–5.
12   *Ibid.* p. 70.

13 E. Fenollosa, *The Chinese Written Character as a Medium for Poetry*, City Lights Books, San Francisco (n.d.) p. 11.

14 J.M. Brinnin, *The Third Rose*, Atlantic Monthly Press, Boston; Weidenfeld and Nicolson, London (1959) p. 64.

15 W. James, chapter IX, 'The Stream of Thought', *Principles of Psychology* (1890) reprinted Dover Publications (1950) vol. I, p. 241.

16 G. Stein, *Selected Writings*, (ed.) Carl Van Vechten, Random House, New York (1946) p. 218.

17 G. Stein, *Narration : Four Lectures*, Chicago U.P. (1935) p. 17.

18 S.K. Kumar, *Bergson and the Stream of Consciousness Novel*, Blackie, Glasgow (1962) p. 105.

19 B.L. Reid, *Art by Subtraction*, Oklahoma U.P. Norman (1958) p. 49.

20 H. Bergson, *op. cit.* p. 143.

21 *Ibid.* pp. 57–8.

22 G. Stein, *Selected Writings*, pp. 230–1.

23 *Ibid.* p. 231.

24 G. Stein, *Lectures in America*, New York (1935) p. 176, 191.

25 R.B. Haas (ed.) *A Primer for the Gradual Understanding of Gertrude Stein*, Black Sparrow Press, Los Angeles (1971) p. 25.

26 G. Stein, *Selected Writings*, p. 407.

27 For these comments, see M. Hoffman, *The Development of Abstractionism in the Writings of Gertrude Stein*, Pennsylvania U.P. Philadelphia (1965) pp. 183–4; R. Bridgman, *Gertrude Stein in Pieces*, Oxford U.P. New York (1974) pp. 127–8; A. Stewart, *Gertrude Stein and the Present* Harvard, U.P. Cambridge, Mass. (1967), p. 93.

28 G. Stein, *op. cit.* p. 408.

29 N. Frye *Anatomy of Criticism*, Atheneum, New York (1966) p. 337.

30 H. Bergson, *Matter and Memory*, pp. 56–7.

31 Letter to William Carlos Williams, October 21, 1908. *The Letters of Ezra Pound*, (ed.) D.D. Paige, Harcourt, Brace, and World, New York (1950), Faber, London (1951) p.6.

32 T.E. Hulme, 'Bergson's Theory of Art', *Speculations*, (ed.) H. Read, Kegan, Paul, London (1924), reprinted Harcourt, Brace, New York (n.d.) pp. 162–3.

33 *Ibid.* pp. 162, 167.

34 T.E. Hulme, 'Notes on Language and Style', *Further Speculations*, (ed.) S. Hynes, Minnesota U.P. Minneapolis (1955); Oxford U.P. London (1956) p. 80.

35 H.N. Schneidau, *Ezra Pound : The Image and the Real*, Louisiana State U.P. Baton Rouge (1969), pp. 77–84.

36 These sentences bring together phrases from the following sources: a letter to Harriet Monroe, January, 1915, *Letters*, p. 49; 'How to Read', *Literary Essays*, p. 21 : and *Guide to Kulchur*, Faber, London (1938) p. 285.

37 E. Pound, 'T.S. Eliot', *Literary Essays*, p. 420.

38 D. Davie, *Ezra Pound : The Poet as Sculptor*, Routledge & Kegan Paul, London; Oxford U.P. New York (1964) p. 177.

39 E. Pound, *Personae*, Faber, London (1952) p. 177. Quotations from this edition will be identified by page numbers included in the text.

40 E. Pound, 'The Wisdom of Poetry', *Forum*, 47 (Apr. 1912) p. 498.

41 E. Pound, 'Vorticism', *Fortnightly Review*, 1914, p. 464.

42 E. Fenollosa, *The Chinese Written Character as a Medium for Poetry*, p. 8.

43 W.C. Williams, 'A Novelette', *Imaginations*, pp. 295–6.

44 W.C. Williams, *Spring and All; Imaginations*, pp. 121, 150.

45   W.C. Williams, Prologue to *Kora in Hell; Imaginations*, p. 19.
46   W.C. Williams, *Spring and All; Imaginations*, p. 150.
47   W.C. Williams, 'Marianne Moore', *Imaginations*, p. 316.
48   W.C. Williams, *Spring and All; Imaginations*, p. 151.
49   W.C. Williams, 'The Avenue of Poplars', *The Collected Earlier Poems of William Carlos Williams*, New Directions, New York (1951) p. 280. Quotations from this volume will be identified by page numbers included in the text.
50   E.E. Cummings, *Poems, 1923–1954*, Harcourt, Brace, New York (1954) p. 62. Quotations from this volume will be identified by page numbers included in the text.
51   I.A. Richards, 'Science and Poetry', *Psyche*, vol. VI, no. 2 (Oct. 1925) p. 260.
52   E. Pound, *Literary Essays*, p. 42.
53   *Ibid.* p. 399.
54   E.E. Phare, 'Valéry and Gerard Hopkins', *Experiment*, I, Undated [November, 1928] pp. 19–23.
55   J. Epstein, 'The New Conditions of Literary Phenomena', *Broom*, II (April, 1922) p. 6.
56   R. Aldington, 'The Poet and His Age', *Chapbook*, No. 29 (September, 1922), p. 8.
57   The resemblances are pointed out by Louis Kampf in *On Modernism*, pp. 3–5, where a description of a Futurist performance in Milan in 1914 is quoted.
58   F. Marinetti, 'Discours futuriste aux anglais', *Le Futurisme*, Paris (1911) pp. 21–32. Most of the Futurist documents are included in *I Manifesti del Futurismo* (Milano, n.d.), 4 volumes (No. 168 of *Raccolta di Breviari Intellettuali*, Istituto Editoriale Italiano, Milano).
59   R.F. Smalley 'Futurism and the Futurists', *British Review*, 7 (Aug. 1914) pp. 222–37.
60   F. Marinetti, *Zang Tumb Tuuum*, Milano (1914) p. 42. 'smoke of the volcano roll-call thrown at the Vesuviuses Strombolis   perfidy of vegetation = disguises of the threatening earthquake of a garden too perfumed with the spicy odor of danger   powder-magazine + will + comfort + mindlessness of nocturnal insemination = Messina'.
61   F. Marinetti, *I Manifesti*, II, 224. 'The sonorous yet abstract expression of an emotion of pure thought.'
62   F. Marinetti, *Zang Tumb Tuuum*, p. 35.
63   S.K. Langer, *Feeling and Form*, Routledge & Kegan Paul, London; Scribners, New York (1953), p. 45.
64   W. Nowottny, *The Language Poets Use*, Athlone Press, London (1965) p. 45.
65   L. Aragon, *Les Collages* Paris, (1965) pp. 29, 45.
66   Quoted in F. Gilot and C. Lake, *Life with Picasso*, McGraw-Hill, New York (1964), p. 77.
67   L. Aragon, *op. cit.* p. 116.
68   W.C. Williams, 'A Novelette', *Imaginations*, p. 300.
69   B. Dijkstra, *The Hieroglyphics of a New Speech*, Chapter 2, Princeton U.P. (1969).
70   W.C. Williams, *Paterson*, New Directions, New York (1949–63) MacGibbon and Kee, London (1964) vol. V, no pagination.
71   R.M. Adams, *Surface and Symbol*, Oxford U.P. New York (1962) pp. 247–8.
72   E. Pound, *Guide to Kulchur*, p. 98.

73 E. Pound, *The Cantos*, New Directions, New York (1970); Faber, London (1975), p. 171. Quotations from the New York edition will be identified by page numbers in the text.

74 See G. Smith, Jr., *T.S. Eliot's Poetry and Plays* (Chicago 1956), pp. 62–3.

75 T.S. Eliot, 'The Modern Mind', *The Use of Poetry and the Use of Criticism*, Faber, London (1933) reprinted (1964) p. 126.

76 R. Shattuck, *The Banquet Years*, Doubleday, Garden City, N.Y. (1961) pp. 329–30.

77 J. Joyce, *A Portrait of the Artist as a Young Man*, The Viking Press, New York (1966) p. 11.

Chapter III : Acts of Mind

1 H. Bergson, *Matter and Memory*, trans. N.M. Paul and W.S. Palmer (1911) reprinted Doubleday Anchor Books, Garden City N.Y. (1959) pp. 177–8.

2 E. Cassirer, *The Philosophy of Symbolic Forms*, trans. R. Manheim (1953) Yale U.P. New Haven and London, 3rd printing (1961) vol. I, p. 113.

3 E. Pound, *The Spirit of Romance* (1910) reprinted Peter Owen, London; New Directions, New York (1953) p. 92.

4 E.E. Cummings, *Poems 1923–1954*, Harcourt, Brace, and World, New York (1954) p. 144.

5 H. Bergson, *op. cit.* p. 116.

6 H. Bergson, *Time and Free Will* (1910) reprinted Harper & Bros. New York (1960) pp. 130–2; 164–5.

7 W. Stevens, *The Necessary Angel* (New York, 1951), p. 36.

8 W. Nowottny, *The Language Poets Use*, Athlone Press, London (1965) p. 186.

9 L. Wittgenstein, *Philosophical Investigations*, p. 82.

10 F. Marinetti, *I Manifesti del Futurismo*, I, 134–44.

11 *Ibid*. II, 85–106.

12 *Ibid*. II, 100.

13 For an account of these performances, see H. Richter, *Dada : Art and Anti-Art*, McGraw-Hill, New York (1965), pp. 19 ff.

14 T. Tzara, *La Première Aventure Céleste de Mr. Antipyrine* (Collection Dada, 1916). The French quotations mean (approximately): 'bitter synthesis on the church of curtains'; 'there is no humanity there are reverberations and dogs'; and 'we have become reverberations, then they left'. The pages in this volume are not numbered.

15 T. Tzara, reprinted in R. Motherwell's, *The Dada Painters and Poets*, Wittenborn, New York (1951) p. 86.

16 M. Foucault, *The Order of Things*, Tavistock, London; Pantheon, New York (1970) p. 103.

17 'Reconnaissance à Dada', *Nouvelle Revue Française*, 15 (1920), p. 221, 234. 'Language, for the Dadas, is no longer a medium; it is a being.' 'Every word, from the moment it is uttered, or even envisaged in a flash by the spirit, has a relationship with it. Every word is therefore justifiable, expressive, no matter what other word it succeeds, no matter when it is offered, no matter what it reveals.'

18 Quoted from Tzara's 'Essai sur la situation de la poésie,' *Le Surréalisme au service de la Révolution*, 4 (1934) in Nadeau, *Histoire du Surréalisme*, Editions du Seuil, (Paris 1945) p. 58. 'Let us denounce immediately a misunderstanding which seeks to class poetry under the heading of means of

expression. Poetry which is not distinguishable from novels by its external form, poetry which expresses ideas or sentiments, interests no one. To it I oppose poetry that is an *activity of the spirit*.'

19 A. Breton, 'Les Mots sans rides', *Les Pas perdus* Gallimard, Paris (1924) pp. 167, 168–9. 'I began by defying words, but suddenly I came to see that they had to be treated differently from those little auxiliaries for which I had always taken them.' 'It is a small intractable world, over which we can only keep an insufficient watch. . . . There are words which work against the idea which they try to express. Finally even the meaning of words is not without admixture, and it is difficult to determine to what degree the figurative meaning progressively affects the proper meaning, since to each variation of the latter must correspond a variation of the former.'

20 A. Breton, 'Premier Manifeste du surréalisme' (1924), *Les Manifestes du Surréalisme*, Paris (1946) p. 55. 'Language was given to man so that he could make a Surrealist use of it.'

21 This information about Desnos, Vitrac and Leiris, together with the examples, is from J.H. Matthews, *Surrealist Poetry in France*, Syracuse U.P. Syracuse (1969).

22 A Breton, 'On Surrealism in its Living Works', *Manifestoes of Surrealism*, trans. R. Seaver and H.R. Lane, Michigan U.P. Ann Arbor (1969) p. 297.

23 T.E. Hulme, *Speculations*, (ed.) H. Read, Kegan Paul, London (1924) reprinted Harcourt, Brace, New York (n.d.) p. 158.

24 T.E. Hulme, 'Notes on Language and Style', *Further Speculations*, (ed.) S. Hynes, Minnesota U.P. Minneapolis (1955); Oxford U.P. London (1956) p. 86.

25 T.E. Hulme, *Speculations*, p. 165. In *Time and Free Will*, Bergson says: 'I smell a rose and immediately confused recollections of childhood come back to my memory. . . . To others it will smell differently.—It is always the same scent, you will say, but associated with different ideas—I am quite willing that you should express yourself in this way; but do not forget that you have first removed the personal element from the different impressions which the rose makes on each one of us; you have retained only the objective aspect, that part of the scent of the rose which is public property and thereby belongs to space.' (pp. 161–2).

26 T.E. Hulme, 'Notes on Language and Style', *Further Speculations*, p. 78.

27 T.E. Hulme, *Speculations*, p. 162.

28 E. Pound, *Guide to Kulchur*, Faber, London (1938) p. 126.

29 E. Pound, *The Spirit of Romance*, p. 14.

30 E. Pound, 'The Serious Artist', *Literary Essays*, (ed.) T.S. Eliot, Faber, London; New Directions, New York (1954) reprinted (1968) pp. 53–4.

31 See R.H. Pearce, *The Continuity of American Poetry*, Princeton U.P. (1961) pp. 71 ff.

32 This formulation is from L.S. Dembo's *Conceptions of Reality in Modern American Poetry*, California U.P. Berkeley (1966) p. 4.

33 'Vorticism', *Fortnightly Review*, 1 September 1914, p. 463.

34 T.S. Eliot, *Complete Poems and Plays 1909–1950*, Harcourt, Brace and World, p. 22. Quotations from this volume will be identified by page numbers included in the text.

35 'Tradition and the Individual Talent', *Selected Essays*, p. 4.

36 See D. Van Ghent, *The English Novel*, Rinehart, New York (1953) pp. 263–76.

37 J. Joyce, *A Portrait of the Artist as a Young Man*, Viking Press, New York

(1966) p. 176. Quotations from this edition will be identified by page numbers included in the text.

38 H. Kenner, 'The Portrait in Perspective', in *James Joyce: Two Decades of Criticism*, (ed.) Sean Givens, Vanguard Press, New York (1948) p. 148. This article demonstrates the complexity of the verbal effects. See also 'The Artist and the Rose' by B. Seward, *University of Toronto Quarterly*, January, 1957.

39 In *Time and Western Man*, Wyndham Lewis disapproved of *Ulysses* because he thought it betrayed the influence of time-oriented thinkers like Einstein and Bergson; S.K. Kumar, in his study of Bergson's influence on fiction regards *Ulysses* and Bergson's works as parallel manifestations of the modern interest in mental reality. See S.K. Kumar, *Bergson and the Stream of Consciousness Novel*, Blackie, Glasgow (1962) pp. 106–7. Kumar quotes Bergson's observation that mental life might be composed of a single unbroken sentence, a description that Joyce might have taken as a model for Molly Bloom's soliloquy.

40 J. Joyce, *Ulysses* New York (1961) p. 42. Quotations from this edition will be identified by page numbers included in the text.

41 S.L. Goldberg, *The Classical Temper*, Chatto & Windus London; Barnes & Noble, New York (1961) p. 252, p. 73.

42 A Goldman, *The Joyce Paradox*, Northwestern U.P. Evanston (1966) p. 98.

43 J. Joyce, *Finnegans Wake*, Faber London; Viking Press, New York (1959) p. 23. Quotations from this edition will be identified by page numbers included in the text.

44 D. Hayman, 'From *Finnegans Wake*: A Sentence in Progress', *PMLA*, 73 (1958) pp. 136–54; and C. Hart, 'The Elephant in the Belly: Exegesis of *Finnegans Wake*', *A Wake Digest*, Sydney (1968) p. 4.

45 E. Cassirer, *Philosophy of Symbolic Forms*, vol. I, pp. 93, 108.

46 H. Bergson, *Time and Free Will*, pp. 133–4.

47 E. Cassirer, *op. cit.* vol. I, p. 92.

48 E. Fenollosa, *The Chinese Written Character as a Medium for Poetry*, City Lights Books, San Francisco (n.d.) pp. 22–3.

49 W. Nowottny, *The Language Poets Use*, p. 83.

50 S.K. Langer, *Feeling and Form*, Routledge & Kegan Paul, London; Scribner's, New York (1953) p. 59.

Chapter IV : Form and Language

1 G. Steiner, 'The Language Animal', *Extraterritorial*, New York (1971) p. 90.

2 F. Budgen, *James Joyce and the Making of Ulysses*, Grayson and Grayson, London (1934) pp. 56–7.

3 R.W. Chambers (ed.) *Form and Style in Poetry*, Macmillan, London (1928) pp. 97, 98.

4 E. Pound, *The Spirit of Romance* (1910) Peter Owen, London; reprinted New Directions, New York (1953) p. 88.

5 W. Lewis, *Time and Western Man*, Chatto & Windus, London (1927) Beacon Press, Boston (1957) p. 116.

6 W.C. Williams, *Spring and All; Imaginations*, New Directions, New York; MacGibbon & Kee (1970) p. 133.

7 *Ibid.* p.134.

8 T.S. Eliot, 'The Music of Poetry', *On Poetry and Poets*, Faber, London (1957); Noonday Press, New York (1961) p. 31.

9   W. Lewis, *op. cit.* p. 121.

10   E.E. Cummings, *A Miscellany Revised*, (ed.) G.J. Firmage, October House, New York; London, Peter Owen (1965), p. 27; originally published in *The Dial*, June, 1920. By 'static', 'a school', etc. Cummings meant Pound and the Vorticist movement, which are attacked in the previous paragraph.

11   T.S. Eliot, 'Reflections on *Vers Libre*', *New Statesman*, 8 (March 3, 1917), 518–519.

12   T.E. Hulme, 'A Lecture on Modern Poetry', *Further Speculations*, Minnesota U.P. Minneapolis (1955) Oxford U.P. London (1956) pp. 74–5.

13   G. Lukacs, *The Meaning of Contemporary Realism*, Merlin Press, London (1963).

14   E. Pound, *Gaudier-Brzeska : A Memoir*, John Lane, The Bodley Head, London (1916) p. 148.

15   'Wireless Imagination and Words at Liberty , The New Futurist Manifesto' trans. Arundel del Re, *Poetry and Drama*, 1 (Sept. 1913) 319–326.

16   F. Marinetti 'Manifesto Tecnico,' *I Manifesti del Futurismo*, II, 101–2. 'We will arrive one day at a more essential art, when we will dare to suppress all the first terms of our analogies, in order to give no more than the uninterrupted sequence of second terms. . . . To be understood is not necessary.'

17   G. Hough, *Reflections on a Literary Revolution*, Washington, DC. (1960) pp. 25–6.

18   See R. Shattuck, *The Banquet Years*, pp. 335–9. Doubleday Anchor Books, Garden City, N.Y., 1961.

19   H. Kenner, *The Pound Era*, California U.P. Berkeley; Faber, London (1972) 54–75. Reprinted from 'The Muse in Tatters', *Arion* 7 (1968) pp. 212–33.

20   V. Larbaud, 'The "Ulysses" of James Joyce', *Criterion*, 1 (Oct. 1922) 102.

21   A.W. Litz, *The Art of James Joyce*, Oxford U.P. London (1961) pp. 4–33.

22   F.M. Ford, 'The Poet's Eye', *The New Freewoman*, 6 (1 Sept. 1913) 109.

23   E. Fenollosa, *The Chinese Written Character as a Medium for Poetry*, City Lights Books, San Francisco (n.d.) p. 32.

24   G. Hough, *op. cit.* p. 32.

25   R.M. Adams, *Surface and Symbol*, Oxford U.P. New York (1962) p. 85.

26   E. Pound, *Guide to Kulchur*, Faber, London (1938) p. 188.

27   F. Marinetti 'Manifesto Tecnico,' *I Manifesti del Futurismo*, II, 89. 'Analogy is nothing else but the profound love which binds together distant things apparently diverse and hostile.'

28   F. Marinetti, 'Wireless Imagination and Words at Liberty', *Poetry and Drama*, 1(Sept. 1913) 322.

29   T.E. Hulme, 'Notes on Language and Style', *Further Speculations*, pp. 80–91.

30   C. Hart, *Structure and Motif in Finnegans Wake*, Northwestern U.P. Evanston (1962) pp. 48–62.

31   Quoted by T.H. Jackson in *The Early Poetry of Ezra Pound*, Harvard U.P. Cambridge, Mass. (1968) p. 32.

32   A.L. Taylor *The White Knight* Oliver & Boyd, Edinburgh (1952) pp. 83–93.

33   C. Brooks, 'The Waste Land: The Critique of a Myth', *Modern Poetry and the Tradition* North Carolina U.P. Chapel Hill; Oxford, U.P. London (1939) pp.136–72.

34   E. Pound 'Dr. Williams's Position', *Literary Essays* Faber, London; New Directions, New York (1954) reprinted (1968) pp. 394–5.

35   E. Pound, 'The Alien Eye', *The New Age*, 12 (Jan. 1913).

36 E. Pound, *Gaudier-Brzeska : A Memoir*, pp. 9–13; first published in *Blast*, 1 (June 1914).

37 E. Pound, *Literary Essays*, pp. 214–26.

38 E. Pound, 'Vorticism', *Fortnightly Review*, 96 n.s. (1 Sept. 1914), p. 469.

39 H. Kenner, *The Poetry of Ezra Pound* Faber, London (1951) pp. 233, 200.

40 For a thorough analysis of Canto IV, in which this passage occurs, see W. Baumann, *The Rose in the Steel Dust* Bern (1967) pp. 19–53.

41 T.E. Hulme, *Speculations*, (ed.) H. Read, Routledge & Kegan Paul, London (1924) reprinted Harcourt, Brace, New York (n.d.) p. 180.

42 G.M. Hopkins, *Letters to Bridges*, Letter XL, May 13, 1878, p. 50.

43 G.M. Hopkins, 'Poetry and Verse', *Journals and Papers*, (eds) H. House and G. Storey, Oxford U.P. London (1959) p. 289.

44 S.L. Goldberg, *The Classical Temper*, chap. V, 'Homer and the Nightmare of History', Chatto & Windus, London; Barnes & Noble, New York (1961).

45 F. Budgen, *James Joyce and the Making of Ulysses*, p. 21.

46 G.M. Hopkins, 'Notes, February 9, 1968', *Journals and Papers*, p. 126.

47 A.W. Litz, *The Art of James Joyce*, pp. 13–17, 22–34.

48 Quoted from *Introduction à la Philosophie de l'Histoire de l'Humanité* in *The Books at the Wake* by James S. Atherton, p. 35. 'History is reflected and inscribed in the depths of our souls in such a manner that he who is truly sensitive to its interior movements would find the whole series of centuries as if enshrouded in his thoughts ... I perceived, for the first time, the nearly infinite number of beings like myself who have preceded me ....'

49 J. Ortega y Gasset *The Dehumanization of Art*, Doubleday Anchor Books, Garden City, N.Y. (n.d.) pp. 8–11.

50 W. Worringer, 'Art Questions of the Day', *Criterion*, 6 (Aug. 1927) p. 112.

51 G.M. Hopkins, *op. cit.* p. 126.

52 F. Budgen, *op. cit.* pp. 171–2.

53 E. Sewell, *The Structure of Poetry*, Routledge & K. Paul, London (1951) pp. 113–20.

54 C. Lévi-Strauss, *The Savage Mind*, pp. 16–22.

55 T.E. Hulme, 'Notes on Language and Style', *Further Speculations*, p. 84.

56 W. Heisenberg, 'Recent Changes in the Foundation of Exact Science', *Philosophic Problems of Nuclear Science*, New York (1952) pp. 15–16.

57 G.M. Hopkins, February 24, 1873, *Journals and Papers*, p. 230.

58 T.E. Hulme, *op. cit.* p. 95.

59 C. Hart, *Structure and Motif*, p. 35.

60 J.S. Atherton, 'Finnegans Wake: The Gist of the Pantomime', *Accent*, 15 (Winter 1955) 14.

Chapter V : Abstraction and Language

1 P. Mondrian, *Plastic Art and Pure Plastic Art*, quoted in *The Forms of Things Unknown* by H. Read, Faber, London (1960) p. 163.

2 W. Lewis, 'A Review of Contemporary Art', *Blast*, 2 (1915) pp. 38–47.

3 T.E. Hulme, 'Modern Art and Its Philosophy', a paper read on 22 January 1914, *Speculations*, (ed.) H. Read, Kegan Paul, London (1924) reprinted Harcourt, Brace, New York (n.d.) pp. 75–109.

4 W. Worringer, *Abstraction and Empathy*, trans. M. Bullock, Routledge & Kegan Paul, London; International Universities Press, New York (1953) p. 40.

5   M. Foucault, *The Order of Things*, Tavistock, London; Pantheon, New York (1970) p. 113.
6   Quoted in Pound's 'Vortex Gaudier-Brzeska', *Gaudier-Brzeska : A Memoir*, John Lane, The Bodley Head, London (1916) p. 20.
7   *Wyndham Lewis and Vorticism*, programme for a Tate Gallery exhibition, October, 1956.
8   W. Lewis, 'The New Egos', *Blast*, 1 (1914) 141.
9   E. Pound *op. cit.* p. 130.
10 E. Pound, *Literary Essays*, (ed.) T.S. Eliot, Faber, London; New Directions, New York (1954) reprinted (1968) pp. 441, 444.
11 Quoted in R. Motherwell, *The Dada Painters and Poets*, Wittenborn, New York (1951) xix.
12 G. Stein, 'Composition as Explanation', *Selected Writings*, (ed.) C. Van Vechten, Random House, New York (1946) p. 458.
13 W.C. Williams, 'Marianne Moore', *Imaginations*, New Directions, New York; MacGibbon & Kee, London (1970) pp. 309, 313.
14 W.C. Williams, 'The Work of Gertrude Stein', *ibid*, pp. 349–50.
15 W.C. Williams, 'Marianne Moore', *ibid*, p. 312.
16 J.H. Miller, *Poets of Reality* Harvard U.P. Cambridge, Mass. (1965) Oxford U.P. London (1966) pp. 311–28.
17 Quoted from Williams in 'Introduction' by R. Jarrell *Selected Poems* New Directions, New York (1949) p. xvi.
18 W.C. Williams, 'Comment', *Selected Essays* Random House, New York (1954) p. 28.
19 C. Norman, *The Magic Maker* Bobbs-Merrill, Indianapolis (1972) p. 309.
20 R.P. Blackmur, 'Notes on E.E. Cummings' Language', *Form and Value in Modern Poetry* Doubleday Anchor Books, Garden City, N.Y. (1957) pp. 287–312. This essay originally appeared in *Hound and Horn* in 1931, and has often been reprinted.
21 E. Pound, 'How to Read', *Literary Essays*, p. 25.

Chapter VI : Imagery and Other Resources

1   H. Bergson, *Matter and Memory*, trans. N.M. Paul and W.S. Palmer (1911) Doubleday Anchor Books, Garden City, N.Y. (1959) p. 20.
2   Aristotle, *The 'Art' of Rhetoric*, trans. J.H. Freese, Loeb Classical Library, III, II, p. 359.
3   V. Shklovsky, 'Art as Technique', *Russian Formalist Criticism; Four Essays*, trans. with intro. L.T. Lemon and M.J. Reis, Nebraska U.P. Lincoln (1965) pp. 3–24.
4   Marinetti, *Zang Tumb Tuuum*, Milano (1914) pp. 37–8.
5   Reprinted in R. Motherwell's *The Dada Painters and Poets*, Wittenborn, New York (1951) p. 226.
6   The phrase "le stupéfiant *image*" occurs in *Le Paysan de Paris*, Paris (1926) p. 81.
7   T.E. Hulme, *Speculations*, (ed.) H. Read, Kegan Paul, London (1924) reprinted Harcourt, Brace, New York (n.d.) pp. 135, 164, 134.
8   *Ibid.* pp. 265–7. Some new poems by Hulme have been published in *Thomas Ernest Hulme*, A.R. Jones, Gollancz, London; Beacon Press, Boston (1960).

9   T.S. Eliot, 'Conclusion', *The Use of Poetry and the Use of Criticism*, Faber, London (1933) reprinted (1964) pp. 144–5.

10 W. Lewis, reprinted in *A Soldier of Humor and Selected Writings*, (ed.) R. Rosenthal, Signet Classics, New York (1966) pp. 74–105.

11 E. Pound, 'Vorticism', *Fortnightly Review*, 96 n.s. (1 September 1914) p. 463.

12 E. Pound, *Literary Essays*, p. 4; 'Vorticism', *Fortnightly Review*, pp. 463, 466.

13 E. Pound, 'Early Translators of Homer', *Literary Essays*, p. 267.

14 E. Pound, 'Cavalcanti', *Ibid*. p. 154.

15 E. Pound, 'Vorticism', *Fortnightly Review*, p. 464.

16 L.S. Dembo, *Conceptions of Reality in American Poetry*, California U.P. Berkeley (1966) pp. 11–13, 46–47.

17 E. Fenollosa, *The Chinese Written Character as a Medium for Poetry*, City Lights Books, San Francisco (n.d.) p. 25.

18 E. Pound, 'Vorticism', *Fortnightly Review*, p. 469.

19 The manner in which this circulation takes place in individual *Cantos* has been examined by a number of critics. See, for example, G. Dekker, *Sailing after Knowledge : The Cantos of Ezra Pound*, Routledge & Kegan Paul, London (1963) pp. 15 ff. for an explication of Canto VII, and W. Baumann, *The Rose in the Steel Dust*, Bern (1967) pp. 19–53 for Canto IV.

20 E. Fenollosa, *op. cit*. p. 22.

21 W.C. Williams, Prologue to *Kora in Hell; Imaginations*, New Directions, New York; MacGibbon & Kee (1970) p. 18.

22 W.C. Williams, 'The Descent of Winter', *Ibid*. p. 247.

23 See L.S. Dembo, *op. cit*. p. 6.

24 W.C. Williams, *Kora in Hell; op. cit*. pp. 81, 35.

25 W.C. Williams, 'Comment', *Selected Essays*, Random House, New York (1954) p. 28.

26 W.C. Williams, 'A Novelette', *Imaginations, op. cit*. p. 281.

27 H. Bergson, *Matter and Memory*, p. 112.

28 V. Mercier, *The Irish Comic Tradition* Clarendon, Oxford (1962) p. 221. See this chapter as a whole, 'James Joyce and the Irish Tradition of Parody', pp. 210–36 for comment on *Finnegans Wake* as well.

29 H. Meyer, *The Poetics of Quotation in the Modern Novel*, trans. T. and Y. Ziolkowski, Princeton U.P. (1968) pp. 3–8, 59–68, 83–5.

30 This aspect of Pound's work is thoroughly ventilated in R.P. Blackmur, 'Masks of Ezra Pound' in *Form and Value in Modern Poetry*, Doubleday Anchor Books, Garden City, N.Y. (1957) pp. 79–112. Blackmur's argument that Pound is successful only when he is borrowing is intended, of course, to be depreciative, but it does confirm the point that borrowing is a crucial feature of his style.

31 Of the numerous exegeses and specialized works on the *Cantos* that have appeared, the ones that I have found most useful are: J.H. Edwards and W.W. Vasse, *Annotated Index to the Cantos of Ezra Pound;* H. Kenner. *The Poetry of Ezra Pound* and *The Pound Era*; D. Davie, *Ezra Pound : The Poet as Sculptor*; C. Emery, *Ideas Into Action*; G. Dekker, *Sailing After Knowledge;* D.D. Pearlman, *The Barb of Time;* W. Baumann, *The Rose in the Steel Dust*.

32 E. Pound, *Letters*, (ed.) D.D. Paige, Harcourt, Brace, and World, New York (1950) Faber, London (1951) pp. 274–5.

33 D.D. Pearlman, *The Barb of Time*, Oxford U.P. New York (1969) p. 37.

34 E. Pound, reprinted as 'Translators of Greek: Early Translators of Homer, II' in *Literary Essays*, pp. 259–67.

35 W. Baumann, *The Rose in the Steel Dust*, pp. 39–40.

36 S. Mallarmé, 'Quant au livre', *Oeuvres Complètes*, pp. 369–87.

37 F. Marinetti, *Zang Tumb Tuuum* Milano (1914) p. 60. 'street going down, going down . . . going up going down stairway of a torrent going down again.'

38 *Ibid.* 'SUN + BALLOON BRAKES villages Turks incendiaries gigantic flames columns of smoke spirals of sparks.'

39 For a survey of these activities in the Post-World War II period, see 'The Changing Guard', *Times Literary Supplement*, 6 August and 8 September 1964.

40 Marjorie G. Perloff attributes a different value to this device, and to the practice of translation and transliteration throughout the *Cantos*. She interprets it as one of the methods Pound uses for seeing things 'from different linguistic perspectives . . . as if to undercut their historicity'. See M.G. Perloff 'Pound and Rimbaud: The Retreat from Symbolism', *Iowa Review* (Winter 1975) vol. 6, 1, pp. 91–113.

Chapter VII : The Language of Finnegans Wake

1 H.E. Rollins (ed.), To Tom Keats, July 17th, 1818, *Letters of John Keats*, Harvard U.P. Cambridge, Mass. (1958) vol. I, pp. 333–4.

2 C. Hart, *Structure and Motif in Finnegans Wake*, Northwestern U.P. Evanston (1962) p. 31.

3 A.W. Litz, *The Art of James Joyce*, Oxford U.P. London (1961) pp. 71–2. Other books that I have found helpful in dealing with *Finnegans Wake* include: C. Hart, *op. cit.*, J.S. Atherton, *The Books at the Wake*; W.Y. Tindall, *A Reader's Guide to Finnegans Wake*; and B. Benstock, *Joyce-Again's Wake*.

4 *Our Exagmination Round His Factification for Incamination of Work in Progress* New York (1962) was first published by Shakespeare and Company in Paris in 1929. An account of the appearance of *Work in Progress* in *transition* and of Joyce's relations with its editors is given by D. McMillan, *transition 1927–38*, Calder & Boyars, London (1975) chapter 13, pp. 179–203. In the following chapter, pp. 204–231, McMillan shows that Joyce used the instalments of the *Wake* to take part in the controversies of the time, making allusions in it to Gertrude Stein, Wyndham Lewis, the contributors to *Our Examination*, the Surrealists, the Dadas and other figures.

5 *Ibid.* p. 16.

6 While they are not systematic, and probably cannot be completely codified, the verbal distortions Joyce commonly employs in the *Wake* are not numerous. C.K. Ogden's Preface to *Tales Told of Shem and Shaun* (published anonymously in *Psyche*, July 1929) lamented the fact that language lagged behind the arts of music and painting in responding to modernism; but Ogden acknowledged that Joyce's work, then appearing serially in *transition*, was interesting, and listed 'ten main ways in which symbolic texture can be complicated and compacted' in language. Most of them are found in *Finnegans Wake* and belong to the repertory of Joyce's usual effects. The list includes: root-cultivation, tongue-gesture, infixation, analogical deformation, onomatopoeia, phonetic and kinetic, puns, select and dialect, Spoonerisms, condensation, mergers, and echoes. Margaret Schlauch also lists the forms of word-distortion in *Finnegans Wake*: 'reduplication,

alliteration, assonance, primitive types of apophony, assimilation, dissimilation, sandhi variants and the like'. ('The Language of James Joyce', *Science and Society*, (Fall 1939) vol. 3, p. 485). To these should be added the use of foreign words, especially in puns ('stammpunct', p. 309), displacement or transposition of letters ('hibat', p. 171 and 'lonestime', p. 319), the occasional internal division of a word ('birth of an otion', p. 309 and 'oura vatars', p. 599), coinings, usually from familar roots ('confusionary', p. 333) and the remarkably varied effects introduced by Earwicker's stammer ('fib fib) fabrication', p. 36). Anthony Burgess's *Joysprick* André Deutsch, London (1973) sheds light on various aspects of Joyce's language; the chapter on the *Wake* (10. 'Oneiroparonomastics') emphasizes puns and the relationship of the *Wake* to Lewis Carroll.

7   G. M. Hopkins, *Journals and Papers*, (eds) H. House and G. Storey, Oxford U.P. London (1959) p. 11.

8   'S. Gilbert, 'Prolegomena to Work in Progress', *Our Exagmination*, p. 60.

9   To Miss Weaver, November 15, 1926, *Letters of James Joyce*, ed. S. Gilbert Viking Press, New York (1957) Faber, London (1966) p. 247.

10 C. Hart, *op. cit.*, pp. 154–60.

11 To Miss Weaver, November 16, 1924, *Letters*, S. Gilbert (ed.) *op. cit.*, p. 222.

12 E. Mason and R. Ellmann, (eds.) *The Critical Writings of James Joyce*, Viking Press, New York (1965) p. 101. Many of the terms used in linguistic discussion ('current', 'drift', 'fluent') suggest that water is an indispensable analogue in thinking about language. Edward Sapir, for example, uses it in *Language*, New York (1921) in speaking of the individual variations that eventually produce general changes in language: 'They themselves are random phenomena, like the waves of the sea, moving backward and forward in purposeless flux. The linguistic drift', on the other hand, ' . . . has direction' (p. 165).

13 E. Pound, *Letters*, To James Joyce, November 15, 1926, p. 202.

14 W.C. Williams, 'A Point for American Criticism', *Our Exagmination*, pp. 184–5.

15 M. Brion, 'The Idea of Time in the World of James Joyce', *ibid.* p. 29.

16 R. Sage, 'Before Ulysses—and After', *ibid.* pp. 155–6.

17 R. Deming (ed.), *Joyce : The Critical Heritage*, Routledge & Kegan Paul, London. First published in *Bravo* (1970), Vol. II, p. 525. Paris (Sept. 1930) and then in *Souvenirs de James Joyce*. The French translation of parts of *Anna Livia Plurabelle* was ultimately completed by a committee consisting of Samuel Beckett, Alfred Péron, Paul Léon, Eugene Jolas and Ivan Goll in addition to Soupault and Joyce himself. It was published in the *Nouvelle Revue Française* and then, together with translations of the first section by André du Bouchet, in *Finnegans Wake : Fragments adaptés par André du Bouchet, suivis de Anna Livia Plurabelle*, Paris (1962). For additional details, see W.V. Costanzo, 'The French Version of *Finnegans Wake*', *James Joyce Quarterly*, 9 (Winter 1971) pp. 225–36.

18 See G. Wagner, 'Wyndham Lewis and James Joyce: A Study in Controversy', *South Atlantic Quarterly*, 56 (Jan. 1957) pp. 57–66.

19 W.I. Thompson, 'The Language of Finnegans Wake', *Sewanee Review*, 72 (Jan. 1964) p. 88.

20 C. Hart, *op. cit.* pp. 69–77.

21 R. Waldrop, *Against Language?*, The Hague (1971) pp. 109–11.

22 'There is joy in sadness, sadness in joy.' This epigraph to Bruno's play,

Il Candelaio, is quoted on p. 19 of J. McIntyre *Giordano Bruno*, Macmillan, London (1903) where Joyce no doubt encountered it.

23 T.F. Staley (ed.) *'Finnegans Wake* in Perspective', *James Joyce Today*, Indiana U.P. Bloomington (1966) pp. 135–65; and C. Hart and F. Senn (eds.), 'The Elephant in the Belly: Exegesis of *Finnegans Wake*', *A Wake Digest* Sydney (1968).

24 B. Benstock, *Joyce-Again's Wake* U. of Washington P. Seattle (1965) pp. 213–14.

25 P. Colum, 'Working with Joyce', *Critical Heritage*, II, 487. Reprinted from the *Irish Times*. 5 October 1956.

26 J. Joyce, To Jacques Mercanton, January 9, 1940, *Letters*, (ed.) R. Ellmann, London (1966) vol. III, p. 463.

27 C. Hart, *ibid.* p. 34.

28 F. Marinetti, *Zang Tumb Tuuum*, Milano, p. 14.

29 F. Marinetti 'New Futurist Manifesto', *Poetry and Drama*, 1 (Sept. 1913) p. 322.

30 F. Marinetti, *op. cit.* pp. 17–18.

31 W.I. Thompson, 'The Language of Finnegans Wake', *Sewanee Review*, 72 (Jan. 1964) p. 83.

32 Quoted by J.L. McIntyre, *Giordano Bruno*, pp. 178, 174.

33 Quoted from *De la causa, principio et uno* in *Bruno : His Life and Thought* by D.W. Singer, Henry Schuman, New York (1950) p. 84.

34 Quoted from *De l'infinito universo et mondi* by McIntyre, p. 221.

35 Quoted from *De l'infinito universo et mondi* by Singer, p. 72.

36 Quoted from *De l'infinito universo et mondi* by Singer, p. 72.

37 S.B. Purdy, 'Mind Your Genderous: Toward a Wake Grammar', *New Light on Joyce from the Dublin Symposium*, (ed.) F. Senn, Indiana U.P. Bloomington (1972) pp. 59–60.

38 J. Derrida, 'Structure, Sign and Play in the Discourse of the Human Sciences', *The Structuralist Controversy*, (eds) R. Macksey and E. Donato Johns Hopkins U.P. Baltimore, (1970, reprinted 1972), pp. 247–65.

39 M. Norris, *The Decentered Universe of Finnegans Wake* Johns Hopkins U.P. Baltimore (1974, reprinted 1976). See especially the chapter on 'Technique'. Derrida's views are applied to Williams's poetry in J.N. Riddell, *The Inverted Bell* Louisiana State U.P. Baton Rouge (1974) pp. 163–6.

40 C. Hart, *op. cit.* pp. 182–200.

41 *Ibid.* pp. 42–3.

42 N. Frye *Anatomy of Criticism*, Atheneum, New York (1966) p. 61.

INDEX